BODIES IN
TREATMENT

RELATIONAL PERSPECTIVES BOOK SERIES

Volume 36

BODIES IN TREATMENT

The Unspoken Dimension

Edited by
Frances Sommer Anderson

Routledge
Taylor & Francis Group
NEW YORK AND LONDON

First published 2008 by The Analytic Press, Inc.

This edition Published 2014 by Routledge
711 Third Avenue, New York, NY 10017
27 Church Road, Hove, East Sussex, BN3 2FA

First issued in paperback 2014

Routledge is an imprint of the Taylor and Francis Group, an informa business

© 2008 by Taylor & Francis Group, LLC

International Standard Book Number-13: 978-0-88163-448-8 (Hardcover)
International Standard Book Number-13: 978-1-138-00589-1 (pbk)

Library of Congress Cataloging-in-Publication Data

Bodies in treatment / [edited by] Frances Sommer Anderson.
    p. ; cm. -- (Relational perspectives book series ; v. 36)
    Includes bibliographical references and index.
    ISBN 978-0-88163-448-8 (hardcover : alk. paper)
    1. Psychoanalysis. 2. Mind and body therapies. I. Anderson, Frances Sommer, 1948- II. Series.
    [DNLM: 1. Psychoanalytic Therapy--methods. 2. Body Image. 3. Mind-Body Relations (Metaphysics) 4. Professional-Patient Relations. WM 460.6 B667 2008]

RC504.B59 2008
616.89'17--dc22
                                  2007015768

Dedication

In memory of
Donald M. Kaplan
With appreciation and affection for
Joyce McDougall

Contents

Preface   ix

Acknowledgments   xv

Contributors   xvii

Introduction   xxi

1   At a Loss for Words and Feelings: A Psychoanalyst Reflects on
Experiencing Bodywork   1
     Frances Sommer Anderson, PhD

Part I. Bodily Experience in Self-Organization: Contemporary Views

2   Self in Action: The Bodily Basis of Self-Organization   29
     William F. Cornell, MA, TSTA

3   The Role of Bodily Experience in Emotional Organization: New
Perspectives on the Multiple Code Theory   51
     Wilma Bucci, PhD

Part II. Psychoanalysts Informed by Body-Based Modalities

4   Learning From Work With Individuals With a History of Trauma:
Some Thoughts on Integrating Body-Oriented Techniques and
Relational Psychoanalysis   79
     Christopher B. Eldredge, MA, LCSW, and
     Gilbert W. Cole, PhD, LCSW

5   The Coconstruction of "Psychoanalytical Choreography"
     and the Dancing Self: Working With an Anorectic Patient   103
        Maria Paola Pacifici, MD

6   Yoga and Neuro-Psychoanalysis   127
        Patricia L. Gerbarg, MD

7   Sweet Are the Uses of Adversity: Psychic Integration Through
     Body-Centered Work   151
        Graham Bass, MA, APRN-BC

8   Coming Into Being: Employing the Wisdom of the Body and
     Mind-Body Therapy   169
        Helen M. Newman, PhD

Part III. Analysts Using Bodily Experience in the Treatment Relationship

9   Tipping Points Between Body, Culture, and Subjectivity: The
     Tension Between Passion and Custom   193
        Steven H. Knoblauch, PhD

10   "We" Got Rhythm: Miming and the Polyphony of Identity in
     Psychoanalysis   213
        Gianni Nebbiosi, PhD, and Susanna Federici-Nebbiosi, PhD

Part IV. The Analyst's Body as Object and Subject

11   When a Body Meets a Body: The Impact of the Therapist's Body
     on Eating-Disordered Patients   237
        Jean Petrucelli, PhD

12   The Analyst's Vulnerability: Preserving and Fine-Tuning Analytic
     Bodies   255
        Adrienne Harris, PhD, and Kathy Sinsheimer, MFT

Index   275

Preface

Patients in pain or distress or confusion who seek the ministrations of psychoanalytic therapists are ipso facto "bodies in treatment," so why has it taken psychoanalysts a century to attend systematically to the somatic dimension of their caregiving? Of course, psychoanalysis, the "talking cure," took shape as a method of overcoming repression and eliciting verbalizable insight. It was to be radically differentiated from hypnosis, which relied on induced trance states as a somatic precondition of the recovery of memories, typically bodily memories. The traditional psychoanalytic method, with its rule of abstinence, its mirror simile, its strictures about neutrality and "evenly hovering attention," and its surgical metaphor, was less a coming together of people, bodies and all, than a disembodied chiropractic of the mind: a verbal manipulation to overcome resistance and release tension with the goal of realigning a system of mental energetics and reestablishing healthy energic flow.

From the mid-1930s on, a second factor reinforced analysts' insensitivity to the bodily dimension of psychological caregiving. To wit, many analysts were uncomfortable with the invasive procedures of the new somatic psychiatry and sought to differentiate the talking cure from them. I have in mind Henry Cotton's operative "defocalization" of the allegedly infected tissue of institutionalized mental patients; Manfred Sakel's insulin-coma therapy; Ladislas Meduna's Metrazol-seizure therapy; Ugo Cerletti's electroshock therapy; and finally and most fatefully, Egas Moniz's prefrontal lobotomy. To be sure, there were analysts who not only endorsed the somatic therapies but also devised ingenious (and strained) psychoanalytic rationalizations of them. But prominent voices in the profession—William Alanson White, Harry Stack Sullivan, and D. W. Winnicott among them—spoke out against all the somatic treatments. They were all too aware of the easy segue from bodies in treatment to bodies chemically, electrically, and surgically mistreated. It is fair to say that most analysts, including those who accepted somatic treatments and worked psychodynamically with post-lobotomy patients, saw their uniquely "mindful" ministrations as a counterpoise to the bodily interventions of their psychiatric colleagues.

Finally, psychoanalytic distance from body-based therapies has been reinforced by ongoing concern with the discomfiting reality of boundary violations. After all, bodies in treatment offer up the possibility of trust bodily betrayed. Instances of such professional malfeasance represent yet another unspoken (and unwanted) dimension of the analytic legacy. Scholars have long been acquainted with the recurrent violations that punctuate the history of analysis: Carl Jung's complicated embroilment with his patient Sabina Spielrein; Sándor Ferenczi's simultaneous romantic involvement with his patient (and future wife) Gizella Pálos and her daughter Elma Pálos; and Margaret Mahler's affair with her first analyst, August Aichhorn, among them. The redoubtable Ernest Jones has the dubious distinction of being the first analyst to settle financially with a patient who accused him of sexual misconduct. For many decades, these and other particulars occupied some dim nether region of psychoanalytic self-awareness. Only with the publication in 1996 of Glen Gabbard and Eva Lester's *Boundaries and Boundary Violations in Psychoanalysis*, which documented the continuing reality of such violations, was the profession spurred to self-examination.

As the contributors to this fine volume bear witness, we have traversed these several historical signposts and are at the juncture of a new comprehension of the bodily dimension, indeed the bodily foundation, of an analyst and a patient talking toward a cure. Clearly, the relational turn of the past two decades has much to do with the distance traveled, for relationality, with its emphasis on interaction and mutual influence, directs us back to the bodily aspects of human communication per se. Relationally speaking, we cannot theorize about the role of the analyst as subject without allowing for the bodily grounding of his or her subjecthood. To speak of two subjective presences in the clinical exchange, that is, is to invite an appreciation of the kind of interoceptive feedback—the bodily awareness of shifting emotional and tension states; the bodily concomitants of mental pain; the bodily analogues of therapeutic empathy—with which embodied subjects are endowed. These insights are beautifully exemplified in Frances Anderson's affecting chronicle of her personal and therapeutic movement from psychoanalysis to body-work. Anderson's odyssey, which deepened her *analytic* sensibility, is a microcosm of the shifting sensibility that brings us to the point of this volume. More than a century after Freud's elaboration of his psychoanalytic method, we are finally able to grasp, in the words of Harris and Sinsheimer, "the porousness of body and mind in analytic encounters, the primitive fears of being possessed, colonized, inhabited, of having one's own life and process leaking, spreading, and transmuting."

So we have come a long way. Of course, even in its dated classical guise, the psychoanalytic method never did justice to psychoanalytic engagement, which is always a meeting of minds both embodied and embodying. We are wont to forget that Freud's "concentration technique," the historical precursor of the analytic method, was a literal laying on of hands to overcome resistance; that he put food in the Wolfman's belly; that his theoretical productivity was linked to the nicotine that suffused his body; and that the souring therapeutic purview of his later years went hand in hand with the painful daily insertion of jaw prostheses into his surgically excavated oral cavity. The excellent contributors to *Bodies in Treatment* will have no difficulty appreciating the significance of such particulars. They remind us of many things, not the least of which is that mental pain is often congealed in the body, whereas the liberating insight that ameliorates pain is often a product of bodies in interaction. The manner in which trauma experiences are not only encoded in the body but accessed and addressed through the analyst's own bodily experiences is not the least of their insights.* Bodily experiences, they show us again and again, are both a reservoir *of* insight and a conduit *to* insight. Indeed, as Pacifici observes, the very dialogue between analyst and patient can be "corporeal"; there is a bodily dimension to the moving around within the analytic space "that allows us to experience internal and external spatiality." More fundamentally still, our sense of self in its cognitive, conative, and emotional dimensions is rooted

---

* They are preceded in this respect by Analytic Press author Elaine Siegel. In *Transformations: Countertransference During the Psychoanalytic Treatment of Incest, Real and Imagined* (TAP, 1996), Siegel, a registered dance therapist and motor development specialist as well as an analyst, explored her sensory and physiological responses to her analysands, which provided a valuable tool in learning to differentiate real from imagined sexual abuse. Siegel was also well ahead of the curve in attending to her own bodily states as aspects of countertransference.

in bodily experience. Our bodies, contributors such as Cornell and Bucci tell us, subtend our very sense of who we are and how we process our emotional worlds.

The prescriptive side of this collection resides in richly informative accounts of the integration of psychoanalytically oriented treatment with body-based modalities. Unsurprisingly, body-oriented techniques are most compatible with relationally oriented approaches, and they have special salience with respect to trauma victims (Eldredge and Cole). Craniosacral therapy (Bass) and polarity therapy (Newman) are among the specialized modalities to which analytic readers are introduced. Gerbarg provides an exemplary account of the adjunctive use of yoga, the effectiveness of which can be grounded neurophysiologically. These and other contributors stress the extent to which somatic interventions, typically subsymbolic or nonsymbolic, can promote depth-psychological change. From the vantage point of their various modalities, the contributors write about mobilizing the capacity for insight from the bodily direction or, more accurately, from the bodily dimension of self experience.

Of course, analysts have bodies of their own, and the final two sections of *Bodies in Treatment* explore the range of ways in which these selfsame bodies enter into treatment relationships and help sustain (and contain) treatment dynamics. The meaning-impregnated rhythmicity of analytic exchanges is brought to the fore in chapters that enlarge on the synchrony and asynchrony of these rhythms from the standpoint of nonlinear dynamic theory (Knoblauch) and mirror neuron systems (Nebbiosi and Federici-Nebbiosi), respectively. Analytic work with eating-disordered patients provides a venue for the heightened salience of body language. Petrucelli insightfully explores the unusual sensitivity of these patients to the therapist's body and shows how this sensitivity fuels unarticulated enactments no less than productive therapeutic dialogue. Finally, we are reminded that the daily weight of "analytic work as work" falls on the analyst's body no less than on her mind, a reality that opens to sensitive meditation on the bodily dimension of analytic vulnerability and of analytic self-care (Harris and Sinsheimer).

I trust this brief synopsis conveys the fact that *Bodies in Treatment* is an admirably unconventional psychoanalytic book. I learned things from it that I have not learned from 30 years of immersion in the psychoanalytic literature. This remark is a negative commentary on the literature no less than a ringing endorsement of the volume at hand. Like Aron and Anderson's *Relational Perspectives on the Body* (The Analytic Press, 1998), it achieves originality by bringing into conceptual focus a dimension of clinical work that has long occupied the shadowy realm of tacit knowledge. By bringing this knowledge to the light of day, by theorizing about it in ways that enlarge the domain of psychodynamic engagement, Anderson and her colleagues contribute to a larger project: the development of integrative treatment modalities that are responsive to who patients are and what they need, not to what any one theory, psychoanalytic or otherwise, suggests they should get. With *Bodies in Treatment*, a long unspoken dimension of psychoanalysis is finally given voice.

Paul E. Stepansky
Upper Montclair, NJ
15 October 2006

Acknowledgments

Lewis Aron was the catalyst for this project, via an e-mail in early April 2005, "Subject: got an idea." Lew suggested that we explore the topic of "bodywork" in a seminar or colloquium. I responded, "How about a book?" After a few e-mail exchanges, we quickly saw that *Bodies in Treatment: The Unspoken Dimension* is a natural expansion of *Relational Perspectives on the Body* (The Analytic Press, 1998), which Lew had invited me to coedit. In that volume, we invited analysts to take up a neglected topic in relational theory and practice—the place of the body and bodily experience.

Thank you, Lew, for inspiration, encouragement, unbounded patience, and a sense of humor as you helped me master the skills of editing solo.

I am also grateful to Lew and Adrienne Harris for their commitment to the Relational Perspectives Book Series at The Analytic Press. They foster analytic writing that challenges and enhances our theorizing and practice.

Paul Stepansky, in his role as managing director of The Analytic Press, received my proposal for this book enthusiastically and offered historical perspective, wisdom, the reality principle, and a warm heart as the project unfolded. Paul left The Analytic Press before the book was published. I asked him to write the preface with appreciative recognition of his encouragement to reach out to other disciplines.

The intellectual community at the New York University Postdoctoral Program in Psychoanalysis and Psychotherapy is always a backdrop for my professional efforts. The National Institute for the Psychotherapies Training Institute (NIP TI) has offered me opportunities to learn as I teach about my work in the area of mindbody theorizing and practice. I am grateful to Sandra Shapiro, director of the Trauma Program at NIP TI, for her interest in my work and her practical suggestions about how to reach my goals.

Collaborating with authors who share my passion for learning about the world of the body is a dream come true. Thank you for your commitment to creating this book and your diligence in meeting the deadlines. It has been a pleasure to learn from you.

Eleanor Starke Kobrin, formerly at The Analytic Press, helped many of us with those details that only a seasoned editor like Lenni can handle.

The staff at The Analytic Press were prodigious in their attempts to make the process of publication an easy one. Kristopher Spring was a thorough editorial assistant and Nadine Simms began production and Michael Davidson patiently saw it to completion.

On the challenge of writing. Twenty years ago my supervisor, Don Kaplan, and Joyce McDougall urged me to write about my treatment of pain. Their belief that I had something useful to say has helped me persevere with writing, weathering administrative changes. My writing teacher, Carole Maso, helped me get unstuck several times during this project with her careful critiques offered with encouragement to be open and unafraid.

Mentors, friends, and colleagues have offered buffering, support, and enthusiasm when I needed it. I will always be grateful to Lawrence Friedman, Philip M. Bromberg, John E. Sarno, Pat Kennedy, Jean Petrucelli, Melinda Gellman, Limer Kaufman, Donna McGill, Lucia Kellar, Virginia Kelley, Eric Sherman, Marcia Lesser, Ron Balamuth, Tamsin Looker, Zeborah Schachtel, Neal May, Pasquel Pantone, Elaine Martin, and Barbara Gold. Judith Langis, Dorothy Hunter, and Evie Weitzer provided excellent body care.

And to the one who is always there, my husband, Bill Sommer—thank you for remaining steadfast and convinced when I waiver and for celebrating when I succeed. Thank you, Sweetie and Fog, for feline affect regulation.

Contributors

Frances Sommer Anderson, PhD (Editor)
Private practice, New York City; faculty, National Institute for the Psychotherapies Training Institute, New York City; clinical assistant professor of psychiatry, New York University Medical School; adjunct clinical supervisor, Clinical Psychology Doctoral Program, City College-City University of New York; psychologist, Bellevue Hospital Center

Graham Bass, MA, APRN-BC
Faculty and supervisor, National Institute for the Psychotherapies Training Institute; private practice, New York City and Westchester County

Wilma Bucci, PhD
Professor, Derner Institute of Adelphi University; chair of Research Associates of the American Psychoanalytic Association (RAAPA); faculty, Research Training Programme of the International Psycho-analytical Association; honorary member, American Psychoanalytic Association, the New York Psychoanalytic Institute and Society, and the Institute for Psychoanalytic Training and Research (IPTAR); director of research, the Bernard L. Pacella Parent Child Center at the New York Psychoanalytic Society

Gilbert W. Cole, PhD, CSW
Faculty, Institute for Contemporary Psychotherapy, National Institute for the Psychotherapies Training Institute; faculty and supervisor, Psychoanalytic Psychotherapy Study Center; contributing editor, *Studies in Gender and Psychoanalysis*; author, *Infecting the Treatment: Being an HIV-positive Psychoanalyst* (The Analytic Press, 2002)

William F. Cornell, MA, TSTA
Certified Radix; Neo-Reichian practitioner; private practice; contributing editor, *The Healer's Bent: Solitude and Dialogue in the Clinical Encounter* (The Analytic Press, 2005), a collection of the psychoanalytic writings of James T. McLaughlin; editor, Transactional Analysis Journal

Christopher B. Eldredge, MA, LCSW
Private practice, New York City; faculty and supervisor, National Institute for the Psychotherapies Training Institute Trauma Program

Susanna Federici-Nebbiosi, PhD
Founding and faculty member, ISIPSé, Istituto di Specializzazione in Psicologia Psicoanalitica del Sé e Psicoanalisi Relazionale, Rome, Italy; member, Advisory Board, International Association for Relational Psychoanalysis and Psychotherapy

Patricia L. Gerbarg, MD
Private practice, Kingston, NY; assistant professor in clinical psychiatry, New York Medical College, Valhalla, NY; member, Boston Psychoanalytic Society and Institute; author, with Richard P. Brown, *The Rhodiola Revolution* (Rodale, 2004)

Adrienne Harris, PhD
Faculty and supervisor, New York University Postdoctoral Program in Psychotherapy and Psychoanalysis

Steven H. Knoblauch, PhD
Faculty and supervisor, New York University Postdoctoral Program in Psychotherapy and Psychoanalysis; faculty and supervisor, Institute for the Psychoanalytic Study of Subjectivity; faculty and supervisor, Institute for Contemporary Psychotherapy; faculty and supervisor, Psychoanalytic Psychotherapy Study Center

Gianni Nebbiosi, PhD
President, founding member, and supervising and training analyst, ISIPSé, Istituto di Specializzazione in Psicologia Psicoanalitica del Sé e Psicoanalisi Relazionale, Rome, Italy; vice president, International Association for Relational Psychoanalysis and Psychotherapy; member, International Council for Psychoanalytic Self-Psychology

Helen M. Newman, PhD
Associate professor of psychology, Hunter College, City University of New York; private practice, New York City, registered polarity practitioner

Maria Paola Pacifici, MD
Psychiatrist; psychotherapist; University of Rome "La Sapienza," Department of Psychiatry; Sant'Andrea Hospital, Rome, Italy

Jean Petrucelli, PhD
Director and cofounder, Eating Disorders, Compulsions and Addictions Service; supervisor of psychotherapy, Teaching Faculty, William Alanson White Institute; contributing editor, *Longing: Psychoanalytic Musings on Desire* (Karnac, 2006); contributing coeditor, *Hungers and Compulsions: The Psychodynamic Treatment of Eating Disorders and Addictions* (Jason Aronson, 2001); psychology consultant, *Shape Magazine*

Kathy Sinsheimer, MFT
Private practice, Oakland, CA; member, the Psychoanalytic Institute of Northern California

Introduction

Welcome to the ineluctable, numinous, often ineffable domain of the body, where visceral, sensory, imagistic modes of processing are dominant. We have taken on the challenge of using words to describe bodily experiences of analyst and patient in the treatment relationship. In our efforts to demonstrate how experiences from body-focused modalities can be useful to psychoanalysts, we ask you to temporarily suspend attempts to integrate the information into familiar cognitive schemas. Our aim is to offer new conceptual schemas that are fully informed by the nonverbal and the subsymbolic.

Our contributions have been enriched by the contemporary interest in interdisciplinary dialogue and integration of research on the developmental neurobiology of attachment, the microprocessing of interchanges between the infant and caregiver, the neuroscience of emotional processing and trauma, body-focused talking treatments for trauma, and research in cognitive science. These findings explicate the nonverbal underpinnings of self-regulation and mutual regulation in the analytic dyad.

From the field of trauma research and treatment, our attention has been drawn to the impact of trauma on the body and heightened further since the terrorist attacks of September 11, 2001. In New York City, at the National Institute for the Psychotherapies Training Institute (NIP TI), Sandra Shapiro and Jennifer Almouli developed a trauma program in early 2002 that incorporates interventions at multiple levels, including a range of body-focused modalities.

In early 2002, Lewis Aron, the director of the NYU Postdoctoral Program in Psychoanalysis and Psychotherapy, initiated a program on Specialization Training in Trauma and Disaster Intervention, enlisting the expertise of NYU postdoctoral faculty Judith L. Alpert, Liz Goren, Nina Thomas, and Isaac Tylim. Although the structure of the program is being formalized, the organizers are offering seminars with yearly overarching themes, for example, witness-ing, reparative processes in trauma, and countertransference issues, including attention to trauma and the body.

Two publications since September 11 have made substantial con-tributions to our understanding of the impact of trauma and how to treat it, including a recognition of neurophysiological sequela: *September 11: Trauma and Human Bonds* (Coates, Rosenthal, & Schechter, 2003) and *Living With Terror, Working With Trauma: A Clinician's Handbook* (Knafo, 2004).

In the chapter that follows, I reflect on my personal attempts to integrate "talking" and "bodily experience." My account provides the personal and professional context in which I created this book. I sought a bodywork practitioner, analytically informed, who could provide an overview of the concept of "bodywork" and distinguish it from body psychotherapy (Cornell). To anchor this exploration in contemporary mindbody theory, I invited a cognitive scientist (Bucci) to write about her information processing model of cognitive and emotional processing, showing how it provides for the integra-tion of bodily experience within the psychoanalytic frame.

My focus on the integration of knowledge from the bodywork modalities is reflected in Part II. I invited analysts who had train-ing in body-focused therapies (Eldredge and Cole; Pacifici; Gerberg), including "hands-on" modalities (Bass; Newman), to write about how their expertise informs their work in the talking frame.

Extending inquiry about the analyst's and patient's bodily experi-ence initiated in *Relational Perspectives on the Body* (Aron & Ander-son, 1998), I invited Knoblauch and Nebbiosi and Federici-Nebbiosi to contribute their innovations. The analyst's body as object (Petru-celli) and as subject (Harris and Sinsheimer) are considered as well.

References

Aron, L., & Anderson, F. S. (Eds.). (1998). *Relational perspectives on the body*. Hillsdale, NJ: The Analytic Press.

Coates, S. W., Rosenthal, J. L., & Schechter, D. S. (Eds.). (2003). *Septem-ber 11: Trauma and human bonds*. Hillsdale, NJ: The Analytic Press.

Knafo, D. (Ed.). (2004). *Living with terror, working with trauma: A clini-cian's handbook*. Lanham, MD: Jason Aronson.

1

At a Loss for Words and Feelings

*A Psychoanalyst Reflects on
Experiencing Bodywork*

Frances Sommer Anderson

It was peony season last year when I committed to write this chapter. It is peony season again, as I struggle to finish. Monday's tightly compressed buds, the size of pink cotton balls, have become Thursday's 13-inch, effusive, exuberant, multilayered wonders, and they're still expanding. Last year, I was in a full-bloom self-state while planning this book. As soon as I tried to use words to describe ineffable, imagistic experiences in bodywork, I tightened into an apprehensive, defiant, compressed-bud state: I was afraid I could not convey what I needed to in narrative form. It seemed like an overwhelming project, and I discovered that I did not want to work so hard. All year, I have felt like one of those oppositional buds that never opens. You know the ones I mean: They have such potential. You can wait forever but they never open. I felt as if I would never open. But I did. What I wrote during the year was self-conscious and stilted, too studious, dead. What helped me open was taking in the beauty and wonder of the peonies, staying with the feelings they evoked, and starting to write from that place.

I have a highly conflictual relationship with words compared with my relationship with imagistic mentation (Fosshage, 1997). I respond readily to color, texture, form, movement, facial expression, and posture and to the pitch, volume, rhythm, inflection, and intonation of spoken language. I grew up in a family who did not graduate from high school. They had native intelligence and abundant common sense but a limited vocabulary and only rudimentary grammar. They seldom put thoughts and feelings into words. I remember a lot of silence: Most family communication was through what was *not* said—through facial expression, gesture, and posture. When they did speak, I relied on intonation and inflection to discern what they really meant. I knew more than I could ever articulate, and I longed for the words to capture and convey my experiences.

I was, and still am, in awe of and envy people who seem to be able to articulate concepts and feelings effortlessly, fluidly, eloquently. I experience an unbridgeable gap between my interoceptive, proprioceptive, and kinesthetic experience and what I can convey about those aspects of experience in words. Often I cannot find the links between what Bucci (1997, 2001, 2003, this volume) calls the subsymbolic mode of experience and verbal and nonverbal symbolic representations of those experiences. (I often use *visceral* to refer to what she calls the subsymbolic mode.) Despite many years of formal education and evidence of mastery in some areas, I still feel at a loss when I confront dense, highly conceptual verbal and quantitative material. In contrast, when I meet someone for the first time or consult with a new patient, I "know" a lot immediately, even though I cannot always articulate what I "know" in my body. I rely heavily on subsymbolic and nonverbal symbolic modes of processing as an analyst and often find it difficult to articulate the complexity of my awareness in discussions with colleagues and when writing.

I resonated recently with a *New York Times* article, "Being Joan Didion" by Campbell Robertson (2006), in which he discusses the ways Ms. Didion and actress Vanessa Redgrave are collaborating on Ms. Redgrave's role as Joan Didion in a play based on Ms. Didion's book, *The Year of Magical Thinking*. The book is a gripping account of the impact of the sudden death of her husband, concurrent with the life-threatening illness of their only child. He quotes Ms. Redgrave,

"I'm thinking about a lot of things in a lot of different ways.... I don't like to put it into words." Ms. Didion supplied, "It freezes it" (p. E2). David Hare, the British playwright who will write the script, contrasts Ms. Redgrave and Ms. Didion as follows: Ms. Redgrave "is the most emotionally expressive actor about a certain kind of extreme feeling.... And one of Joan's extraordinary qualities is this glacially perfect prose which contains fantastic feeling underneath a formal surface" (p. E2). There's my challenge—I wish to be emotionally expressive about extreme feeling in glacially perfect prose.

My difficulties in the realm of verbal communication, discovered in my personal analysis and in my treatment of people in pain, together with my discoveries about personal trauma through bodywork modalities, are the sources of my passion for integrating verbal symbolic, nonverbal symbolic, and subsymbolic modes of processing. Writing from my perspective as a psychoanalyst reflecting on 30 years of experiencing body-based treatments, I hope to illustrate how I discovered experience that is difficult to represent in words but that I symbolized in images and eventually integrated into my biographical narrative. I also attempt here to identify conditions that can facilitate accessing feelings when the narrative lacks a connection with the subsymbolic realm. Finally, I wish to convey what I have learned about the advantages and limitations of verbal and nonverbal modes of treatment and how we can build bridges between self-states elicited in each.

The Beginning of My Quest

What began as an intellectual, academic pursuit became a passionate personal journey, fueled by each discovery I made along the way. My quest began in 1975, after I had finished my dissertation, received my doctoral degree, and completed my clinical psychology internship. I joined the psychology staff at my internship site—Rusk Institute of Rehabilitation Medicine at NYU Medical Center—diagnosing and treating children and adults with progressive neuromuscular diseases and doing research on sexuality and neuromuscular disease (Anderson, Bardach, & Goodgold, 1979). I have elsewhere described the impact of working as an analytically oriented clinician in physical rehabilitation medicine, where the material body dominates the physical environment and is the focus of one's work every day (Anderson & Gold, 2003).

Eager to learn, I began studying in a private group with a psychologist, Camilla Kemple. She was renowned for diagnostic acumen and a creative approach to the interpretation of projective techniques—figure drawings and the Rorschach, among others. Having studied with Flanders Dunbar, a prominent figure in the field of psychosomatic medicine, Camilla had developed distinctive ideas about the relationship between mind and body, psychosomatic medicine, and how the Wechsler scales and projective tests could be used to detect difficulties in these areas. I had serendipitously found in Camilla someone from whom I could learn more about the mind-body connection, an interest dating back to my first undergraduate course in psychology. I first heard about "bodywork" from Camilla. She knew a seasoned Alexander teacher, and I, who had always been a very serious academic student, was ready to learn in a completely different modality. Thus, in 1976 I began to experience bodywork out of intellectual curiosity.

I chose to begin Alexander lessons without doing research on the technique; I relied only on Camilla's descriptions. I wanted to enter from a place of curiosity, open to discovery, not from my "head." Being goal oriented and practical, however, I found myself justifying the lessons: I knew that the Alexander technique focused on improving one's posture, so I decided that I needed to correct my posture. That is where the trouble, and the unanticipated discoveries, began.

What was wrong with my posture? All I knew was that as far back as I could remember, Aunt Sadie had made harsh criticisms of it, such as, "What's wrong with you? Hold your shoulders up." Or, "Don't slouch. You look like your daddy when you do that." I continue to deal with the emotional reverberations of her critical voice, still audible within and capable of making me cringe as I write this. Having learned to avoid further castigation from her by being compliant, I never considered asking her to explain what she meant. Being precociously resourceful, I determined that I should lift my shoulders straight up to my ears. I hoped that would correct my problem, please Aunt Sadie, and literally get her off my back. Well, no matter how hard I tried to be perfect in order to avoid her criticism and to get her approval, my shoulders did me in. I just couldn't remember to "hold them up" every single moment.

Thus, I brought my "poor posture" and "slumping shoulders" to my Alexander teacher, Patricia, fully intending to correct it. The sessions were about an hour long, and I was fully clothed. My first discovery was that, unlike my teacher, I was impatient with the painstakingly slow pace at which we worked. I had always taken pride in being diligent and patient. The body awareness Patricia required was very subtle and precise. Two thirds of each one-hour session was spent standing, turning, and bending, very slowly, with keen attention to doing it correctly. I quickly suppressed my feeling that this exercise was very tedious, boring, and, to my surprise, infuriating. I was angry that I had to be so conscious of every movement—what happened to spontaneous movement? What about the majority of people who never heard of Alexander lessons and seemed to be just fine without them?

The last part of the session, I lay on my back on a massage table, fully clothed, with my head off the table, supported only by my teacher's hands. This posture was absolutely wonderful. I had never experienced anything like it. Her supporting my head was blissfully soothing. For about 3 years, I went for a class once a week, enduring the first part in order to get to the second part so that I could experience her holding my head. I had no idea why that was so important, and I never asked for the rationale for that part of the lesson.

I made two discoveries about myself that I had not yet made in my talking treatment: 1) I was very impatient and silently furious about having to work hard, in contrast to my conscious pride in being able to endure and persevere without complaint no matter what I had to do, and 2) it was very important for me to let go, to allow myself to be held, to be soothed: I hadn't been aware of wishing for or needing that. These self-states, accessed first through "hands-on" body treatment, would prove to be fundamental in my process of integration and self-healing, to echo Krystal (1988). Neither my analyst nor I understood the significance of these self-states.

Treating Pain, Finding Myself

In 1979, I began working with a physiatrist, John E. Sarno, MD, at Rusk Institute, NYU Medical Center, treating people with chronic musculoskeletal pain. He was the only mainstream physician who recognized, from a psychoanalytic perspective, the role of emotions in creating and curing pain (Sarno, 1991, 1998, 2006). I have written a detailed case presentation of my treatment of Ellen, a patient referred by Dr. Sarno (Anderson, 1998).

My patients were exquisitely attuned to pain sensations in their bodies. Before long, I became aware of my own somatic sensations. I had hardly noticed them before, or I had paid scant attention to them if I did. Family and cultural norms had constrained and devalued bodily experience. I grew up on a working farm in the South, where we used our bodies for manual labor to make a living. We gave little thought to taking care of the body, except to feed it properly and to rest so that we could work. We had no concept of soothing the body, nor a concept of pleasure or leisure. My family also required Fundamentalist religious training, in which I was taught that the body was to be used to work and to do good deeds. I had much to learn about the body.

In the pioneering years of collaborating with Dr. Sarno, we treated people who had usually been suffering with pain for years. Many had had numerous unsuccessful medical procedures, including surgeries and injections. They had come to him as a last resort, placing great faith in and pressure on all of us who treated them. In the rehabilitation medicine field, they were thought of as "difficult," even "untreatable," except by the use of cognitive behavioral techniques to "manage," not cure, the pain. That attitude prevails today, even though Dr. Sarno's approach has gained national and international attention. My patients were not easily soothed; it was difficult to get them to talk about anything but their bodily pain, and they usually could not speak easily about their emotions. I was fascinated with the challenge of helping them but had no idea how much I had in common with them and how profoundly I would be affected by working with them.

As I worked with my pain patients, I began to feel that I needed a different kind of bodywork. Perhaps the Alexander technique had helped my posture, but more important were my discoveries that I hated working tediously at correcting my posture and that I craved the time I spent on the table "letting go." I was eager to learn more about letting go through hands-on bodywork and in the talking situation.

What do I mean by letting go, recommended in many kinds of bodywork and meditation? Let me return to Monday's peony buds. If you don't know peonies, imagine a tight new rosebud. Can you locate within yourself the visceral experience of the tightly compressed buds? Here I use *visceral* to refer to sensory information from the internal organs of the body that reaches the brain by way of the spinal cord and to refer to our verbal concept of "gut feeling." A technical term for this awareness is *interoception*. What do you sense in your body when you try to find that closed, compressed-bud self-state? Imagine the tightly compressed bud and notice what happens in your body. I call that the OPPOSITE of letting go. Now, imagine Thursday's 13-inch peonies, or a voluptuous rose, and notice what you feel in your body. What sensations, images, feelings, and thoughts arise when you try to access your peony/rose-in-full-bloom self-state? I call this a form of letting go, or opening up—a process that took my peonies about a week.

The "open" state that happens when we "let go" comprises cognitive, emotional, imagistic, and visceral elements difficult to convey precisely in words. Another image of letting go is to imagine holding a small rubber ball that will fit in the palm of your hand so that you can wrap your thumb and fingers around it. Imagine squeezing that ball very tightly, as tightly as you can, and notice all sensations, images, feelings, and thoughts that arise as you "hold on" very tightly. Now imagine suddenly letting go of the ball, suddenly releasing it—I call that letting go. What do you feel in your hand and in the rest of your body now that you have "let go"? Can you express in words what you feel in your body?

In 1979, I knew that my pain patients could not let go. And working with them forced me—allowed me—to discover that letting go was difficult for me also. Continuing to seek methods of experiencing feelings I could not access in talking treatment alone, I worked with a woman, Samantha, trained as a psychomotor therapist, focusing on how the body moves. I hoped to be able to discover how I could feel free to move and also understand what psychological processes interfered with moving freely. I also hoped that moving freely would generalize to feeling free to move cognitively and emotionally as well.

As I had anticipated, the work with Samantha was much more active than the Alexander lessons had been. It involved a lot of stretching and breath awareness while I was fully clothed. Some of it was done standing and some lying on the floor. I loved my teacher—she was warm, had a great sense of humor and a lovely voice, and was remarkably patient. I felt good being in her physical presence. I was amazed that, unlike Aunt Sadie, she did not criticize me or pressure me, even though I was not being a good student.

When I first wrote the preceding three sentences, I felt embarrassed, like a child in grade school talking about her favorite teacher. Awareness of feeling ashamed alerts me to recent writing by Schore (1994, 2003a, 2003b) and Bromberg (2003, 2006) about the significance of shame regulation in the development of trauma and in its treatment. My feeling ashamed that I had expressed loving feelings toward my teacher indicates that I still have dissociated shame about spontaneous expressions of affection that must have origins in what Bromberg (2006) calls "the early failure of responsiveness by the mother or father to some genuine aspect of the child's self." This "nonrecognition" or "masked withdrawal from authentic contact" with the child can lead to a "*structural* dissociation of a part of the self," which may interfere with the "early attachment process and in the capacity for mutual regulation" (p. 139). Other analysts (e.g., Corrigan & Gordon, 1995) have drawn on and elaborated Winnicott's (1960) formulation of a false self, which unfolds to make possible the survival of what Bromberg (2006) has referred to as nonrecognition. I could easily identify with this form of developmental trauma.

I see now that I needed Samantha's warm, accepting attitude because I was still very impatient with my body's limitations and deficiencies: I was still carrying around images of my "bad posture," and I felt physically inept, not well coordinated, and weak. I felt like a failure—I was not perfect and, for a child in my family system, being perfect was a survival strategy. I did not acknowledge to Samantha the importance of this relational dimension of the treatment. It was implicit; but my explicit recognition of it as I was writing evoked embarrassment, indicating that I still have dissociated shame around spontaneous, authentic expressions of self-experience.

In the sessions, I quickly discovered that I did not want to do the exercises, just as I had felt during the Alexander lessons. I rarely did my homework. This time, I was acutely aware that I wanted my teacher to "fix" me. "I need fixing and I don't want to have to do it myself!" This wish was not explicit, but we were enacting it in the sessions. Clearly, the transference and countertransference are vitally important in bodywork. Much is enacted and not understood as such because the frame does not allow it. I knew that I had been searching for a treatment arrangement that would help me to process psychologically my need to let go and my wish to be fixed. With Samantha, I was aware of this wish as I never had been in my talking treatment. There was something about her "presence" that facilitated my experiencing these feelings.

Years later, I realized that I was experiencing at a visceral level what Krystal (1988) and McDougall (1980, 1985, 1989) identified as common fantasies in people who have somatic symptoms and addictions. They speak about the fantasies as resistance to "owning" one's body in the belief that the body belongs to a powerful other such as God or Mother. In their view, these difficulties arise from developmental trauma in the relationship with the primary caregiver, severe trauma in adult life, or both. Prior to participating in bodywork, I had not "known" that I had such fantasies and resistance. At the time of the sessions with Samantha, I did not think of myself as having experienced trauma, so I was very puzzled by my "resistance to self-care."

I worked with Samantha for about 6 years. My posture changed—I was able to keep my chest open by *lowering* my shoulders and moving them backward. I learned, finally, that what my family had really been critical of was my natural tendency to curl my shoulders forward. Aunt Sadie could not criticize me any longer. I gained an intimate appreciation of how one's image of one's body parts becomes entwined with relationships with authority figures: I am still self-conscious of where my shoulders are resting, and I am very attuned to where other people's shoulders are positioned.

As I worked with Samantha and my analyst, I searched the analytic literature to locate help in treating my "difficult" patients—and found myself. A colleague who knew about my work with pain recommended one of Henry Krystal's early papers on alexithymia (1982/1983). His conceptualization validated my experiences with my patients who could not speak in words about their emotions and who often could not recognize that they had feelings. I realized that I had similar difficulty, although most people would never guess that I did. Winnicott's (1960) concept of false-self development pertained to the experiences of many of my patients. His understanding of the formative impact of the facilitating environment on the infant's development was richly supportive (Winnicott, 1965). I read all his work that I could find. *Playing and Reality* (1971) became a transitional object, given to me by my analyst to use during her two-and-a-half-month summer vacation.

I was particularly intrigued by Winnicott's (1949a) statement that infants remember every second of the birth process and by his description of the significance of the pressure on the head, and the need to relive that process in analytic treatment. I thought of the story my mother had told many times as I was growing up about her 48 hours of labor before I was delivered. I don't know if forceps were used. I thought of the comfort I felt in having my head held. I began to feel that I *needed* to have my head held, to feel pressure on my head, as Winnicott described. Discussing the impact of prolonged labor, he stated, "There can very easily be delay at a time when there is constriction round the head, and it is my definite view that the type of headache which is clearly described as a band round the head is sometimes a direct derivative of birth sensations remembered in somatic form" (1949b, p. 186).

My analyst, Dr. L, and I were working with the feelings of constriction that I experienced emotionally. In the fifth year, she broached the subject of how stuck we were and suggested that I consult with other analysts with whom I might more easily access my feelings, in particular, my negative feelings toward her and others. I was resistant for some time because I felt like a failure and I still idealized her. I was barely aware that I envied her, but we never dealt with my envy. I consulted with two male analysts she recommended, chose one, and we set a termination date for the end of that fifth year.

I was eager to have a termination dream. We had worked with dreams productively, she valued them, and I had come to value them. The night before my last session, I dreamed that I found a mutilated, murdered body hidden underneath my multigenerational family's dining room rug. I was trying to discover the identity of the body, a man, and to learn who had murdered him. I was stunned, perplexed, and disappointed by my dream. I felt that it revealed that I had failed in the analysis.

Over the years, I have come to appreciate the richness of that dream. Daily meals at my family's dining table were accompanied by long silences interspersed with harsh, gossipy critiques of all members of the extended family who were not present. At times, they would lash out at one another as well. Everyone was afraid of and utterly dependent on my stern, maternal grandmother, the family matriarch. I rarely said a word. Rather, I listened carefully to calculate exactly what I needed to do, or not do, to prevent such criticisms of me. Viscerally soaking up the aggression, I became a supersaturated sponge, as I sat silent, unmoving, and afraid.

I was shocked at the way my termination dream blatantly depicted my long-standing, compliant, goody-two-shoes adaptation, which I had refined so as to survive and, eventually, escape from my family circumstances. Dr. L and I "knew" the narrative very well: I was still hiding my murderous rage at my family for their aggression toward one another. I remained a supersaturated sponge. We had tried hard to bring that directly into our relationship.

As I learned more about trauma and its impact on the body, I realized that I was reflexively using my shoulders to protect myself from those tension-filled dynamics. My shoulders seemed to be curling forward as if to ward off those dangerous verbal assaults I had witnessed in family interactions and that I sought to avoid at all costs. My sympathetic nervous system was conditioned to respond reflexively to aggression, and my right shoulder is still hypervigilant. I have an exaggerated startle response as well, which I now understand as a response to sensory and emotional overstimulation at an early developmental stage.

The dining room rug in my dream belonged to my analyst; it was out of place in my family's dining room, which was covered with linoleum. She and I agreed that we had been unable to destabilize what Dr. Sarno refers to as "goodist," "people pleasing," perfectionistic behaviors that cover feelings of inferiority, fear, rage, and other threatening emotions. Together, Dr. L and I had hidden them under her Oriental rug, just as I had hidden "not nice" feelings from my family to avoid their disapproval and criticism. I ended the analysis feeling grateful for how much she had helped me, yet feeling that I had failed to learn how to tolerate and regulate my aggression. Nor had I touched on the envy underlying my idealization of her. I have found myself in Dr. L's shoes many times with my patients and appreciate how difficult a challenge I was to her.

Many years later, I met Dr. L in the lobby of a building while I was on my way to an appointment. We greeted each other amicably, and she asked how I was doing. I gave her a sketch. Then, to my surprise, she asked, "Are you still holding yourself so tightly?" as she scrunched her shoulders into the position I had worked so hard to change! Her question revealed that she had been very affected and regulated by my posture, but we had never discussed it. We had not created a space in which we could welcome my protective armor masquerading as slumping shoulders into the talking situation. I have had similar reactions to aspects of my patients' posture and have not always been able to bring these reactions into our relationship.

Developing a Somatic Symptom

By 1983, I had developed a symptom—tension headaches. Until then, I had not had somatic symptoms. I could remember only one headache in my life—a vivid memory. It occurred during my junior year of high school when I made a less-than-perfect score on a chemistry exam. I relied exclusively on my academic performance to escape the clutches of my insular family system and repressive Southern culture. I had always had the highest GPA in my class, and I intended to keep it that way. But the chemistry instructor had given an exam that had nothing to do with the material covered in class. Unable to feel furious, I was devastated; I could not stop thinking about my poor grade and the lost opportunities it heralded. I felt an endless loop playing in my head. Two days later, I got a headache that required a family member to take me home from school, a first. I was nauseated and extremely sensitive to light. It was probably a migraine, but I was not given a diagnosis and no one knew how upset I was about my bad grade.

The life context in which I gradually developed a pattern of headaches was fraught with similar dynamics: Like many of my pain patients, trying my best to do a "perfect job," I was putting extraordinary pressure on myself in a situation that placed objective external limitations on what I could accomplish. I knew I was furious but was not able to use my anger effectively enough to have an impact on the system in which I was working. After a few years, I chose to leave the situation, a move that relieved my symptoms for a few months. I took my perfectionism and its companion, rage, with me, however. My headaches returned as I created more and more impingements.

In my new analysis with Dr. W, recommended by Dr. L, I quickly developed an idealizing father transference—he was very smart and must have all the answers. Certainly he could "fix me." The analysis was intense but my emotions were still difficult to access. I looked for a "more powerful" bodywork to complement the talking process. I wanted to have bodily experiences that would give me easier access to my feelings.

A friend recommended her bodyworker, Monique, who combined bioenergetic techniques with kundalini yoga breathing to open areas of "energy" blocked by emotional "holding" in different areas of the body (see Bass & Newman, this volume, regarding the concept of energy). I did not know what all that meant, but I wanted to try it, hoping that this mode of experiencing would enhance my talking analysis. I made a point of not researching bioenergetics and kundalini yoga beyond the basics I already knew because I wanted to enter the work openly, still trying to counter a tendency to overconceptualize, to have everything already worked out in my "head."

Monique was quiet and calm. Her voice was soothing and her hands were remarkable—surprisingly small, powerful, and boundaried are the best descriptors I can find. She worked as I lay on my back on a massage table, wearing only underpants. She would have treated me fully clothed but explained that it was easier for her to see my breathing and changes in blood circulation if I wore fewer clothes. Her explanation made me feel comfortable working this way. She directed my breathing into different areas of my body where she sensed that energy was blocked: She was the authority about what was happening in my body. I hated the breathing. In fact, I did not want to have to breathe. I complied, however, because I always felt better after a session. The last 10 minutes or so of each session, I could breathe naturally while she worked on my head as she listened to sounds in my belly with a stethoscope. She was aiming to stimulate normal peristalsis in the lower gastrointestinal tract. I never asked her why this method worked nor why it was important. This was my favorite part of the session.

After three sessions, I had a dream that contained disturbing, vivid body imagery. I remember it as clearly as if it had happened last night. I still get chills if I tell it. Although Monique encouraged me to work with dreams and incorporate talking in the sessions, I did not tell her the dream because she was not trained as a therapist. Dr. W and I worked on the dream but with little success.

The emotional impact of the bodywork with Monique, in the context of an intense, idealizing transference to my analyst, proved unmanageable. Specifically, my idealized analyst became openly exasperated with me in reaction to my constant complaints about insurmountable limitations in current primary relationships, including my relationship with him. I was appalled that I was becoming a "difficult" patient, much more openly than with Dr. L.

We conceptualized what was happening as my "acting out." I think of it now as an "enactment" that was unfolding, like a screenplay. His open, verbal response of being fed up was much like my mother's when I pressed her too hard to get what I wanted. With my mother, I felt guilty. With my analyst, I felt criticized. For the first time, I reacted by being a "bad girl," both inside and outside the treatment. I was breaking rules, defiantly—something I had never done. I was reacting to feeling unrecognized and misunderstood by him and by significant people in my life. I was certainly *feeling* more intensely than ever, but my analyst did not recognize the hurt, disappointment, and rage that I barely disguised by my rebellious behavior. After 8 months of combined treatments, I ended both. I felt that the bodywork was too intense and unboundaried; I was afraid of what might emerge next. I felt jarred and disillusioned with psychoanalysis. My idealization of Dr. W was shattered, and I lost hope and trust that he could "fix" me. We could not repair the rupture in our relationship, although we tried.

Looking back, I can see that Dr. W and I had entered what Bromberg (1998) has referred to as the "messy" part of the analytic relationship. While writing this chapter, I thought of a conversation I had a couple of months ago with Bromberg on the topic of being "difficult." He is comfortable with being difficult and likes to work with difficult patients. I found myself saying, "Philip, I aspire to tolerate being thought of as difficult!"

I have come a long way since the enactment that disrupted my analysis in 1985. For the next several years, in the same month I had had that powerful dream, I had a dream with the same theme, which I have come to articulate as "Learning to stay in the room when something dreadful is happening." (More about this dream later.) On two occasions, I awoke from the dream unable to move because of pain in my lower back. Eight years later, when I began to study the impact of emotional and physical trauma on the mindbody system, I came to think of the dream as containing information about trauma and dissociation. In the dream, the body images represented trauma— "The body keeps the score" (van der Kolk, 1994)—just as my dream about the mutilated murdered body under my family/analyst's carpet was conveying information about traumatic affect that could not be

easily regulated and integrated into family, interpersonal relationships, and my relationship with my idealized analyst.

After I ended that analysis, for the next couple of years I tried
to figure out what had happened in the chemistry of my idealizing analytic transference and the bodywork. Trusting that I would
find my way, I read voraciously, had consultations with analysts of
varying orientations, and paid a lot of attention to my dreams. For
a while, I thought I was incapable of being analyzed. I now think of
this period of solo exploration as one of building a sense of agency. I
continued to look for literature to help me treat my patients who had
chronic pain, and I continued to puzzle about my headaches. When
I discovered Joyce McDougall's (1980) work, I felt understood and
relieved as analyst and patient. She describes an enactment in which
she and her patient became mutually exasperated and hopeless. Her
patient lashed out at her. This rupture opened her patient up to previously inaccessible feelings. It shed some light on what had triggered
the enactment with Dr. W.

As I read more, I felt hopeful again because of what Dr. McDougall
had to say about how experiencing and not experiencing affect was
related to the development of somatic symptoms. I consulted her
for a referral to an analyst, Dr. G, with whom I began treatment. I
continued to study in supervision with Dr. McDougall. I was fascinated with the psychoanalytic concept of affect as a link between
mind and body and used Krystal's (1988) information-processing
model of affects in my discussion of the psychoanalytic treatment of
pain (Anderson, 1998).

Affect regulation has become a key construct in understanding
the development of the mindbody system (Schore, 1994, 2003a) and
the impact of trauma (Schore, 2003b; van der Kolk, 1994; van der
Kolk, McFarlane, & Weisaeth, 1996). This literature gave me a new
perspective on my own development and symptom. Through the lens
of trauma, I could now begin to answer a question I had posed to
my analyst, "Why do I have somatic symptoms?" I didn't experience
developmental trauma severe enough to be affecting me somatically.

Prompted by the literature on attachment trauma, I asked my
family for details about a traumatic separation that they had always
mentioned casually, even matter-of-factly, as I was growing up. The
narrative was that I had been separated from my mother in a marital
dispute when I was about a year and a half old. No one could remember
how long the separation had lasted or how it had affected me or them.

As I was gathering details about this calamity, my mother mentioned that, again in the context of a dispute between my parents, I had been separated from her, against her will, when I was about 10 days old. As she told me the details, I remember getting chills, then feeling frozen, and suffering a strong visceral sense of dread. I wanted and yet did not want to know more (Laub & Auerhahn, 1993). She could not remember how long the separation had lasted but said that, when we were reunited, "Everybody was worried about you. All you did was sleep. You didn't move." I was stunned. I tried to ask some questions, get some details, but she could not remember how long I was in this separation-induced traumatized state.

A year prior to getting this information from my mother, I had spent several months on the analytic couch, four sessions a week, feeling like "petrified wood," not wanting to move, not feeling anything, not wanting to speak. Dr. G tried every possible way to engage me, but without success. We could not make sense of my unreachable state. As soon as I heard my mother's answers to those questions about my developmental trauma, that period in my analysis began to make sense. I gained a new appreciation of the concept of "ownership" of one's body. I understood better the deficits that interfere with ownership and the resistance to ownership I had experienced in bodywork, in analytic treatment, and in trying to take care of myself.

On reflection 15 years later, I feel that I was reliving what I think of as a "layering" of traumatic states in an enactment with my analyst: birth trauma, infantile trauma in the second week of life, and separation trauma when I was about 18 months old. She tried very hard to reach me but she failed. I remember that the "petrified wood" period had been triggered by my feeling that I could not make her understand why I had felt so keenly "abandoned" in an important relationship. I gave up and lapsed into an unmoving, unreachable state. Eventually she told me that she had become aware of a traumatic experience she had survived that she thought contributed to her difficulty reaching me. It was not her theoretical orientation to elaborate further, and I was not assertive enough to ask her to tell me more. I eventually began speaking and continued in the analysis without our understanding the significance of the "petrified wood" state.

I believe that it was inevitable that traumatized states, which I had been contacting in bodywork, would emerge in my analytic relationship. The bodywork facilitated their emergence. The vivid dream I had in 1985 in the context of bodywork and an intense transference now began to make sense. The dream contained an image of an alive but immobilized preadolescent girl who was being physically traumatized as I watched. Her pale, unmoving body, frozen in a protective reaction to traumatic stimulation, carries information about residues of trauma that can still cause the cognitive and affective paralysis I experience, so aptly described by Laub and Auerhahn (1993). The traumatized preadolescent body, along with the narrative of the infantile traumatized state I experienced in the early weeks of life when I "didn't move," have helped me understand why I can become exhausted, immobilized, and frozen, conceptually and somatically, in response to sensory, emotional, and cognitive stimulation. For instance, it sheds light on the constricted, compressed-bud, cognitive state I described at the beginning of this chapter. I have come to realize that I can easily be overstimulated when I have overworked, and that I usually need a period of prolonged, silent rest, preferably meditation or bodywork, in order to recover. Bodywork and meditation, combined with analysis, have made it possible for me to make contact and gradually integrate dissociated frozen, unmoving, immobilized states. I am still learning how to self-regulate in order to feel restored and revitalized. The willingness to do so is slowly developing. I am still processing the images in that dream as I continue learn about the lasting impact of developmental trauma.

Additional Bodywork Experiences

In the past 15 years, I have continued to explore different kinds of bodywork/treatment. For example, having read about biofeedback as treatment for a variety of physical symptoms, I decided to experience it. The practitioner monitored tension in my forehead muscles and the temperature in my index finger. I could easily change the tension and temperature by using an image of my deaf cat, Herzog, resting on my chest while my yoga teacher, Alicia, sat behind me and held my head.

This was an impressive demonstration of the power of "relational" imagery to regulate internal, visceral states. Specifically, my emotional relationship with Herzog was based entirely on communication through visual and tactile cues. My husband and I referred to him, affectionately, as our "healing" cat because of his ability to seek us out when were feeling despondent or ill and soothe us with his presence. In the image I created in the biofeedback session, I placed Herzog on my chest and recalled an incident 20 years earlier when he had "healed" me. Herzog had found me weeping in bed, inconsolable because of a distressing phone call from my husband, hospitalized for several weeks due to postsurgical complications. I was lying on my back when Herzog jumped on the bed and climbed onto my chest. Aligning himself perfectly along the midline of my chest, he rested his nose on my chin. He remained there long after I had stopped crying. This is the most powerful bodywork experience I have ever had.

I returned several times to do bodywork with Monique. Noting that she had to work very hard to get my energy to flow, she observed many times during the sessions that it was "sluggish." I did not tell her that I felt criticized and ashamed—I did not work with her in that way, even though she was open to doing body-oriented psychotherapy (versus only bodywork; see Cornell, this volume). In the sessions, she could always help me change my somatic/emotional state. I always felt better after the session. I craved that release. The problem was that I could not, or would not, do it for myself. I felt completely dependent on her, which made me feel ashamed, helpless, and furious. She gave me exercises to do on my own, but I still did not want to have to self-regulate.

I was stunned when she announced that she was retiring, giving only 2 months' notice. I felt abandoned and desperate. Fleeing from these feelings, I tried another kind of treatment I had heard about from friends—craniosacral therapy (see Bass, this volume). I consulted the practitioner, Janine, whom they had highly recommended. One friend had been recommending her for more than a year. I had called Janine for an appointment several times but never left a message because her voice seemed closed and dismissive. Now I felt desperate, so I made an appointment. When I saw her, I had a sinking feeling about the expression in her eyes. That, combined with her restrained manner, which was consistent with her voice quality and intonation on the phone, made me wary. I went forward with the session anyway. She took a developmental history and reported that she could see evidence of birth trauma during the prolonged delivery in my face and head. This was on target and gave me hope.

She conducted the hands-on treatment as I lay on a massage table wearing underpants. Gently holding and moving different parts of my body, she focused a great deal on my head—wonderful! A skilled practitioner, she could take me into states of "letting go" that I had never experienced. In these open states, I found myself sharing associations and images with her, disclosing details that made me feel ashamed immediately because of her perfunctory, dismissive response. My longing to be taken care of was awakened again, and I started to feel acute dependency on her to change my state, despite my negative reactions to her nonverbal cues. She did not consciously invite dependency in the interpersonal realm. In fact, she seemed to discourage it.

I was in a bind: I felt invited to let go and open but felt unsupported and rejected when I accepted the invitation. We did not create a safe, contained space in which I could integrate what the bodywork was unleashing. Unfortunately, I left the sessions disoriented, ungrounded, longing, craving more sessions, and feeling very dependent on her to change my state. I started to feel angry and had to find a way to dissociate it in order to continue the work. Once, after a particularly powerful session, I tripped on the sidewalk a couple of blocks down the street from her office, barely escaping serious injury. This kind of event can happen to anyone, anytime, anywhere, but I am convinced that it happened because I had not made a transition to an alert, awake, grounded state. I realized that I did not feel safe enough to continue to work with her.

Boundaries in Bodywork

Explicitly, boundaries can be particularly difficult to define when one is working in an area where words cannot easily be used as markers, as limit-setters. In contrast to the talking situation, where "Do not touch" is explicit, in body-focused treatments I have experienced, I relied on the implicit, usually unarticulated, judgment of the bodyworker. When the work is "hands-on," the bodyworker's judgment is particularly more important because he or she may not be able to verbalize what is being done and why. Such an unbounded space can "open" the patient to dissociated self-states that the patient is not prepared to integrate. The bodyworkers' conscious and unconscious intention, as well as their skill, becomes very important. Often it is unacknowledged or addressed because the bodyworker has not been trained to incorporate this dimension of the treatment.

For example, take my right shoulder, which prefers to curve in slightly, after all these years. Every bodyworker I have consulted has noted it immediately and tried to get it to open, usually without asking "permission" (see Bass, this volume). I remember a session with a highly skilled massage therapist and bodyworker, recommended by a trusted friend. She incorporated a variety of hands-on techniques in her treatments. Consciously, I was ready to participate in this session, even though there was something about her nervous laugh that had unsettled me from our first conversation on the phone. I had taken a group workshop with her and felt unsettled there as well, for the same reason. In the individual session, when I was open and disclosing, she made lighthearted, joking remarks, which were jarring. I experienced her as pushing me away, and I felt bad about myself. Her hands-on work was excellent, however. She worked very gently with my shoulder, almost not touching it. My shoulder cooperated—she was able to take it into an open, properly aligned position that I never recall having attained. I "felt" very open and amazed that such a state was possible. I rushed from the session back to my office. Within half an hour my right shoulder had rebounded into a position far tighter than ever, and I had a severe headache. I, the patient, had participated willingly in the treatment, which had nonetheless produced a result that neither of us had anticipated. I have had similar experiences with practitioners of other modalities, for example, bioenergetic therapy.

What we did not do in the session I just described was inquire about why my shoulder seems to need to be in the curved in position all the time. I have not worked with a practitioner who inquired about what my shoulder is communicating through its preferred position. Rather, I have given over my body to the authority of the bodyworker. In the talking situation, we might think not of my shoulder as "resisting" but as the body expressing an unsymbolized, or subsymbolic, self-state in reaction to traumatic overstimulation—an embodiment that has become chronic and unmoving. My study of the impact of trauma on the mindbody system has helped me appreciate how my body was affected by my family's emotional violence manifested in their harsh critiques around the dining table. Unfortunately, my bodyworker did not have this information about me. In the talking frame, it is the therapist's job to respect and inquire about a bodily state such as this before trying to change it. That was not my experience in the bodywork modalities I have described. This omission led to some of the intense reactions I experienced, e.g., the pronounced opening of my right shoulder followed quickly by its retraction once the session was over. In the new body-based talking therapies, such as Somatic Experiencing (Levine, 1997, 2005; Eldredge & Cole, this volume) and Sensorimotor Psychotherapy (Ogden, Minton, & Pain, 2006), the practitioner, respecting my shoulder's position, would recognize the possibility that it had assumed this chronic "poorly aligned" position as a protective response to trauma of some kind. The practitioner would inquire in detail about my sensory experience of my shoulder before collaborating with me to make interventions to change its position.

Another consideration regarding bodywork interventions is that changes in the body's position and movement can quickly evoke affect-laden self-states that neither the practitioner nor the patient may be able to regulate adequately. For example, I worked in individual sessions with a yoga teacher, Alicia, mentioned earlier. I had an instantaneous positive transference from the moment I heard her voice on the phone. When I saw her, I felt completely open, filled with hope and longing to be soothed and healed by her. Her calm, focused attention to breathing work on the floor, without touching me, "held" me in a way I had never experienced. At the end of our first session, when we did a brief silent meditation, she was simultaneously completely silent and fully present in a way no one else ever had been.

I was in bliss when we worked on the floor. As soon as I had to stand, to our surprise, I became overwhelmed and would start to cry. Neither of understood what was happening. She instinctively suggested that I move into "child's pose" (kneel, sit on your heels, fold your torso forward to rest it on, or between, your thighs, hands on the floor alongside the torso with palms up) on the floor. She sat beside me, rested her hand on the middle of my back, and left it there until I stopped crying. What had happened? I knew a good deal about what was unfolding, but we did not have a way to integrate the "meaning" of this emotional experience in our treatment relationship. I was looking for an integrative experience that she was not trained to provide.

Those examples, among others, have led me to realize that it is crucial to choose carefully when and with whom to open, and how far to open. This discernment is particularly important for people who know that they have a history of trauma. When I began bodywork, I did not "know" about the developmental traumas I had experienced. I knew that some of my experiences had been challenging but I had no idea *how* challenging. Choosing a bodyworker is as important a decision as choosing an analyst.

I cannot emphasize strongly enough how important the transference and countertransference are in bodywork. I tell people who ask for recommendations that they need to check their gut reaction to the bodyworker. I tell them to ask themselves, "When I think of X, what do I feel in my body? Do I feel like opening up or closing down? What is it about X that makes me feel that way?" Feeling like opening up may not necessarily be a good thing, unless the practitioner is prepared to work with eruptions of affect and help the patient regulate and integrate it. Feeling like you are closing down is usually not a positive indicator: Why would you put yourself in a treatment situation where opening is usually a goal when your visceral sense is, "No, don't go there."

I now give the same recommendations to people when they are choosing an analyst. At the end of the initial consultation, I invite patients to be aware of and to feel free to share their visceral reactions to me—to my body, to my voice, to my office. When I teach physical therapists, yoga teachers, and other bodyworkers about pain, trauma, and the treatment relationship, I focus on the significance of the transference–countertransference configuration and the importance of openly setting up communication about boundaries.

Conclusions

When I was at a loss for words and feelings, I sought experiences in the nonverbal, subsymbolic realm to help me find words for what I could not speak about and to access feelings that I could link with the words in my verbal narrative. In the world of moving and breathing—the sensory, motoric, and visceral domain—I made contact with what Winnicott (1960) referred to as the true self, the source of the spontaneous gesture. I conceptualize these experiences as authentic self-states, dissociated long ago in an effort to survive.

Transferences to my bodyworkers proved more affective-laden than transferences to my psychoanalysts. The physical presence of the bodyworker and the immediacy of body contact, without the boundaries provided by words and interpretations, activated previously unconscious feelings of longing to be held, soothed, healed, and fixed. My understanding of Bucci's (1997) model is that this treatment modality quickly engaged the affective core of emotion schemata, the prototypic images of the self interacting with others: "The emerging image of the caretaker is the crucial, enduring prototypic symbol about which the emotion schemata are organized from the beginning of life" (p. 162). The affective core is dominated by sensory, motoric, and visceral elements, and in normal emotional development, these must be integrated into the emotion schemas.

Bodywork, combined with traditional analysis, helped me discover developmental trauma at a visceral and affective level, through transferences to my bodyworkers and analysts and through imagery in dreams. My tranferences to bodyworkers opened the portal to intense experiences evocative of birth trauma and separation trauma, previously dissociated. In two instances—my mother's prolonged labor and the separation from her when I was a year and half—the traumatic events were part of my narrative, but I did not have affective connections with the narrative. In another instance, a separation in the second week of life, I did not know the narrative of the event but discovered that I had been carrying the residues in somatic memory. The residues in bodywork manifested in my attitude of not wanting to "do my homework" and in wanting to be "fixed," "soothed," and "healed." In an enactment with my analyst, a residue was my feeling like "petrified wood" and not moving or speaking.

Bodywork can be a powerful adjunct to psychoanalysis. The unbounded space of bodywork can, however, enable access to affect-laden self-states that are alarming and difficult to regulate and integrate. Such self-states elicited in the bodywork domain often are not easily accessed in the analytic frame, which makes it difficult to integrate them. Both bodyworker and psychoanalyst need to be prepared to collaborate in these instances. When the analyst and the patient "know" about trauma, they need to carefully consider the type of bodywork, and the bodyworker needs to be aware of the narrative. Ideally, bodyworkers need training about psychological mechanisms, trauma, transference, and countertransference. Psychoanalysts need to know more about the body and to experience bodywork themselves to expand their awareness of the complexity of the mindbody system. I hope that our efforts in this volume will stimulate interest in learning from each other.

References

Anderson, F. S. (1998). Psychic elaboration of musculoskeletal pain: Ellen's story. In L. Aron & F. S. Anderson (Eds.), *Relational perspectives on the body* (pp. 287–322). Hillsdale, NJ: The Analytic Press.

Anderson, F. S., Bardach, J., & Goodgold, J. (1979). *Sexuality and neuromuscular disease* (Rehabilitation Monograph No. 56). New York: Institute of Rehabilitation Medicine & the Muscular Dystrophy Association.

Anderson, F. S., & Gold, J. (2003). Trauma, dissociation, and conflict: The space where neuroscience, cognitive science, and psychoanalysis overlap. *Psychoanal. Psychol., 20,* 536–541.

Bromberg, P. M. (1998). *Standing in the spaces: Essays on clinical process, trauma, and dissociation.* Hillsdale, NJ: The Analytic Press.

Bromberg, P. M. (2006). *Awakening the dreamer: Clinical journeys.* Mahwah, NJ: The Analytic Press.

Bucci, W. (1997). Symptoms and symbols: A multiple code theory of somatization. *Psychoanal. Inq., 17,* 151–172.

Bucci, W. (2001). Pathways of emotional communication. *Psychoanal. Inq., 21,* 40–70.

Bucci, W. (2003). Varieties of dissociative experience: A multiple code account and a discussion of Bromberg's case of "William." *Psychoanal. Psychol., 20,* 542–557.

Corrigan, E. G., & Gordon, P. (1995). The mind as an object. In E. G. Corrigan & P. Gordon (Eds.), *The mind object* (pp. 1–22). Northvale, NJ: Aronson.

Fosshage, J. (1997). The organizing functions of dream mentation. *Contemp. Psychoanal., 33,* 429–458.

Krystal, H. (1982/1983). Alexithymia and the effectiveness of psychoanalytic treatment. *Internat. J. Psychoanal. Psychother., 9,* 353–388.

Krystal, H. (1988). *Integration and self-healing.* Hillsdale, NJ: The Analytic Press.

Laub, D., & Auerhahn, N. (1993). Knowing and not knowing massive psychic trauma: Forms of traumatic memory. *Internat. J. Psycho-Anal., 74,* 287–302.

Levine, P. (1997). *Waking the tiger: Healing trauma: The innate capacity to transform overwhelming experiences.* Berkeley, CA: North Atlantic Books.

Levine, P. (2005). *Healing trauma: A pioneering program for restoring the wisdom of your body.* Boulder, CO: Sounds True.

McDougall, J. (1980). *A plea for a measure of abnormality.* New York: International Universities Press.

McDougall, J. (1985). *Theaters of the mind: Illusion and truth on the psychoanalytic stage.* New York: Basic Books.

McDougall, J. (1989). *Theaters of the body.* New York: Norton.

Ogden, P., Minton, K., & Pain, C. (2006). *Trauma and the body: A senso-rimotor approach to psychotherapy.* New York: Norton.

Robertson, C. (2006, May 26). Being Joan Didion. *The New York Times,* pp. E1–E2.

Sarno, J. E. (1991). *Healing back pain.* New York: Warner Books.

Sarno, J. E. (1998). *The mindbody prescription.* New York: Warner Books.

Sarno, J. E. (2006). *The divided mind: The epidemic of mindbody disorders.* New York: Regan Books/HarperCollins.

Schore, A. N. (1994). *Affect regulation and the origin of the self.* Hillsdale, NJ: Lawrence Erlbaum Associates.

Schore, A. N. (2003a). *Affect regulation and disorders of the self.* New York: Norton.

Schore, A. N. (2003b). *Affect regulation and the repair of the self.* New York: Norton.

van der Kolk, B. A. (1994). The body keeps the score: Memory and the evolving psychobiology of posttraumatic stress. *Harv. Rev. Psychiat., 1,* 253–265.

van der Kolk, B. A., McFarlane, A. C., & Weisaeth, L. (Eds.). (1996). *Traumatic stress.* New York: Guilford.

Winnicott, D. W. (1949a). Mind and its relation to the psycho-soma. In *Through paediatrics to psycho-analysis* (pp. 243–254). New York: Basic Books, 1975.

Winnicott, D. W. (1949b). Birth memories, birth trauma, and anxiety. In *Through paediatrics to psycho-analysis* (pp. 174–193). New York: Basic Books, 1975.

Winnicott, D. W. (1960). Ego distortion in terms of true and false self. In *The maturational processes and the facilitating environment* (pp. 140–152). New York: International Universities Press, 1965.

Winnicott, D. W. (1965). *The maturational processes and the facilitating environment.* New York: International Universities Press.

Winnicott, D. W. (1971). *Playing and reality.* New York: Basic Books.

Winnicott, D. W. (1975). *Through paediatrics to psycho-analysis.* New York: Basic Books.

Part I.

Bodily Experience in Self-Organization: Contemporary Views

2

Self in Action

The Bodily Basis of Self-Organization

William F. Cornell

> From the start of life, a newborn infant moves to communicate "interest."
> ... Face, voice, hands, the whole body display the dynamic impulses of
> seeking for conscious awareness and for testing changes in reality "out-
> side." ... thus the infant shows us it has a "self" that intends. (Trevarthan,
> 2004, pp. 3–4)

> The mature mind, not a body-free structure of logic and rationality, is a
> body-based organization of increasingly sophisticated and nuanced pat-
> terns of experience in which the personal and emotional are of continuing
> importance. (Fast, 2006, p. 275)

There were but two early childhood memories, both in the upstairs
living room of my maternal grandparents' house, a second-floor flat
in which my mother, father, and I lived until I was nearly 4 years
old. The first memory was a visual image of the brown slats of a
wooden playpen. There was no narrative, no sequence of events, only
the image of the slats and the sensation of my back pressing against
the wood. The other memory, taking place in the same room, was the
music of the refrain of "Hernando's Hideaway," and the sensation of
being carried in my mother's arms as she danced.

I presented these memories in a workshop at the beginning of
my training as a psychotherapist. The workshop leader, Christopher
Whitmont (1972, 1973), a Jungian analyst, noted that my memories
were held as physical sensations rather than as stories or images.

He explained that in working with early memories or dreams, he attended to the primary mode of experience in the memory/dream: be it somatic sensation, visual imagery, or narrative. He then worked to explore the material, using Jung's concept of active imagination, within the primary mode of experience with which the memory or dream was organized.

He suggested we work with my memories as sensate experiences and see what we might discover. He asked that I sit with my eyes closed, centering my attention on the sensation of the slats against my back, and notice any inclination of my body to move. He encouraged me to inhabit each sensation and movement. The sensations were startlingly vivid and profoundly disturbing. I found myself standing, arching backward, pressing into the air with my back, the sensation of the slats sharpening. I wanted to bang my head. I wailed. The only movement available to my body was to press backward and against. With these sensations came a deep and familiar ache of loneliness. I finally collapsed to the floor in tears, feeling lonely to the core.

Whitmont waited in silent attention for my distress to subside. He then pointed out that I had presented two memories and asked if I would like to move into the other. Again he asked not that I remember and tell the memory, but that I move into it, that I let it move within me. He asked that I hear the music and feel the sensation of the music in my body. It was immediate. In my mental recall of this experience, I remembered the music sweetly. I had associated it with older childhood memories of dancing the jitterbug with my mother, to an LP that I still have. But the experience in my body as I moved into this music was not so sweet. I felt a deep tenderness toward my mother. I felt the sensation of the dance, held to my mother's body. And I felt the intense, melancholic loneliness of her body. I wept again and felt lonely still. I felt loneliness alone and loneliness with and in my mother.

I had entered psychotherapy training after a highly intellectual graduate program in phenomenology. I was in a phase of overworking, overly responsible early adult life, following an adolescence of drug dependency and heroin addiction. In these embodied memories I got my first glimpse of the functions of both my manic and my addictive efforts to ward off this profound loneliness.

It was in that singular piece of bodywork early in my training that I learned something about myself that I would return to again and again over the course of my body psychotherapy and subsequent psychoanalysis. The sensations of that bodily exploration of those two memories informed me of something fundamental about myself. I remembered it in my body, I explored it through my body, and the experience shaped my development as a psychotherapist. I did not yet know the theory or the techniques of body psychotherapy or bodywork, but I knew that the direct engagement of the body would be an essential element in my work as a psychotherapist.

It is not uncommon, in the midst of deep relational psychoanalysis, for the body—be it that of the client or the therapist—to present itself in the therapeutic playing field, often unbidden and unsettling in its arrival (Bucci, 2001; Knoblauch, 2000, 1999; La Barre, 2005, 2001; Lyons-Ruth, 1999; McLaughlin, 2005; Wayne, 1999; Wrye, 1999). In the classical analytic model of the "talking cure," mind was privileged over body in the enduring expectation that everything that "comes to mind" (the patient's mind) was to be put into language, and the analyst (should she offer any response at all) should respond in kind with language. When language "fails" and the somatic takes over, it was assumed that the therapeutic dyad had fallen into some mutual enactment or, even worse, regression. Contemporary models of psychoanalysis—object relations, neo-Kleinian, and relational—have opened up new therapeutic terrain in their deepening attention to the relational field.

In contemporary relational models, patient and analyst alike have the option of speaking their minds and emotions. The unconscious relational field tends to inevitably cast patient and analyst alike into states of affective and somatic experience, raising the question "What comes to body?" in addition to that of what comes to mind.

When the body shows up (for the patient or the therapist) in the consulting room, what is an analyst to do with it? Ignore it and hope that it goes away? Talk faster? Interpret more brilliantly? Seek supervision? Refer out? This chapter is designed to inform an analytic audience of some of the primary body-centered modalities that can supplement the psychoanalytic process in providing systematic attention to somatic patterns or that can be incorporated within the psychoanalytic endeavor, drawing upon sensate experience or exploratory movements so as to deepen self-awareness and more fully inhabit what we have come to understand as implicit/procedural knowledge and subsymbolic processing.

In a mode of therapy such as psychoanalysis that has historically valorized the capacities for language and verbal symbolization, the emergence of the body is often, I suspect, more disturbing to the analyst than to the patient. Contemporary relational paradigms increasingly see the experience of nonverbal, somatically centered experiences in the consulting room as informative and communicative (Anderson, Resnick, & Glassman, 2005; Aron & Anderson, 1998; Beebe, 2004; Dorpat, 2001; Knoblauch, 2000; La Barre, 2001; McLaughlin, 2005; Rick, 2001; Shapiro, 1996) in sharp contrast to the more traditional analytic understanding of bodily manifestations within the analytic dyad as regressive or defensive acting out.

In this chapter, I will speak primarily about "the body" in human development and psychoanalysis, in keeping with the title of this volume. In so doing, I am maintaining a cultural artifact and an artifact of the dominant attitude toward "the body" over the course of psychoanalytic history. The body is, of course, never actually without a mind, and the mind is never without the body. These are in lived reality and neurophysiological processing a functional unity, no matter how persistently (and inadvertently) we split them apart in our language and theories (Aisenstein, 2006; Bucci, 1997a, 1997b; Fast, 2006; Johnson, 1987; Mancia, 2006; Pally, 1998).

Relational sensibilities and the growing influence of parent/infant research seek to describe and emphasize dyadic and intersubjective experience, be it that of parent and infant or analyst and patient. To my mind, however, what the relational perspective too often overlooks is the fact that we as infants, children, and adults spend significant amounts of time *alone*, in a solitary relation to our own thoughts, affect states, reveries, and bodies. And when alone, we are not simply waiting desperately for someone else to show up so that we can be engaged in some sort of dyadic completion. An enormous amount of learning, of psychic growth, of self-organization and dis-organization happen through our bodily experience when alone, engaged with one's self in the tasks of psychomotor mastery and in interaction with the physical environment.

One's relation to one's own body, at all phases of life, is central in the development of a cohesive sense of self agency (Brewer, 1995; Butterworth, 1995; Goldfield & Wolff, 2004; Krueger, 2002). As Shaw observes, "The body is not merely an imbiber of external stimuli. ... Our bodies are the means by which we engage with the world; they are how we come to understand our environment and make sense of our place in the world" (2003, p. 40).

Seen from a body-centered perspective, human development swings constantly, throughout the course of life, between the body in relation to others (Cornell, 1997, 2000, 2004, in press) and the body in relation to itself—that is, the realm of sensation, sensorimotor organization, and bodily movement. Psychomotor development precedes and underscores the life of the mind and is foundational in the development of self-agency as well as interpersonal relatedness (Downing, 1996). Subsymbolic learning and organization are never fully replaced by cognitive and symbolic processes. These dual realms of intrapsychic and interpersonal organization remain in constant dialogue, often in a dialectal tension.

Within the diverse range of modalities characterized as body-centered psychotherapy and bodywork, the body itself is the primary field of therapeutic endeavor. The therapeutic process may well be brought into language, but the direct work with bodily movement and sensate experience is understood to be a central mechanism of self-learning and change. Body-centered modalities seek to stress self-learning through direct exploration and experience of the body, assume a life-long plasticity of sensorimotor and psychomotoric systems, and understand the work to be accessing systems of implicit memory (Aposhyan, 2004; Cornell, 2003; Fogel, 2004) and subsymbolic organization (Bucci, 1997a, 1997b). It is beyond the scope of this single chapter to present comprehensive overviews of both body-centered psychotherapy and bodywork. Body-centered psychotherapy, most often anchored in a neo-Riechian or Gestalt foundation, views bodily experience and expression from a psychodynamic perspective as a mirror to the mind and as providing avenues of intervention in intrapsychic and characterological structure and self-understanding. As this chapter focuses on the role of the body in self-organization and psychoanalytic self-investigation, my primary attention here will be to models of bodywork. Bodywork seeks to provide avenues for direct exploration of sensory, postural, and movement patterns. Bodywork practitioners seek to inform and enliven a client's body through altering chronic patterns of breathing, posture, and muscular configurations through body awareness, experiments with novel and exploratory movements, and hands-on physical manipulation of the client's body.

The history of psychoanalysis and the history of bodywork have run in precarious parallels of mutual interest and suspicion. Vienna, Baden-Baden, Budapest, and Berlin were all sites of psychoanalytic excursions into bodywork. With their bold and rather poorly informed experiments with direct somatic interventions in the treatment of hysteria, Freud and Breuer seemed to have frightened (if not traumatized) themselves. The body, as a result, was increasingly banished to the sidelines of the psychoanalytic endeavor.

But attention to the body did not disappear altogether. Groddeck, at his spa and residential clinic, incorporated massage, deep tissue work, sensory awareness, hot baths, special diets, exercise, and his own brand of psychoanalytic inquiry into his therapeutic regimens. He maintained a friendly relationship with Freud, and his work influenced Ferenczi and Reich. Ferenczi, Horney, and Fromm-Reichmann, among other analysts, were visitors to Groddeck's clinic.

Ferenczi experimented constantly. Initially, he actively discouraged the patient's bodily movements, which he understood as a defense against free association, imagining that this stilling would facilitate the verbal associative processes at the heart of the talking cure. He noticed that this did not necessarily work as he'd had expected, so he began to experiment and, influenced by his contact with Groddeck (Downing, 1996; Ferenczi, 1917/1955, 1921/1955 ; Rachman, 1997), began to work actively with the patient's body process, intervening directly in patterns of body movement and expression (Ferenczi, 1920/1955, 1928/1955, 1930/1955). His experimentation was not well received by many of his analytic peers. Once at the center of the psychoanalytic universe as a beloved friend and colleague to Freud, Ferenczi's immersing himself into the analytic endeavor as a deeply personal and emotional enterprise (with his risk taking and the consequent errors in so doing) seems to have threatened those in the analytic community committed to a more distant, observer/surgeon position. Ferenczi and his colleagues in Budapest found themselves gradually relegated to the periphery of analytic orthodoxy.

And then there was Reich, first in Vienna and later in Berlin. Always an analyst with a deep fascination with the body (1949, 1961, 1982, 1983), it was in Berlin where he was deeply influenced by the body awareness and dance therapy movements in Germany. In Berlin, and subsequently in Norway, the body itself became the primary field of Reich's therapeutic intervention and correction, leaving free association and verbal interpretation as secondary forms of treatment.

But for the experiments of Groddeck, Ferenczi, and Reich, the lived, breathing, moving body of patient and analyst received little attention for decades.

To bodyworkers, the traditional psychoanalytic attitudes toward the body and the hands-off prohibitions seem rather strange. Johnson, a Rolfer, bodyworker, and historian of bodywork modalities, comments rather humorously on the psychoanalytic attitude toward the body:

> There is a psychoanalytic body. Despite Freud and Jung's immersion in bodily experience, the body that surfaces in much of the later psychoanalytic literature is freighted by images of the erect penis, full breast, Greek murderers, Hindu devas: dramatic, meaningful, but with little reference to sweat, blood, and the muscular stresses of daily work. One searches hard for simple expressions of what it might be like to experience the primal waves of breath from moment to moment; or the knees, elbows, and shoulders of the everyday walking body; or the peristaltic waves of grief; or the cerebrospinus fluid leaps for joy. (Johnson & Grand, 1998, p. 9)

From her perspective as a relational psychoanalyst, Shapiro (1996) captures this sense of the body as she describes "the whole range of somatosensory phenomena: our breath, pulse, posture, muscle strength, fatigue, clarity and speed of thought, sense of boundedness, our skin, mucous membranes, bodily tension, facial expression, taste, smell, pulse, vitality" (p. 298), arguing against the standard analytic view of "these experiences as more primitive and pathological than verbally symbolized experience" (p. 299), suggesting that the welcoming of somatosensory phenomena has the potential to interanimate and interpenetrate the therapeutic process. Krueger (2002) stresses the self-organizing functions of bodily experience:

> The body is the primary instrument through which we perceive and organize the world. We regularly return to the body as a frame of reference throughout development. Subsequent learning and experiences are referred to what has already been sensorily experienced for confirmation and authentification. (p. 23)

In turning our attention now to the evolution of bodywork modalities, we return first to Berlin. As in Vienna, Berlin at the time of the Weimar Republic was a center of artistic, intellectual, psychoanalytic, and somatic experimentation (Danto, 2005). As in many periods of fervor and creativity, it is difficult to delineate a simple narrative of the evolution of the body awareness movement and its interface with psychoanalysis.

A central figure in the body awareness movement was Elsa Gindler (Downing, 1996 ; Weaver, 1994, 2004), a gymnastics teacher who developed a system of "movement and breathing experiments for sensing our way" (Weaver, 2004, p. 39). Gindler married Heinrich Jacoby, an experimental musician and educator with a deep interest in psychoanalysis. Through Jacoby, Gindler's body methods drew the interest of analysts in Berlin, especially the Fenichels (Danto, 2005). Friends of the Fenichels, Wilhelm and Annie Reich, learned of Gindler's work. Elsa Lindenberg, a dancer and Reich's long-term companion after he divorced Annie, studied with Gindler and further influenced the development of body-centered psychoanalytic techniques. At the same time, Rudolph Laban, a dancer and choreographer, was the central figure in the dance therapy movement (Bartenieff, 1980; Laban, 1971; North, 1972), seeking to help students experience habitual patterns of movement, which can then evolve into freer, more "authentic" patterns of movement and self-expression. In 1931, a major psychotherapy conference in Dresden brought together psychoanalysts, psychotherapists, and body awareness teachers. Groddeck presented a paper there on "Massage and Psychotherapy" (1977, pp. 235-240). Had events unfolded differently in Germany, one must wonder what influence these creative experiments might have had on the evolution of psychoanalysis and psychotherapy. In Germany, these originators laid the basis for a variety of models of sensory awareness and therapeutic dance (Becker, 1986; Boris, 2001; Dahlman, 1986; Muller-Braunschweig, 1986; Proskauer, 1968; Trautmenn-Voight, 1991).

As with the psychoanalysts, many of these teachers were forced to leave Germany. One important émigré in the body awareness movement was Charlotte Selver, a student of Gindler, who continued and further developed the work in the United States, calling it "sensory awareness" (Brooks, 1974). Selver, who wrote very little, was widely influential through her teaching. Erich Fromm was a devoted student, giving a joint paper with Selver at the New School for Social research in the mid-1950s. Clara Thompson, an analysand of Ferenczi, studied with her, as did Fritz and Laura Perls (who originally studied with Gindler in Germany), Christopher Whitmont, Alan Watts, and Judith Weaver.

Parallel to the evolution of sensory awareness models, dance therapy and "authentic movement" therapy (Chodorow, 1991; Pallaro, 1999) have gained wider recognition. These approaches to working with the body emphasize process over content, offering the student the opportunity to notice habitual, unconscious ("subsymbolic"; Bucci, 1997a) patterns of body organization, moving in a rather meditative fashion from the initial noticing of patterns to the allowing of more spontaneous movement. Movement therapists may begin a session with a series of simple, open-ended, inner-directed awareness and movement exercises, or they may move from current life situations, recurrent body sensations, dreams, or images that the student brings to session. Patterns of both inhibited and spontaneous movement are explored. Deeply influenced by the work of Jung, this style of somatic exploration is understood to open the student to unconscious desires:

> Powerful images, feelings and memories may arise out of self-directed movement and out of the relationship which contains it. Because the process involves the use of the body to express the imagination, it tends to take the mover to complexes that can be traced back to the sensory-motor period of infancy and early childhood. ... Rather than attempting to evoke behavioral change, this approach to dance therapy relies on the natural development of internally-generated cues. It sees the body as the primary guide to the unconscious. (Chodorow, 1999, p. 258)

The "psychoanalytic body" has been imbued with decades of bias framed in various theories of primitive modes of experience, acting out, projection, regression, and developmental failure or trauma. Bodyworkers are well aware that many of our bodies have troubled histories and are highly sensitive to areas of disturbance and disorganization. Most are well trained to identify and work with patterns of both hyperfunctioning (manic or rigid) and hypofunctioning (depressive or collapsed). But bodyworkers are also trained to see the rich potentials of the body as a resource for self-agency, passion, resilience, and creativity. It is particularly in this regard that I think psychoanalysts have much to learn from bodyworkers and body-centered psychotherapists.

It is difficult to capture work of movement therapy or sensory awareness on the written page. It is taught in an oral and experiential rather than a written and academic tradition (Johnson, 1995, 1997). The written literature in many of these modalities is extremely limited; Else Gindler (1926/2004), for example, wrote but one article her entire career. Johnson (1995, 1997; Johnson & Grand 1998), a Rolfer and somatics practitioner, has edited three books of articles and interviews to provide a written history of some of the founding creators of bodywork methodologies. He captures something of the quality of their work in this way:

> They worked quietly, wrote very little. Typically, they spent their lives outside of the vociferous worlds of university and research clinics. ... These pioneers in embodiment are typically a feisty lot, unwilling to take at face value a poor medical diagnosis, a dull exercise class, ordinary states of consciousness. Rejecting the bleakness of conventional wisdom, they have chosen to survive outside the mainstream, like artists who often struggle to make a living by doing something other than their heart's work. (1995, pp. ix and xi).

In the typical sensory awareness experience, the student is sitting, lying down, or standing up in a quietly relaxed position, breathing softly but consciously, often with eyes closed. Now you, as a reader, are most likely seated and your eyes are most definitely open. So, as a little experiment, I will take you through a standard body awareness exercise, though we shall have to bypass the standard opening instruction to close your eyes:

Give yourself some time to notice the rhythm of your breathing. Don't change it, just notice it. Can you sense the moment of transition from the inhalation to the exhalation? Notice that moment of stillness as your breath shifts from inhalation to exhalation, from exhalation to inhalation. Allow the pause. Perhaps you'll notice that while you are "sitting still," your body is actually moving in subtle ways. Perhaps you'll notice that your body wants to move more, shift in some way. Perhaps there is a way you can sit, shift your posture, that frees your breath. If your breath flows more freely, what happens to your body? Perhaps it is a little more still. Perhaps it wishes to move more. Allow your body to do what it wishes. Don't direct, don't push, don't expect, just allow and notice. Where in your body do you feel your breathing? When your attention wanders from your body, where does it go? Don't change or judge it, just notice where your attention goes. Perhaps your body slips out of awareness. Perhaps your body senses go one way, your thoughts another. Now actually close your eyes, stay with your experience of your body, accept whatever happens.

As perhaps you have discovered, it is not easy to maintain body awareness while reading. The bulk of bodywork training is not through the written text—quite a contrast to the psychoanalytic educational style. Typically, of course, in an actual sensory awareness or movement experience, the instructions would be spoken, you would hear them, not read them. The voice of the teacher would be nonintrusive, permissive, and paced to what was emerging in your body. I offer two brief vignettes to illustrate how sensory awareness and movement interventions might be incorporated into ongoing psychotherapy.

Abby was one of four siblings, two sons and two daughters, born to ambitious, upper middle-class parents. The family prided itself on its social and political accomplishments, the children pressured to be outgoing, independent, socially competent, and academically accomplished. Abby, both as a child and as an adult, felt she often fell short of the mark. Her therapy tended to focus on professional concerns and self-doubts and the stresses of being a professional woman while raising very active children. In discussing struggles with colleagues or family members, Abby was intensely self-critical, rarely feeling or expressing anger or disappointment toward those around her. She was able to express anger and disappointment toward me, though with considerable apprehension and difficulty. Our sessions were productive, and yet no underlying theme seemed to emerge. Abby remained uncertain as to why she was "really" in therapy, whether she could justify the time and expense.

During one session, she was talking about her growing pleasure in drawing and painting and mentioned, quite in passing, that she had become preoccupied with a photograph she'd seen in a magazine, one that both fascinated and disturbed her, which she kept wanting to draw. She had thought several times of bringing it up with me but hesitated, feeling embarrassed and uncertain of what to say about it. She finally decided to draw it, hoping she could then discover its meaning. After drawing, redrawing, and reworking the image several times, she asked to bring the drawing to a session.

The image was of three football players walking off the field, hunched over, soaked in rain and covered with mud. The figures were somewhat obscured in the rain and mist, their faces hidden by their helmets. The figures communicated both a menace and a fatigue. The men were physically close, touching each other, clearly part of a team. The drawing was very finely rendered and quite moving as a drawing in and of itself.

As Abby began to associate to the picture, she thought of her father, his pride in his body and his athleticism, his preference for his sons over his daughters, his narcissistic bullying and self-righteousness. All of this was familiar material from her previous therapy,

Abby reported, and she expressed bewilderment at not being able to get through to whatever it was that made the image so compelling for her. I suggested that rather than talking about the image, she *become* it physically, literally taking it on with her body.

A series of sessions ensued in which she worked standing up, mimicking each of the figures, gradually entering the posture of each, walking and moving in the way she imagined they would move. We spoke very little. I stood near her, offering no interpretations, simply asking her to express in words what she experienced if she was so inclined. She *did* a lot and *said* very little, occasionally commenting on sensations in her body, on what she was feeling, on what she sensed the men in the picture might be feeling. She felt keenly that the enormous energies she sensed within and between the bodies of the men in the picture had been forbidden to her. She felt anger, longing, and envy. She began having a new sense of her own body. She began to notice a different sense of herself between sessions, feeling more substantial in herself with her thoughts and feelings. She realized she felt angry more often. She was moving into the way of being that had captivated her in the photograph, one that had been denied to her as a daughter in the family. Language and insight gradually followed, informed and enriched by her bodily activity and exploration. I made no observations of possible transference/countertransference implications of her work. I did not bring the experience into the field of our therapeutic relationship. I saw this work as a fundamental exploration of self-organization. I served largely as a witness. I was mostly silent but deeply attentive. She, too, was largely silent but deeply attentive to herself in this process of somatic inquiry and gradual reorganization.

Fogel (2004), in his discussion of implicit (or procedural) body memories and explicit (narrative) verbal memory, introduces the concept of "participatory memory," defined as "lived reenactments of personally significant experiences that have not yet become organized into a verbal or conceptual narrative" (p. 209), arguing that "participatory memories arise from unconscious implicit memories and, under certain social relational conditions (during psychotherapy, for example), may become transformed into explicit verbal memories ... and may become resolved and integrated into a more complex and expanded autobiographical sense of self through time" (p. 210). Fogel concludes that "implicit memory forms the core self, the unconscious processes that regulate our response to the sensory and motor aspects of the environment, the interpersonal world, and emotion" (p. 223) and characterizes the emergence of participatory memory as "unexpected, nonrational, spontaneous, and emotional" (p. 223), quite consistent with the descriptions afforded in the writing and training about sensory awareness and authentic movement.

The second clinical vignette was one truly unexpected and for me very disturbing. I saw Ann as she entered the movie theater. It was a shock. I had been working with Ann for several years in weekly psychotherapy, but our paths had never crossed outside of my office. In the office, I saw a woman who was deeply anxious, hypersensitive to approval or disapproval, and often withdrawn. She was also sweetly naïve and maintained a subtly ironic sense of humor about the struggles in her lonely life. I knew that she was profoundly lonely, but I never quite understood how she kept herself so socially isolated.

In the theater, I barely recognized this woman hunched down into her overcoat, arms held tightly at her sides, unkempt hair over her face, moving like a street person with the thorazine shuffle. She walked up and down the aisle several times before choosing a seat far from others. I could not tell if she had seen me. As I watched Ann, I was seeing someone very different from the woman I saw in the familiarity of my office; I suddenly had a glimpse of the mechanisms that kept her so alone. I sat wondering whatever would I be able to do with the information I had unexpectedly come upon.

In the next session, Ann asked, "What did you think of the movie?" I told her that I found it disappointing and rather insipid. She agreed. I told her that I had seen her in the theater but couldn't tell if she had seen me. "It looked like you were with a friend," she replied, "so I didn't want to intrude. I was alone, as usual." With considerable trepidation, I ventured, "I think I learned something important about you. I'd like to talk with you about it." She agreed. I told her that if I hadn't known her, I'd have found her way of coming into the theater rather scary, that her whole demeanor seemed to emanate "Leave me the fuck alone." "Even knowing you," I went on, "I didn't feel I could approach you to say hi. All I could see said, 'Stay the fuck away!'" I asked if that was what she was feeling coming into the theater and if that was what she wanted to convey.

Ann was startled: "NO! Is that really what I look like? What I'm feeling is that everybody else is at the movies with a friend, a partner, a boyfriend, a family, and I'm alone, always alone, and people are staring at me. I hate it. I try to find a seat where I won't bother anybody, and where I don't have to see the couples. I hate it so much that most of the time I can't even get out the door to go to the movie. But I didn't know I looked so weird."

I could see her anxiety rise and shame cloud her face. "It felt important to tell you what I experienced, but I was worried that it might shame you. I think there's a lot we can learn here." She asked how, and I suggested that we bring the body that was in the theater into my office. I suggested that she put her coat back on, hunch into it, and shuffle into the office. I felt sick to my stomach as I watched. I wanted to move to her, to tell her to pull the hair out of her face, to look at me, to do or say something kind to her. I asked her to notice any feelings that came up in her and to allow her body to move in any way it needed. Gradually, she became still and then slumped to her knees, curling over, pulling her coat over her head. She looked to me now like she was awaiting a beating. I thought of her stories of beatings by her father, the teasing and taunting by her brothers, the delusional ravings of her mother. But I did not feel compassionate. I felt irritated. She just knelt there, curled over and inert. I wanted to kick her. I got bored. I started thinking ahead to my evening after work. My bladder began to ache. I wanted the session over. I felt I'd made a mistake in talking to her about the theater, in intervening this way. Still, she did not move. I forced myself to look at her inert form. She looked like a supplicant. I began thinking of my Catholic upbringing (Ann was also raised Catholic)—forced to genuflect, to kneel, to pray for forgiveness, awaiting the sound of the nuns' clickers informing us we could stand up and move on. Submission. Defeat. Hatred. An object of derision and disgust. Do I speak to Ann? Do I wait? I waited in silence.

Ann began to stir. She placed her hands on the floor and pushed herself upright, brushing the hair out of her face. "This is a relief," she said. "This is what I feel all the time, but I've been afraid if you knew it you would give up on me. Did I scare you this time, too? I feel like a freak when I'm outside. But I'm glad we did this. I'm glad I could show you this. This is how my body feels all the time. This is why I'm late for work. You know, I try to remember what we talk about in here. I write it down after the sessions, but I can't use it. It's like my body lives in a different world. I hide it from you, so it's a relief you've finally seen it."

What Ann did not know at that moment was not only that I had seen it, but I had felt it, endured it, hated it in her, hated it in me. Perhaps this could (and likely would) be understood as a projective identification. My experience could also be understood as a somatic resonance. I did not bring my own emotional or bodily experience to her attention in that session. I had learned a great deal through *my* body about *her* body. Was this a form of communication from Ann to me? In part, I think, yes, as Ann clearly felt she had communicated something to me that had been long hidden. But it was also an exploration of her somatic self-organization, of her shaping of herself *in* the world, and her shaping of herself *against* the world. She was focused on her relationship to her own body, *knowing* something about herself through her body, and *showing* me something about herself through her body. In time, I have been able to bring that experience of her body into the relational work between us: I now see in some sessions the subtle hunchings-down, her dread of visibility coupled with her longing to be seen and taken up, and can speak to it in a way that allows us to examine what is happening between us as well as within her.

These clinical vignettes are offered to illustrate how body awareness and movement can be utilized within a more traditional psychotherapeutic arrangement. There are, however, many approaches to bodywork, some of which involve direct hands-on interventions by the practitioner, that can be compatible with psychoanalysis as a collateral form of treatment. At the risk of overlooking some modalities, I will list those that I have seen as valuable adjuncts to verbal psychotherapy and psychoanalysis: massage (Green & Goodrich-Dunne, 2004), sensory awareness (Brooks, 1974; Hanna, 1988, 1993; Weaver, 2004), dance and authentic movement (Chodorow, 1991; Caldwell, 1997; Pallaro, 1999), structural integration (Johnson, 1977; Rolf, 1989), the Feldenkrais method (Feldenkrais, 1950, 1981; Bartal & Ne'eman, 1975), the Alexander technique (Jones, 1979; Gelb, 1981; Maisel, 1989), Rosen Method Bodywork (Rosen, 2003; Rosen & Brenner, 1991), and body-mind centering (Cohen, 1993; Aposhyan, 2004; Hartley, 2004).

Although the practitioner's primary attention in working with a student (the more common term in bodywork than client or patient) is to body process, the work develops within the context of a relationship. I have found many of my analytic colleagues reluctant to refer out for bodywork both out of concern for giving advice and suggesting action (still a common analytic taboo) and out of fears of splitting the transference. In my own experience, the transferential relationships may become more complex, but often in a way that can be informative, rather than inevitably defensive and splitting. I rarely consult directly with the bodyworker practitioner, preferring instead to leave the responsibility for communication within the working triad to the client. I have found it extremely important to present such referrals in the context of the client's attention to self- and somatic organization, collateral to an ongoing, psychodynamic psychotherapy.

Informed and systematic attention to one's body can greatly enhance the psychoanalytic endeavor. Bodywork can provide a means for deep self-exploration and the possibility of a somatic reorganization of myself in relation to my self. While done in the presence of another (a teacher or facilitator), there is an essential privacy of the self in these somatic explorations. It is my personal hope that as the psychoanalytic process evolves into an evermore deeply affective and intimate exploration between two curious beings, thereby bringing bodily experience increasingly into the analytic field, psychoanalysts will seek their own bodywork and body-centered training.

References

Aisenstein, M. (2006). The indissociable unity of psyche and soma: A view from the Paris Psychosomatic School. *Int. J. Psychoanal.*, 87, 667–680.

Anderson, S., Reznik, I., & Glassman, N. (2005). The unconscious relational self. In R. Hassin, J. Uleman, & J. Bargh (Eds.), *The new unconscious*. Oxford: Oxford University Press.

Aposhyan, S. (1999). *Natural intelligence: Body-mind integration and human development*. Baltimore: Williams & Wilkins.

Aposhyan, S. (2004). *Body-mind psychotherapy*. New York: W.W. Norton.

Aron, L., & Anderson, F. S. (1998). *Relational perspectives on the body*. Hillsdale, NJ: The Analytic Press.

Aron, L., & Harris, A. (1993). *The legacy of Sandor Ferenczi*. Hillsdale, NJ: The Analytic Press.

Bartal, L., & Ne'eman, N. (1975). *Movement, awareness, and creativity*. New York: Harper & Row.

Bartenieff, I. (1980). *Body movement: Coping with the environment.* New York: Gordon & Breach.

Becker, H. (1981). *Konzentrartive Begegunstherapie: Integrationsversuch von koperlichkeit und handeln in den psychoanalytishen prozess.* Stuttgart: George Thieme.

Becker, H. (1986). Body experience and alienation: Psychoanalytically oriented concentrative movement therapy as an introduction to psychotherapy of psychosomatic patients. In E. Brahler (Ed.), *Body experience: The subjective dimension of psyche and soma* (pp. 77–90). Berlin: Springer-Verlag.

Beebe, B. (2004). Faces in relation: A case study. *Psychoanal. Dial.,* 1–52.

Brewer, B. (1995). Bodily awareness and the self. In J. L. Bermudez, A. Marcel, & N. Eilan (Eds.), *The body and the self* (pp. 267–290). Cambridge, MA: The MIT Press.

Brooks, C. (1974). *Sensory awareness: The rediscovery of experience.* New York: Viking Press.

Bucci, W. (1997a). *Psychoanalysis and cognitive science: A multiple code theory.* New York: Guilford.

Bucci, W. (1997b). Symptoms and symbols: A multiple code theory of somaticization. *Psychoanal. Inq., 17,* 151–172.

Bucci, W. (2001). Pathways of emotional communication. *Psychoanal. Inq., 21*(1), 40–70.

Butterworth, G. (1993). Dynamic approaches to infant perception and action: Old and new theories about the origins of knowledge. In L. B. Smith & E. Thelan (Eds.), *A dynamic systems approach to development: Applications* (pp. 171–187). Cambridge, MA: The MIT Press.

Butterworth, G. (1995). An ecological perspective on the origins of self. In J. L. Bermudez, A. Marcel, & N. Eilan (Eds.), *The body and the self* (pp. 87–105). Cambridge, MA: The MIT Press.

Caldwell, C. (Ed.). (1997). *Getting in touch: The guide to new body-centered therapies.* Wheaton, IL: Quest Books.

Chodorow, J. (1991). *Dance therapy and depth psychology.* New York: Routledge.

Chodorow, J. (1999). Dance/movement and body experience in analysis. In P. Pallaro (Ed.), *Authentic movement* (pp. 253–266). London: Jessica Kingsley Publishers.

Cohen, B. B. (1993). *Sensing, feeling, and action.* Northhampton, MA: Contact.

Cornell, W. F. (1997). If Reich had met Winnicott: Body and gesture. *Energy & Character, 28*(2), 50–60.

Cornell, W. F. (2000). Transference, desire and vulnerability in body-centered psychotherapy. *Energy & Character, 20*(2), 29–37.

Cornell, W. F. (2003). Babies, brains, and bodies: Somatic foundations of the Child ego state. In C. Sills & H. Hargaden (Eds.), *Key concepts in transactional analysis, contemporary views: Ego states* (pp. 28–54). London: Worth Publishing.

Cornell, W. F. (2004). Body, self, and subjectivity: Discussant paper to Lewis Aron's relational psychoanalysis, the emergence of a tradition. Pittsburgh Psychoanalytic Society & Institute, April 2, 2004.

Cornell, W. F. (in press). A stranger to desire: Entering the erotic field, *Stud. Gend. & Sexual.*

Dahlman, W. (1986). Exercises in concentrative body perception: A psychophysiological therapy technique. In E. Brahler (Ed.), *Body experience: The subjective dimension of psyche and soma* (pp. 104–118). Berlin: Springer-Verlag.

Danto, E. A. (2005). *Freud's free clinics: Psychoanalysis and social justice, 1918–1938.* New York: Columbia University Press.

Dorpat, T. (2001). Primary process communication. *Psychoanal. Inq., 21,* 448–463.

Downing, G. (1996). *Korper und Wort in der Psychotherapie.* Munich: Kosel Verlag.

Dupont, J. (1988). *The clinical diary of Sandor Ferenczi.* Cambridge, MA: Harvard University Press.

Fast, I. (2006). A body-centered mind: Freud's more radical idea. *Contemp. Psychoanal., 42*(2), 273–296.

Feldenkrais, M. (1950). *The body and mature behavior.* New York: International Universities Press.

Feldenkrais, M. (1981). *The elusive obvious.* Cupertino, CA: Meta.

Ferenczi, S. (1917/1955). Review of Groddeck's 'Die psychische bedingtheit und psychoanalytiche behandlung organischer leiden.' In *Further contributions to the theory and technique of psycho-analysis, Vol. III* (pp. 342–343). New York: Basic Books.

Ferenczi, S. (1920/1955). The further development of an active technique in psycho-analysis. In *Further contributions to the theory and technique of psycho-analysis, Vol. II* (pp. 198–216). New York: Basic Books.

Ferenczi, S. (1921/1955). Review of Groddeck's 'Der Seelensucher'. In *Further contributions to the theory and technique of psycho-analysis, Vol. III* (pp. 344–348). New York: Basic Books.

Ferenczi, S. (1925/1955). Contra-indications to the 'active' psycho-analytic technique. In *Further contributions to the theory and technique of psycho-analysis, Vol. II* (pp. 217–229). New York: Basic Books.

Ferenczi, S. (1928/1955). The elasticity of psycho-analytic technique. In *Further contributions to the theory and technique of psycho-analysis, Vol. III* (pp. 87–101). New York: Basic Books.

Ferenczi, S. (1930/1955). The principles of relaxation and neocatharsis. In *Further contributions to the theory and technique of psycho-analysis, Vol. III* (pp. 108–125). New York: Basic Books.

Fogel, A. (2004). Remembering infancy: Accessing our earliest experiences. In G. Bremner & A. Slater (Eds.), *Theories of infant development* (pp. 204–232). Malden, MA: Blackwell Publishing.

Fortune, C. (Ed.). (2002). *Ferenczi-Groddeck correspondence 1921–1933*. New York: Other Press.

Gelb, M. (1981). *Body learning: An introduction to the Alexander technique.* New York: Delilah Books.

Gindler, E. (1926/2004). Gymnastic. *The USA Body Psychother. Jour., 3*(1), 48–55.

Goldfield, E. C., & Wolff, P. H. (2004). A dynamical systems perspective on infant action and development. In G. Bremner & A. Slater (Eds.), *Theories of infant development* (pp. 3–29). Malden, MA: Blackwell Publishing.

Greene, E., & Goodrich-Dunn, B. (2004). *The psychology of the body.* Philadelphia: Lippincott, Williams & Wilkins.

Groddeck, G. (1977). *The meaning of illness: Selected psychoanalytic writings.* London: Hogarth Press.

Hanna, T. (1988). *Somatics.* Reading, MA: Perseus Books.

Hanna, T. (1993). *The body of life: Creating new pathways for sensory awareness and fluid movement.* Rochester, VT: Healing Arts Press.

Hartley, L. (2004). *Somatic psychology: Body, mind, and meaning.* London: Whurr Publishers.

Johnson, D. H. (1977). *The Protean body.* New York: Harper Colophon Books.

Johnson, D. H. (Ed.). (1995). *Bone, breath, and gesture: Practices of embodiment.* Berkeley, CA: North Atlantic Press.

Johnson, D. H. (Ed.). (1997). *Groundworks: Narratives of embodiment.* Berkeley, CA: North Atlantic Books and California Institute of Integral Studies.

Johnson, D. H., & Grand, I. (Eds.). (1998). *The body in psychotherapy: Inquiries in somatic psychology.* Berkeley, CA: North Atlantic Books.

Johnson, M. (1987). *The body in the mind: The bodily basis of meaning, imagination, and reason.* Chicago: University of Chicago Press.

Jones, F. P. (1979). *Body awareness in action: A study of the Alexander technique.* New York: Schoken Books.

Knoblauch, S. (1999). Absorbing maternal erotics: A slippery affair—Commentary on papers by Wrye and Wayne. *Gend. & Psychoanal., 4*(1), 35–46.

Knoblauch, S. (2000). *The musical edge of therapeutic dialogue.* Hillsdale, NJ: The Analytic Press.

Krueger, D. W. (2002). *Integrating body self and psychological self.* New York: Brunner-Routledge.

Laban, R. (1971). *The mastery of movement.* London: Duckworth.

La Barre, F. (2001). *On moving and being moved.* Hillsdale, NJ: The Analytic Press.

La Barre, F. (2005). The kinetic transference and countertransference. *Cont. Psychoanal., 41*(2),, 249–280.

Lyons-Ruth, K. (1999). The two person unconscious: Intersubjective dialogue, enactive relational representation, and the emergence of new forms of relational organization. *Psychoanal. Inq., 19*(4), 576–617.

Maisel, E. (Ed.). (1989). *The Alexander technique: The essential writings of F. Matthias Alexander.* New York: University Books.

Mancia, M. (2006). Implicit memory and early unrepressed unconscious: Their role in the therapeutic process (How the neurosciences can contribute to psychoanalysis). *Int. J. Psychoanal., 87,* 83–103.

McLaughlin, J. T. (2005). *The healer's bent: Solitude and dialogue in the clinical encounter.* Hillsdale, NJ: The Analytic Press.

Muller-Braunschweig, H. (1986). Psychoanalysis and the body. In E. Brahler (Ed.), *Body experience: The subjective dimension of psyche and soma* (pp. 19–34). Berlin: Springer-Verlag.

North, M. (1972). *Personality assessment through movement.* London: MacDonald & Evans.

Pallaro, P. (1999). *Authentic movement: Essays by Mary Stacks Whitehouse, Janet Adler and Joan Chodorow.* London: Jessica Kingsley Publishers.

Pally, R. (1998). Emotional processing: The mind-body connection. *Int. J. Psychoanal., 79,* 349–62.

Proskauer, M. (1968). Breathing therapy. In J. Mann & H. Otto (Eds.), *Ways of growth.* New York: Grossman.

Rachman, A. W. (1997). *Sandor Ferenczi: The psychotherapist of tenderness and passion.* Northvale, NJ: Jason Aronson.

Reich, W. (1949). *Character analysis.* New York: Orgone Institute Press.

Reich, W. (1961). *The function of the orgasm.* New York: Farrar, Straus & Giroux.

Reich, W. (1982). *The bioelectrical investigation of sexuality and anxiety.* New York: Farrar, Straus & Giroux.

Reich, W. (1983). *Children of the future: On the prevention of sexual pathology.* New York: Farrar, Straus & Giroux.

Rick, C. (2001). Movement and meaning. *Psychoanal. Inq., 21,* 368–377.

Rolf, I. P. (1989). *Rolfing.* Rochester, VT: Healing Arts Press.

Rosen, M. (2003). *Rosen method bodywork.* Berkeley, CA: North Atlantic Books.

Rosen, M., & Brenner, S. (1991). *The Rosen method of movement.* Berkeley, CA: North Atlantic Books.

Shapiro, S. A. (1996). The embodied analyst in the Victorian consulting room. *Gend. & Psychoanal.*, *1*, 297–322.

Shaw, R. (2003). *The embodied psychotherapist: The therapist's body story.* Hove, East Sussex, UK: Brunner-Routledge.

Thelan, E. (2005). Dynamic systems theory and the complexity of change. *Psychoanal. Dial.*, *15*(2), 255–284.

Thelan, E., & Fogel, A. (1989). Toward an action-based theory of infant development. In J. J. Lockman & N. L. Hazen (Eds.), *Action in social context: Perspectives in early development* (pp. 23–63). New York: Plenum Press.

Thelan, E., & Smith, L. B. (1998). *A dynamic systems approach to the development of cognition and action.* Cambridge, MA: The MIT Press.

Trevarthan, C. (2004). Intimate contact from birth: How we know one another by touch, voice, and expression in movement. In K. White (Ed.), *Touch: Attachment and the body* (pp. 1–16). London: Karnac Books.

Wayne, D. J. (1999). The male analyst on the maternal erotic playground. *Gend. & Psychoanal.*, *4*(1), 23–34.

Weaver, J. O. (2004). The influence of Elsa Gindler on somatic psychotherapy and Charlotte Selver. *The USA Body Psychother. Jour.*, *3*(1), 38–47.

Whitmont, C. (1972). Body experience and psychological awareness. *Quadrant*, *12*, 5–16.

Whitmont, C. (1973). *The symbolic quest: Basic concepts of analytical psychology.* New York: Harper & Row.

Wrye, H.K. (1999). Embranglements on the maternal erotic playground: "They aftly gang awry." *Gend. & Psychoanal.*, *4*(1), 7–22.

3

The Role of Bodily Experience in Emotional Organization

New Perspectives on the Multiple Code Theory

Wilma Bucci

Through all the changes and controversies of this first century of psychoanalytic thought, there are several core ideas that have endured and that continue to define the field. Among these fundamental concepts of psychoanalysis are a view of treatment as the "talking cure" and a view of the human psyche as characterized by mind-body interaction. Psychoanalytic treatments in their various forms are characterized by the intersection of these two concepts.

What was remarkable in the discovery of the "talking cure" was not the emphasis on verbalization, but the discovery of systematic treatment based on *psychological* functions of communication between people, rather than chemical or surgical or other physical means. What was remarkable in the intersection of this discovery with the emphasis on mind-body interaction was the recognition that words and other forms of emotional communication have the power to interact with biological systems, to bring about change in bodily symptoms, not only in ideas.

Although these concepts were seminal for psychoanalysis, they could not be adequately explained within the psychoanalytic theory of the psychical apparatus, as it was formulated a century ago. We can come somewhat further in understanding these concepts in the context of the psychology and neuroscience of today.

My framework for understanding these processes is the theory of multiple coding and the referential process. Current developments in cognitive science and affective neuroscience converge in a view of the human organism as inherently a multilevel, multiformat system, with substantial but limited integration among the components of the system. This corresponds in a broad sense with the psychoanalytic formulation of the psychical apparatus, although with significant differences. The psychical apparatus, as conceptualized in the metapsychology, is inherently a multiple-component system. The basis for Freud's distinctions shifted in the development of his thought from a system based on level of awareness—*unconscious, preconscious,* and *conscious*—to one based on structure—*id, ego,* and *superego*; but the premise of multiple components remained. Both models, the topographical and the structural, retain an underlying distinction between more primitive, irrational, infantile systems driven by wish fulfillment, and characterized by the primary process mode; contrasting with more mature, rational reality-oriented functioning, operating via the secondary process. In both models, the goal of treatment is a unified system developed through the more rational and reality-oriented systems replacing the lower-level primitive ones: "to make the unconscious conscious" or "where id was there ego shall be."

Whereas Freud's deep and generative insight concerning the multiplicity of the human psychical apparatus remains valid, the psychoanalytic premise of lower or more primitive systems—unconscious, nonverbal, irrational—being replaced by more advanced ones needs to be revised in the light of current scientific knowledge. We now recognize that diverse and complex processing systems exist, function, and develop side by side, within and outside of awareness, in mature, well-functioning adults throughout life. Unconscious processes are not necessarily primitive and driven by wish fulfillment; rational, organized information processing may occur outside of awareness. Although some degree of dissociation is inherent in a multiple code system, adequate integration is needed in service of the individual's overall goals. The goal of treatment is better formulated as the integration, or reintegration, of systems where this has been impaired, rather than as replacement of one system by another.

Multiple Coding and the Referential Process

I will present here the multiple code theory that I have developed based on current work in cognitive psychology, neuropsychology, and related fields. Like all theories, this is a work in progress, a guide to investigation that needs to be elaborated and revised on the basis of new observation.

The human emotional information processing system comprises two major subsystems of psychic functioning, *subsymbolic* and *symbolic*. The symbolic system is further divided into *nonverbal* forms, which we know as imagery, and *verbal* forms, the words of language; thus yielding three major subsystems: *symbolic verbal*, *symbolic nonverbal*, and *subsymbolic*.[1]

Symbols: Words and Images

Symbols are defined here in the semiotic rather than psychoanalytic sense: They are discrete entities with properties of *reference* (referring to entities outside of themselves) and *generativity* (the capacity to be combined to make an essentially infinite variety of forms). Symbols may be images or words.

Language is the quintessential symbolic form. Words can be combined to generate the essentially infinite variety of phrases and sentences that we speak and write; words and their combinations have reference to the events of life and to knowledge of many forms. Language has specific powers of discrimination, generalization, and logical filtering of many types; it is efficient in certain ways in chunking and categorizing information; it is also the mode of representation over which we have the most control. Language is also *arbitrary* and *abstract*. Words do not resemble the entities that they represent (with the unique example of onomatopoeia in the auditory mode). They carry the same meaning in different sensory forms: through hearing them spoken, by many different voices; seeing them visually in many forms; or through the tactile sense of braille.

Imagery is also a symbolic form: Images *refer* to the entities they represent; elements of images can be combined to *generate* new images. We have images of people, places, and things, and images constitute elements that we can combine in mind in different ways, as

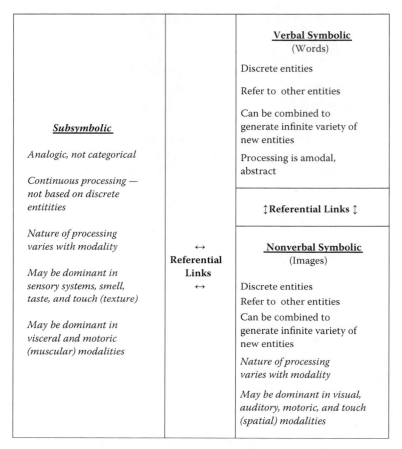

Figure 3.1 Components of the Multiple Code System

we do in dreams. What came in with the advance from Neanderthal to homo sapiens was not only verbal language but advances in the symbolic function in general, for example, communication through visual images such as cave drawings. The field of photography has developed powerful means of producing creative (or deceptive) composite images through this generative function of imagery. In contrast to language, imagery is *sensory specific*, appearing in specific sensory modalities, including auditory, and even olfactory or tactual modalities, as Helen Keller (1908) describes; for most sighted people, the visual modality dominates. Images combining sensory modalities can also be constructed, as in some new art forms or in the performance arts; when we imagine the Willis dancing in the second act of *Giselle*, we will see the visual imagery and hear the music in an integrated way, but the elements appear in their individual sensory modalities.

The Subsymbolic System

The subsymbolic system is less familiar conceptually and hard to describe technically, but most familiar to us in our daily lives. In contrast to the discrete representational entities of the symbolic mode, subsymbolic processing is characterized technically as continuous, that is, not discrete or digital, and analogic, that is, based on similarity of pattern or structure.

We know this processing as intuition, the wisdom of the body, and in other related ways. The crucial information concerning our bodily states comes to us primarily in subsymbolic form, and emotional communication between people occurs primarily in this mode. Reik's (1948) concept of "listening with the third ear" relies largely on subsymbolic communication, as I have discussed in detail elsewhere (Bucci, 2001).

The phenomenon of affective attunement described by Daniel Stern is an example of analogic and continuous emotional communication. In the following example with a 10-month-old girl, the mother provides a nonverbal analogy or similarity of pattern, in continuous format, not formed of discrete elements, that corresponds to the infant's emotional expression:

> The girl opens up her face (her mouth opens, her eyes widen, her eyebrows rise) and then closes it back, in a series of changes whose contour can be represented by a smooth arch (*a continuous function*). Mother responds by intoning "Yeah" with a pitch line that rises and falls as the volume crescendos and decrescendos: ... The mother's prosodic contour has matched the child's facial-kinetic contour (*an analogic response*). (Stern, 1985, p. 140; parenthetical comments added)

Subsymbolic processes occur in motoric and visceral forms, and in all sensory modalities. In contrast to the primary process as characterized in psychoanalytic theory, subsymbolic processes are not chaotic, not driven by wish fulfillment, or divorced from reality. They are organized, systematic, and rational forms of thought that continue to develop in complexity and scope throughout life. They are involved in a wide and diverse array of processes, such as the rapid, implicit computations we do to decide whether it is safe to enter a highway, the sensory decisions of the winemaker or perfume blender or chef, the processes involved in dance or sports or musical performance, or the processing that is needed to recognize changes in vocal or facial expression. Such processes operate as well in creative mathematical and scientific thought, operating on dimensions that have not yet been formulated, and categories that have not yet been constructed, as Poincaré and Einstein have described.[2] The systematic analogic and continuous computations of the subsymbolic mode are modeled in cognitive science by connectionist or parallel distributed processing (PDP) systems (McClelland, Rumelhart, & Hinton, 1989), with the features of dynamical systems (Bucci, 1997). The nature of this processing is also compatible with the findings of neuroscience.

Subsymbolic processes may operate either within or outside of awareness. In some cases, they may be directed by intention; in some cases, particularly in the cases of bodily functions, or aspects of emotional communication, we have limited ability to direct or control these functions intentionally. In that sense, they may be experienced as outside of the self.

What Donnell Stern (1997) has talked about as *unformulated experience,* what Philip Bromberg (2006) talks about as nonlinear thought, and from a different perspective the type of emotional communication that has been characterized as projective identification may all be accounted for in terms of the properties of subsymbolic processing, in some cases dissociated from the symbolic mode (Bucci, 2001). We are not accustomed to thinking of nonsymbolic processes, including somatic and sensory processes, that cannot be verbalized or even symbolized and that may operate outside of intentional control, as systematic and organized thought. It changes our understanding of pathology and treatment when we are able to make this shift.

The Referential Process

The three formats, with different contents and different organizing principles, are connected, partially and to varying degrees, by the referential process. Imagery is the pivot of this connecting process: In its sensory features, imagery connects to the subsymbolic processes; as generative and discrete entities, images can potentially be connected to words. This pivotal function of imagery is crucial to the psychoanalytic process. I will describe this function in the therapeutic context, following the introduction of the multiple code formulation of emotion schemas and their development.

The Emotion Schemas[3]

Based on the understanding of multiple processing systems, we can develop a more specific view of the psychological organization of emotional functioning, in adaptive functioning and in pathology. The fundamental organizing structures of human emotional life—and probably of other species—are characterized in multiple code theory as particular types of memory schemas that are termed *emotion schemas*. In using the concept of the *schema*, we emphasize the constructive and active nature of perception and memory. Memory schemas determine how we see the world and are themselves changed by each new interaction. Memory is not an inert bin in which we place and hold representations; perception is not a reproductive lens. We see all things through the lens of our memory schemas; there is no other way. There is no need to turn to postmodernism or constructivism to make this basic point; the cognitive psychologist Bartlett (1932) demonstrated the constructive nature of memory and perception in his classic work more than 70 years ago.

Emotion schemas are particular types of memory schemas that develop on the basis of repeated interactions with others from the beginning of life and that form the basis of personality organization. They share the active and constructive nature of all memory schemas; they determine what we desire and expect from other people, how we perceive them, and how we act in response; and are themselves continuously affected and changed by new interpersonal experience. From this perspective, the processes underlying *transference, countertransference,* and *enactment* are ubiquitous in all human interaction; the psychoanalytic terms represent the specific ways in which these pervasive, constructive processes play out in the therapeutic encounter.

Emotion schemas incorporate all components of the multiple code theory, including nonverbal subsymbolic representations and imagery; words are later added to some degree. The simple emotion terms cannot begin to capture the complexity of these structures. We can be *unhappy* in many different ways; contrary to Tolstoy's famous opening line in *Anna Karenina,* we can be *happy* in different ways as well.

Development of Emotion Schemas in the Interpersonal Context

The emotion schemas differ from other types of memory schemas in the dominance of the *affective core*—the bodily, visceral, sensory, and motoric components of the emotion schema that are largely subsymbolic. The elements of the affective core are activated in response to different people, in different contexts, and the organizing schemas of the emotions are built through those activations. Images play a central role in the emotion schemas as they do in all psychic organization; for the emotion schemas, the central organizing images are the significant people of our lives.

Daniel Stern's concept of the representation of interactions that have been generalized (RIG) is essentially a version of this type of emotional organization, as illustrated in his description of the development of a schema of joy:

> Mother's making faces, grandmother's tickling, father's throwing the infant in the air, the babysitter's making sounds, and uncle's making the puppet talk may all be experiences of joy. What is common to all five "joys" is the constellation of three kinds of feedback: from the infant's face, from the activation profile, and from the quality of subjective feeling. (Stern, 1985, p. 90)

The interpersonal context is crucial to the development of these schemas. The baby who feels joy and laughs and smiles can see and hear the other person also using the smiling and laughing muscles and making the corresponding sounds; just as the child who cries may hear sympathetic sounds and see a particular facial expression along with a soothing touch. We may say that the other person's expressions and actions operate as external referents for the baby's internal experience. The child's own expressions and actions—the affective core of its schema—make emotional sense and derive emotional meaning through this correspondence. In this sense, the fundamental meanings of an emotion include external referents, the response of the other, as well as internal and subjective feelings.

We are now beginning to know more about the wiring that connects internal experience with perception of the expressions of

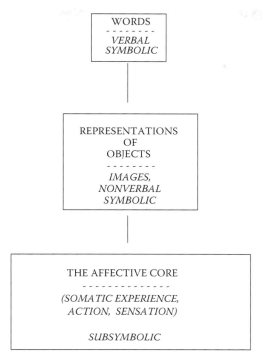

Figure 3.2   Contents of the Emotion Schemas

others. Neurons, termed *mirror neurons,* have been found in the frontal cortex of monkeys and humans that represent, in an individual's brain, the movements that the brain sees in another individual and produce signals toward sensorimotor structures so that the corresponding movements are either "previewed" in simulation mode, or actually executed in trace form by the viewer (Rizzolatti, Fadiga, Gallese, & Fogassi, 1996; Rizzolatti, Fogassi, & Gallese, 2001). New research indicates that the "mirroring function" can be executed in many areas of the neocortex; which area is activated depends on the nature of the empathic demand, or task. Thus, motor neurons fire when imitation of action is involved; insular cortex neurons (gustatory cortex) fire when disgust is involved (Wickers et al., 2003); affective components with pain (Singer et al., 2004). The implications of these new findings are potentially enormous, in understanding emotional communication in development and throughout life. I have to put two caveats here: First, to recognize that this neurological research is at a relatively early stage and many questions and controversies remain. Second, we need to recognize that we really do not require knowledge of the exact anatomy to validate the psychological functions of emotional communication in various nonverbal forms, which have been observed at least since Darwin (1872), James (1890), and Reik (1948).

The basic process—in which individuals have the feelings and actions associated with their own affective core, and perceive the expressions and actions of other people in relation to these—plays out for all emotions, painful as well as pleasurable. The affective core of fear incorporates a range of sensory and somatic and motoric activation including arousal of physiological components of the stress response—rapid breathing and heartbeat, and changes in the general homeostatic environment. These emotion-induced effects are often truly physically painful for the infant, even experienced as a threat to life.

In healthy-enough development, the parent recognizes the child's feelings, is not overwhelmed by them, and provides responses such as soothing mechanisms that diminish the threat or modulate the activation that occurs in response to the threat. The emotion schema of fear will then be elaborated to incorporate potential representations of others who can provide protection and comfort, and to incorporate mechanisms of self-care and self-regulation derived from these representations.

Integrated emotion schemas—negative or positive—are built in this way, incorporating representations of other people validating the child's responses, and also modulating and regulating them. When fear schemas are activated throughout life, the child will then potentially be able to take in new information about the situation in relation to its own powers. Representations of the sources of fear or anger or other affects, and the responses to them, can then change as the child's situation and powers change, and the emotion schemas will develop to incorporate and reflect these new connections.

Adequate integration within the emotion schemas provides the necessary basis for adequate organization of the multiple schemas of others and the self. Each important object, each important person in an individual's life, connects to a range of different affective experiences, different components of the affective core. The baby has satisfaction and pleasure in its mother's arrival, anger at her frustrating its needs, fear when mother appears different than expected or when she is harsh—and, of course, many more affective responses specific for each experience. In adaptive development, these are incorporated in an overall schema of mother with multiple subschemas.

Schemas of self in relation to others build as the center, the spine, of this development; we have multiple self-states, activation of different elements of the affective core, connected in psychic organization to different objects. In normative development, these multiple self-states are registered on a subjective autobiographical time line, in a shared subjective space.

The focus of attention in working memory is constantly shifting, depending on interpersonal context and inner state, including some experiences within and some outside of consciousness. We have different personas with different people and in different contexts. Sometimes, we wish to keep our worlds separate; it can be uncomfortable to activate different self schemas at the same time. (Women who have moved through phases of child rearing to an active career are deeply aware of these multiple personas, in the past, and also in the present, as they interact with their adult children.)

Nevertheless, in adaptive and reasonably healthy functioning, whatever comes into working memory comes in with a kind of subjective time and space marker that tags it as part of the schema of self. There are several theories as to how this core integration occurs and is represented: Damasio (1994, 1999) talks of a representation of the body self, like a map in the brain, as a means of continuity across different states; I would refer to the essential continuity of the quality and range of the affective core. The gradually, imperceptibly changing image that we see in the mirror; the image of oneself in the old photographs; the feelings inside that perhaps do not change as much as the image in the mirror; the responses to different people in past and present that change and also stay the same; for most people, these can exist as components of a shared autobiographical organization, what Damasio calls the autobiographical self. *This is what happens when things go well enough.*

Development of Pathology

The integration of the emotion schemas may be compromised in many different ways. The most obvious is through specific and acute trauma and abuse. A schema of the caretaker as a threat or predator, activating a response of terror in the child, is unbearable—in part because of the intensity of the experience itself, overwhelming the child; also because the caretaker is the one to whom the baby must turn for protection in time of danger. The schema of mother as a danger to oneself is incompatible with the schema of mother as protector; the child is under attack and there is no place to turn.

The child then attempts to deal with the threat in some way. She cannot realistically attack or escape physically; she is small and weak and fears being abandoned. What she can do is turn attention away from the threat and from the perception of the caretaker as the source of terror; dissociation within the emotion schemas occurs through such a process.

Bromberg writes about a patient who says:

> When I was little and I got scared—scared because Mommy was going to beat me up—I'd stare at a crack in the ceiling or a spider web on a pane of glass, and pretty soon I'd go into this place where everything was kind of foggy and far away, and I was far away too, and safe. At first, I had to stare real hard to get to this safe place. But then one day Mommy was really beating on me and without even trying I was there, and I wasn't afraid of her. I knew she was punching me, and I could hear her calling me names, but it didn't hurt and I didn't care. After that, any time I was scared, I'd suddenly find myself there, out of danger and peaceful. I've never told anybody about it, not even Daddy. I was afraid to because I was afraid that if other people knew about it, the place might go away, and I wouldn't be able to get there when I really needed to." (2001, pp. 904–905)

Damage to the integration of the emotion schemas may also occur through chronic failure of connection between the child's inner experience and the patient's response. Parental coldness and neglect or failure to acknowledge or respond to the child's feelings will also lead to dissociation of the schemas, and the effects of specific trauma and chronic developmental issues will interact. In her research on childhood experiences as affecting later psychological disorders, using her childhood experience of care and abuse interview and questionnaire, Antonia Bifulco and her colleagues (Bifulco & Moran, 1998) found that parents' simple failure to observe the child and the child's general experience of neglect and being ignored were at least as powerful in leading to affective and other disorders as sexual or physical or psychological abuse.

Attempts at Repair

While dissociation among systems is the root of emotional disorders, this is only the beginning of the story of what troubles people and brings them to treatment. Much of the symptomatology of pathology results, not directly from the dissociation itself, but from the individual's attempts at its repair. A person who experiences overwhelming affect, whose source cannot be acknowledged, will try to provide some meaning for this and regulate emotion in this way. A young woman suffers from severe lower body pain, including stomach or menstrual cramps. She also has memories of sexual abuse by her brother, largely devoid of affect. She does not connect her current bodily experiences with her memories of abuse and cannot acknowledge other emotional issues associated with this. She visits a series of gynecologists for this condition, seeking one who is willing to do a surgical intervention, although no organic basis has been found for her discomfort. A young star athlete remembers being beaten by his father and is grateful to his father for the discipline; he performs very well for a while, then makes a mistake in a crucial game, is depressed and angry with himself, and goes into an extended slump that endangers his career. He continues to appreciate his father's discipline and is angry with himself for not being able to live up to his father's standards.

The many complex constructions of pathology, including somatization and displacement of anger, as seen in these examples, as well as addictions, phobias, and eating disorders, and even psychotic symptoms, may be accounted for as dissociations at different levels and of different types within the emotion schemas, and different strategies of managing the experiences of affective arousal whose source cannot be acknowledged. Such attempts at self-regulation add layer after layer to the onion of pathology that must be addressed before the initial avoidance can be understood. But these layers are also part of the schema of the individual's self and need to be recognized as such; this adds great complexity to therapeutic work, as I will discuss later in this chapter. The characterization of pathology as based on dissociation and spurious repair applies for all types of patients in different ways, not limited to specific diagnoses.

Neurophysiological Model of the Emotion Schemas

Here I want to turn briefly to some neurophysiological observations that provide support for the psychological processes that have been described here and that have important implications for treatment. An emotion schema can be activated directly by sensory features in

Wilma Bucci

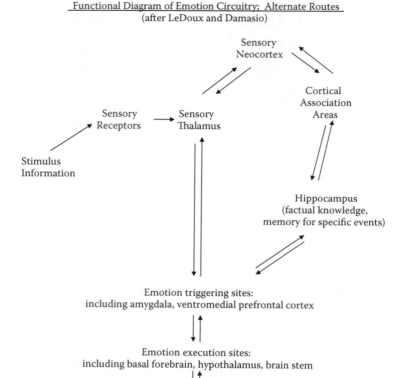

Figure 3.3   Functional Diagram of Emotion Circuitry

perception or from memory; we see something that frightens us, we get bad news, something makes us angry; a smell or a song arouses a set of feelings; some fragment of imagery comes to mind in a memory or a dream. This is what Damasio has called the *emotionally competent stimulus* (ECS). Whether presented as actual perceptions or recalled from memory as images, the stimulus information must be represented in one or more of the brain's sensory systems. Once the ECS has occurred, the emotion will play out in some form and to some degree. Two different general processing routes may be identified; LeDoux (1998) has studied these routes focusing on the fear response as illustrated in Figure 3.3.

The Direct Route

One route, which LeDoux (1998) has characterized as the low road, passes directly from the sensory stimulus through the *sensory thalamus* to the *emotion triggering sites* including the amygdala and prefrontal cortex, which then activate a number of *emotion execution sites*. These initiate the somatic and motoric and visceral components of the emotion response, the affective core of the schema, including changes in body chemistry, heart rate, blood pressure, and respiration; also including expressive functions such as facial, body, and hand movements, and vocalizations; and also including organized behavior patterns with innate features such as freezing and flight, courting and nurturing. Once the trigger has been activated, these components of the emotion response will play out, although the context and intensity may vary.

These responses may be experienced as playing out automatically, without intentional direction: "I am attracted to someone, or I feel fear or repulsion, I don't know why" or "I found myself arguing with her, I know it is useless, I'm always doing that." When we use the expression "the body knows," this refers to mentation in this part of the emotion circuitry. These are the processes of what we call the unexamined life that perhaps do not need to be examined if they are working well.

The bodily functions of the affective core also feed back as stimuli that affect cognition. Our feelings provide crucial information concerning the significance of the events of life, and we work in various ways, sometimes useful, sometimes damaging, to provide a reasoned context for them.

The Cortical Loop

The other route, characterized by LeDoux (1998) as the high road, also is initiated by the emotional stimulus and passes through the thalamus, but then includes an indirect bypass, through the cortical association areas and hippocampus. This permits appraisal of a situation and delay, modulation, regulation, and redirection of the immediate affective response: "I understand what attracts me to this person and I know from past experience that this relationship will not be good for me." This indirect route may itself become automatic through repeated life experiences and may affect the operation of the trigger itself, thus actually modulating the emotional response: "He actually doesn't turn me on anymore."

The hippocampus and related processes constitute the pivot of a well-operating integrated emotion system that permits us to take in new emotional information, from within our bodies, and from the external world, throughout life, and to use this new knowledge adaptively to affect how we respond. The hippocampus connects to the cortical association areas, the source of general knowledge and personal autobiographical memory. The hippocampus also connects to the emotion triggering and emotion execution sites of the amygdala, limbic systems, and brain stem; sends signals to them; and receives feedback from them. The two pathways join here; the cortical hippocampal system enables regulation and modulation of the more direct and immediate thalamic-amygdalar activation, based on the experience of life.

Stressor events, whether chronic or traumatic and acute—neglect or abuse in childhood, early loss of parents, the traumas of war—specifically impact this integrative process, through direct impairment of the hippocampal and related functions, and through disturbance in their modulation of the amygdalar functions. The physiology of the effect of stress on the hippocampus is well known. There are dense concentrations of stress hormone receptors in the pivotal hippocampal system, and abnormally high or low levels of stress hormones (glucocorticoids) can disrupt hippocampal function. Chronic stress may be at least as damaging as specific acute events, and the physiological effects of chronic and acute stressors will interact (Payne, Nadel, Britton, & Jacobs, 2004).

The pivotal function of the hippocampal (and related) systems is directly related to the operation of the referential process and has direct implications for therapeutic work, as I will discuss below. This pivotal function operates through representation of specific events in a time and space context—what cognitive scientists and neuroscientists talk about as event-specific knowledge or episodic memories, in contrast to general or semantic memory. Specific events occurring in the present, and also images of past events that are activated in working memory, have powerful cognitive-emotional impact. They are experienced and processed in multiple systems, including all sensory modalities, motoric action systems, and visceral and autonomic activation, and also potentially connect to the cortical association areas.

Hippocampal dysfunction induced by stress, whether chronic or acute, particularly affects the registration and retrieval of episodic memory. Moderate levels of circulating glucocorticoids appear to enhance episodic memory, whereas maximal or minimal levels appear to disrupt it. We see this effect in the memories reported by abuse victims or persons diagnosed with PTSD. Rather than reporting contextually specific memories with specific source information as to persons involved, time, and place, they frequently report schema- or knowledge-based narratives, lacking context and detail (McNally, Lasko, Macklin, & Pitman, 1995). The young woman remembers that her brother abused her ("It started when we were kids") but does not report specific memories with time and place context. The general memories represent schemas in autobiographical memory, processed in the cortical association areas, but lack the connections to sensory modalities, actions, and visceral and autonomic activation; they remain flat and without affect. Specific memories ("There was this one day, he came home from school, I heard him come into the house, I was in my room doing my homework, my mother was in the kitchen, I heard him come up the stairs and he came into my room . . .") are likely to activate components of the affective core. They are also likely to connect to aspects of the schema she does not want to remember: for example, where her mother was while this was happening, what her mother knew.

The high levels of the stress hormone cortisol that disrupt hippocampal function and impair episodic and spatial memory, at the same time facilitate the amygdala. This intensifies the painful emotional and physiological responses and also has the function of contributing to the "stamping in" of fragmented emotional memories, not oriented in time and space. Arousal of the subsymbolic components of the affective core, without recognition or acknowledgment of the object that is the source of the activation, is seen in the fragmentary memories with vivid, intrusive, unmodulated affect, not oriented as to space and time, or generalized feelings of anxiety, anger, fear, or uneasiness that van der Kolk (1994) has referred to as body memories. The intrusive vivid playbacks and the terrifying dreams, which are the other side of the coin of traumatic memories, may be accounted for this way. Other zones including the prefrontal cortex play a role in regulation of the amygdala and other components of emotional experience, but in this general schematic view, we focus on the hippocampal pivot, where the neurophysiological evidence is clearest.

The direct route is necessarily faster than the cortical loop; when a threat is perceived, the triggering and execution sites will play out, leading to immediate and instinctual responses of avoidance, primarily freezing and flight. This is the case throughout the animal kingdom.

In instances of well-functioning life, the execution of the bodily response may occur in trace form only; the activation of the cortical-hippocampal connection will occur in time to modulate the emotion execution sites and will ultimately feed back to alter the perception of the stimulus to some degree. Where this does not happen, where the threat is real or continues to be experienced as real, the expectation is reinforced and the execution of the response pattern will continue to play out.

In the normal course of events, again across all species, when the threat is experienced as past, the response patterns cease; adaptive recuperative behaviors, including self-care and soothing, as well as appeal to social supports, may occur. The organism then returns to the prethreat state, the normal way of being.

In some cases, however, where pain is overwhelming, or stress is chronic, the individual does not return to the prethreat state. The extreme reactions to threat remain and are enhanced. This may happen in different ways for someone who was at the site of the World Trade Center, or who was in Iraq, or for someone who experienced chronic childhood neglect or abuse. When stimuli associated with the stressor occur, in life or in memory, the instinctual patterns will play out again. Through repetition of this pattern in different contexts, the zones of threat, the categories of stress-inducing stimuli, proliferate; new and complex means of avoidant and dissociative responses will proliferate as well. The zone of adaptive emotional functioning and the flexibility of response patterns will be correspondingly limited. The protective responses that the individual has developed—the somatizing, avoidance of intimacy, addictions to food or alcohol or drugs, and many others—themselves become the problems that interfere with life.

Goals of Therapeutic Work

For all psychic disorders, the goal of therapeutic work is to bring about actual change in the organization of the emotion schemas, so that the painful activation is reduced, the patterns of reaction are changed, and the individual is enabled to return in a more flexible manner to a prethreat state. Different treatment forms may enter the circuitry of the emotion schemas at various levels to achieve this goal. For example, in general and oversimplified terms, supportive treatments may operate by substituting interpersonal means of emotion regulation for the self-damaging mechanisms the individual has developed, thus perhaps entering new objects in the emotion schemas and altering them in such respects, but often without opening connections to the actual source of the arousal. Methods of exposure and desensitization may operate to modify the connection of the emotional stimulus to the response execution mechanism; psychotropic medications operate on the physiological response circuitry itself. Alternate methods such as meditation and yoga may be seen as modifying the response circuitry by psychological rather than chemical means.

I suggest that the essence of psychodynamic and other exploratory treatments, in their various forms, lies in enabling change in the emotion schemas through more accurate perception of the events of the interpersonal world, in relation to the individual's current state and powers. The reorganization of the emotion schemas constitutes reorganization of the self. This process must involve engagement of the cortical association areas as well as activation of the affective core and depends on their connection through the hippocampal pivot.

The Referential Process in the Therapeutic Context

Elsewhere, I have talked about how such change may occur in terms of the referential process (Bucci, 1997, 2002). The many different psychodynamic approaches—relational, classical, and short- and long-term treatments—use this route in different ways, for different patients at different times of treatment. Some of these features may also be shared with other treatment forms as well. The referential process has the following phases:

1) *Arousal:* Activation of elements of the affective core of the dissociated schema in the new interpersonal context of the relationship. This requires that the patient experience, in vivo, both the affective core of the dissociated schema and the protective processes that she has developed throughout life to shield herself from the dreaded affect: disowning, somatization, displacement of anger or

terror. The patient has chosen to put herself into this new relational situation of the therapy; she wants to change although she doesn't know how or what it means; this offering, this opening, represents a chink in the protective devices and invites further entry into the schema.

2) *Symbolizing:* This will lead to representation of specific events associated with the schema, in memory or in the relationship. The individual will report an episode, memory, or fantasy whose connections to the schema may not be recognized and will also enact elements of the frozen relationship that the schema represents; it is here in these specific events brought into working memory, activating the hippocampal pivot, that the possibility of actual change in the schema exists.

Here is the minefield, the potential Catch-22: One cannot bring about change in the emotion schema without the connecting process, but as the connections come alive, the avoidance is weakened, the pain increases. We need to recognize and respect the power of the activation of a specific event in memory or enactment. The painful arousal that occurs in response to imagery is physical and real. The memory operates as an emotionally competent stimulus that triggers the playing out of an emotion, similar to the perception of the actual threat itself.

3) *Reorganizing:* The patient and analyst reflect on the events that have been retrieved from memory, or that have occurred in the relationship; by this means, new categories and new connections are formed. The verbal system plays a central role in this phase.

4) *Iteration:* In treatment, if the connecting process is working, the schema of threat and the processes of protection and avoidance will play out to a relatively intense degree, in the relational context. In the patient's current life, the processes of protection and avoidance are more damaging than the initial threat, but they are his life-preserving achievements of the past, and they are now intrinsic components of his self schema, his sense of self, and his view of the world in relation to the self. The patient may experience any challenge to these protective processes not only as threatening his life, but also as threatening his sense of self, evoking dread of a different sort. As all this plays out, there is continuous danger that the new context will be drawn into the schema, rather than the schema being perceived as new; the therapist may be seen as the predator, the aggressor, the seducer, the humiliating agent, as Chefetz (2005) and Bromberg (2006) have discussed. This is an opportunity as well as a threat; what happens next is the question, how is this activation used? This iterative process—connection,

leading to pain and avoidance, followed by further enactments—
provides the multiple code definition of *working through*.

Clinical and Theoretical Implications

Change in an emotion schema occurs through operation of the referential process in the context of the therapeutic relationship. This
involves activation of the subsymbolic bodily and sensory experience
of the affective core in the session, associated with ongoing events in
the therapeutic relationship, triggering memories of the past, leading optimally to changes in the emotional meaning of the activated
imagery, and modulation of the bodily and emotional responses
themselves. This is a basic premise of psychodynamic treatment.
This basic process is characteristic of psychodynamic treatment but
may also be recognized as operating in different ways, and on different levels, in any type of *talking* (or *communicative*) treatment form.
    The major premise of this formulation is an emphasis on disso-
ciation rather than repression as the basic process of defense and as
constituting the roots of pathology. Other points follow from this:
an emphasis on the activation of affective experience in the session;
revision of the concepts of regression and resistance; and a reexami-
nation of the role of language in bringing about therapeutic change.

Dissociation Versus Repression

Contents that are "warded off" are understood psychologically as dissociated rather than out of awareness; this applies for all forms of
neurosis, not only for specific diagnostic categories such as dissociative identity disorder or conditions of trauma and abuse. Memories of
people and events associated with an activated schema may come into
awareness but not as connected to the painful bodily experience of the
affective core; conversely, bodily experiences may be in awareness, but
without being associated to their source, in memory or in the present, or the bodily experiences may be associated to displaced meanings. We can understand the intellectualizing or somatizing patient,
or the patient who tells stories of events that appear to be dramatic
and vivid, but that somehow lack emotional connection, in terms of
particular types of dissociation within the emotion schemas.

Activation of the Affective Core in the Session

The activation of the dissociated painful experience in the session itself is central to the therapeutic process. The implications of this point for therapeutic technique are potentially broad and need to be explored. In the session, the threatening dissociated affect needs to be activated to some degree, but in trace form, regulated sufficiently so as not to trigger new avoidance, and with some transformation of meaning. The questions of how much and when to facilitate or permit this activation, so as to repair the dissociation rather than to reinforce it, must be addressed specifically for each patient. The relationship plays a unique role in this respect. The power of the relationship is in the evocation of the patient's emotion schema in relation to the therapist in the here and now. The therapist may be recognized as standing for other people, but the persona of the therapist is a present factor that changes the balance and context of the interaction.

New Perspectives on Regression, Resistance, and Related Concepts

Once subsymbolic processing is recognized as systematic and organized *thought*—not verbal, not symbolic, but organized nonetheless—it follows that concepts such as regression and resistance need to be revised as well. In the standard view of the psychical apparatus, according to the metapsychology as formulated by Freud, expressions outside of the verbal mode, including focus on somatic experience, enactments, and use of imagery, were characterized as more primitive or regressed modes of processing. In the context of the referential process, these are seen as potential steps in the process of reintegration of components of an aroused emotion schema that have been dissociated. The patient feels that she is hot, or her stomach hurts, or the therapist's office smells strange, then becomes aware that she is angry or afraid, then may come to recognize what it is in the current situation that has triggered her fear. The bodily activation provides information to patient and therapist, and the recognition that these processes are occurring provides an opening to the development of further emotional meaning, where the connection to language or even to imagery is not yet available.

Expressions that have traditionally been characterized as *resistance,* such as apparently irrelevant, even obsessive descriptions of details in the immediate environment or in past events, and many types of derivative and displaced narratives, as well as enactments, may play a related role in the process of exploration.

The Role of Language

From its initial characterization as the *talking cure,* psychoanalysis has assumed a privileged role for language in bringing about change. If, however, change ultimately requires connection to bodily experience that has been dissociated, and new integration of such experience, the role of verbal interventions needs to be reexamined. The difficulties in using verbal instructions to direct and change subsymbolic bodily functions are apparent to anyone who has ever taken a dance or tennis lesson; the use of language to effect changes in the emotion schemas is necessarily far more difficult and complex. Alternate treatment forms such as music, dance, and art therapies, as well as eye-movement therapies, yoga, and meditation, are all designed to access the subsymbolic system more directly, in different ways. If we take seriously the endogenous organization of the subsymbolic and symbolic nonverbal systems, we need to examine the possibility that subsymbolic modes of communication themselves may be sufficient in some cases to bring about therapeutic change, and we need to identify the ways in which this may occur. Once this perspective is opened, alternate treatment forms may be examined as to the elements of the referential process that they employ in relation to the emotional circuitry; for example, do they work entirely in the subsymbolic domain, or through accessing imagery that would operate in the symbolic, but not verbal, processing mode?

At the same time, we also need to recognize the power of the verbal mode. In earlier times, in a different analytic zeitgeist, my argument for the systematic operation of multiple nonverbal modes in the therapeutic process was seen as a radical position. Now I find myself in the position of defending the role of verbal symbols in the treatment process. From the standpoint of psychic function, symbols have the power to categorize and focus experience, enabling the speaker to retrieve and hold more of the selected information in working memory; language has particular powers in this regard. Language is also the vehicle of logical analysis, enabling both explicit discrimination among events that have been inaccurately associated, and generalization over instances not previously seen as related. As signs and markers, verbal expressions also have special powers to access certain types of information stored in autobiographical memory. The stories of one's life, told in a context of time and place, with specific detail and imagery, have the power to connect memory and emotion, linking the individual's autobiographical memory to his current affective state. Whereas nonverbal representations of experience and nonverbal communication may be sufficient when emotional life is proceeding well, verbal reports and verbal interventions, with their particular powers, may play a unique role in facilitating change.

It is also true that the power of language in treatment depends on how it is used, whether to enhance exploration or to defend against it. In my research on the referential process, my colleagues and I are working to identify and distinguish the features of language that enable connection to subsymbolic, including bodily, experience, thus enabling the patient to hold memories of the past together in working memory with experiences of self and other in the present and to distinguish these from the features of language that function in an intellectualized and dissociated mode. We are also studying paralinguistic aspects of discourse, including speech rhythms and pausing, and nonverbal vocalizations such as laughter, sighs, and many others, and attempting to see how the verbal and nonverbal processes interact in sessions characterized as more or less clinically effective.

The therapeutic situation is by its nature a multichannel communicative context. Psychoanalysis is more accurately characterized as a *communicative* than a *talking* cure. The power of this communicative context depends on integration of the multiple channels *within* each participant, as well as connection *between* the participants. When the discourse concerns emotions, the body speaks, processes, and listens, in its own multiple formats; these body messages are also connected to imagery and words. The therapeutic discourse requires incorporation of the messages of the body. To bring about change, the messages and the responses to them need also to be at least partially expressed in symbolic forms. The challenge of therapeutic work is to enable all voices to be heard, ultimately in new ways.

Endnotes

1. We should note that there may also be subsymbolic aspects of the verbal code; this opens new questions concerning the features and functions of language, including rhythm and tonal qualities, that we are beginning to study in poetry and literature as well as in naturalistic discourse (Wallace, 2006).
2. See their comments as reported in Hadamard (1945).
3. The emotion literature does not distinguish systematically among the terms "emotion," "affect," and "feeling"; different definitions and different bases for the distinction have been used by different writers. I use the terms *emotion schema* and *affective core* for the psychological constructs as explicitly defined in this chapter, and the term *feeling* in a more general sense, usually to refer to the subjective experience.

References

Bartlett, F. C. (1932). *Remembering: A study in social psychology.* Cambridge, U.K.: Cambridge University Press.

Bifulco, A., & Moran, P. (1998). *Wednesday's child: Research into women's experience of neglect and abuse in childhood and adult depression.* London: Routledge.

Bromberg, P. M. (2001). Treating patients with symptoms and symptoms with patience. *Psychoanalytic Dialogues, 11,* 891–912.

Bromberg, P. M. (2006). *Awakening the dreamer: Clinical journeys.* Mahwah, NJ: The Analytic Press.

Bucci, W. (1997). *Psychoanalysis and cognitive science: A multiple code theory.* New York: Guilford.

Bucci, W. (2001). Pathways of emotional communication. *Psychoanalytic Inquiry, 20,* 40–70.

Bucci, W. (2002). The referential process, consciousness, and the sense of self. *Psychoanalytic Inquiry, 22,* 766–793.

Bucci, W. (2003). Varieties of dissociative experiences: A multiple code account and a discussion of Bromberg's case of William. *Psychoanalytic Psychol., 20*(3), 542–557.

Chefetz, R. A. (2005). A cognitive psychoanalytic perspective on the treatment of complex dissociative disorders. *Psychiatr. Ann., 35,* 657–665.

Damasio, A. R. (1994). *Descartes' error: Emotion, reason and the human brain.* New York: Avon Books.

Damasio, A. R. (1999). *The feeling of what happens.* New York: Harcourt Brace.

Darwin, C. (1872). *The expression of the emotions in man and animals*. New York: Philosophical Library.

Hadamard, J. (1945). *The psychology of invention in the mathematical field*. New York: Dover Publications.

James, W. (1890). *Principles of psychology*. New York: Holt.

Keller, H. (1908). *The world I live in*. New York: The Century Co.

LeDoux, J. (1998). *The emotional brain: The mysterious underpinnings of emotional life*. New York: Touchstone Books.

McClelland, J. L., Rumelhart, D. E., & Hinton, G. E. (1989). The appeal of Parallel Distributed Processing. In D. E. Rumelhart, J. L. McClelland, & the PDP Research Group (Eds.), *Parallel distributed processing: Explorations in the microstructure of cognition* (Vol. 1: Foundations, pp. 3–44).

McNally, R. J., Lasko, N. B., Macklin, M. L., & Pitman, R. K. (1995). Autobiographical memory disturbance in combat-related posttraumatic stress disorder. *Behav. Res. and Ther., 33,* 610–630.

Payne, J. D., Nadel, L., Britton, W. B., & Jacobs, W. J. (2004). The biopsychology of trauma and memory. In D. Reisberg & P. Hertel (Eds.), *Memory and emotion,* Oxford: Oxford University Press.

Reik, T. (1948). *Listening with the third ear: The inner experience of a psychoanalyst*. New York: Pyramid Books.

Rizzolatti, G., Fadiga, L., Gallese, V., & Fogassi, L. (1996). Premotor cortex and the recognition of motor actions. *Cognitive Brain Res., 3,* 131–141.

Rizzolatti, G., Fogassi, L., & Gallese, V. (2001). Neurophysiological mechanisms underlying the understanding and imitation of action. *Nat. Rev. Neuroscience, 2,* 661–670.

Singer, T., Seymour, B., O'Doherty, J., Kaube, H., Dolan, R., & Frith, C. (2004). Empathy for pain involves the affective but not the sensory components of pain. *Science 303,* 1157–1162.

Stern, D. B. (1997). *Unformulated experience: From dissociation to imagination in psychoanalysis*. Hillsdale, NJ: The Analytic Press.

Stern, D. N. (1985). *The interpersonal world of the infant*. New York: Basic Books.

van der Kolk, B. A. (1994). The body keeps the score: Memory and the evolving psychobiology of postraumatic stress. *Harv. Rev. of Psychiatry, 1,* 253–265.

Wallace, J. (2006). The special language of suicide in the life and art of a poet: The referential process in the poetry and letters of Anne Sexton (Doctoral dissertation, Adelphi University, 2006). *Dissertation Abstracts International*.

Wickers, B. Keysers, C., & Plailly, J. (2003). Both disgusted in my insula: the common neural basis of seeing and feeling disgust. *Neuron 40,* 655–664.

Part II.

Psychoanalysts Informed by Body-Based Modalities

4

Learning From Work With Individuals With a History of Trauma

Some Thoughts on Integrating Body-Oriented Techniques and Relational Psychoanalysis

Christopher B. Eldredge and Gilbert W. Cole

Our thinking about working with and through the body in psycho-analysis extends a conversation already under way between psy-choanalysis and traumatology. A recent paper by Ogden, Pain, Minton, and Fisher (2005) maps out some of the problems addressed in this nascent conversation, with the goal of enabling psychoanalytically oriented psychotherapists to include a body-oriented approach in order to deepen and make more effective their clinical work. Trau-matologists such as Pat Ogden et al. (2005) or Peter Levine et al. (1997) have developed clinical techniques to work with people who have endured significant trauma that aim to enable the release of blocked responses to trauma that are encoded somatically. Their work rests on the proposition that the blocked trauma response stored in the body is most readily reached through attending to the body experience of both patient and therapist. Attention to mutual influence, although operationalized differently, is evident in inno-vative thinking about clinical practice including recent relational work on concepts such as the co-construction of experience (Stolo-row & Atwood, 1992), mutual regulation (Beebe & Lachman, 2002), implicit relational knowing (Lyons-Ruth, 1998; Stern, 1998), mutual recognition of subjectivities in thirdness (Benjamin, 1988; Ogden, 1994), and, crucially, multiple self-states and a dissociation model of the mind (Bromberg, 1998; Davies & Frawley, 1994).

A psychoanalytic approach has traditionally emphasized the construction of a narrative, thus engaging the part of the brain, the neocortex, where language is stored and processed. It must be noted that the trajectory of this process begins with the word applied to the body sensation and leads to the body's relief. Knowing that traumatically experienced material is not encoded in a symbolic, but in a procedural, way suggests that we might rethink this. To that end, the work we attempt to describe here reverses this trajectory. P. Ogden et al. (2005) refers to this reversed trajectory as "bottom-up," distinct from the "top-down" direction of creating a narrative that will provide more coherency. Memory, affect, and image arise from a deep, somatic source, not a verbal or a narrative source. The body experience is allowed to remain a body experience until its qualities can be felt fully, perhaps for the first time.

The traumatologists' work suggests that a primary focus on the sensate experience of the client, rather than one emphasizing the cognitive or affective features of experience, enables the completion of a blocked response to trauma because the blocking and subsequent "storage" of the response to trauma is neurophysiologically determined. It is how our bodies work. This is not to say that cognitions and affects are neglected in the work. An emphasis on the sensate experience provides an organizing principle that creates reliable clinical traction because of an altered stance toward difficult transference/countertransference enactments.

A bodily focused technique might be described as a mechanistic approach and, as such, may be unappealing or troublesome to analytically oriented clinicians because we are challenged to take seriously the limits imposed by the ways our nervous systems are structured and function. Yet the proposition that changes in psychological state do in fact occur through unsymbolized, somatic intervention is hardly remote from most people's daily lives. Most of us have firsthand experience of reaching a different quality of consciousness through concrete, mechanistic processes. The endorphin rush that one gets through vigorous exercise is perhaps the most common one; many have noted improvements like a more buoyant mood, clearer thinking, and a reduction of anxiety. The ancient Eastern Yogic tradition is another example. The physical practice of yoga postures produces a change in psychological state regardless of any ideological or spiritual commitment.

What we wish to point out is that these arguably mechanistic processes produce psychological benefits, through which an individual experiences herself in a different way without a cognitive, verbally encoded component. The symbolized component may follow the beneficial effect, but that symbolizing aspect of the experience is unlikely to be the sole cause of the beneficial effect.

We think it ought to be possible for psychoanalytically oriented therapists to benefit from this phenomenon, too. The benefits we have in mind are not limited to the patient. One of our concerns is the therapist's self-care. Clinical work with individuals who have suffered significant trauma exposes the therapist to vicarious traumatization, the "negative transformation of the therapist's inner experience as a result of empathic engagement with and responsibility for traumatized clients" (Saakvitne, 2002), a process that is not always obvious or easy to acknowledge for a range of reasons. We have found it all too easy to dissociate from our own needs for self-care. It has come to the attention of a number of professionals (e.g., Saakvitne) that there is little explicit support or guidance for remedying this lack. Therefore, our engagement of this conversation between psychoanalysis and traumatology explicitly includes developing ways to attend to the needs of both the therapist and the client to insure that the work is not injurious to either.

The conversation we hope to engage and to further here involves four distinct strands of inquiry. We have in mind contemporary researchers on attachment theory including, among others, Beebe and Lachman (1994, 2002), Tronick (1989), Stern (1985), and Lyons-Ruth (2005); research on affect, ranging from Tomkins (1962) to Schore (2003a, 2003b) and Fonagy, Target, Gergely, and Jurist (2002); neurological researchers Porges (2001), van der Kolk, McFarlane, and Weisaeth (1996), and Siegel (1999); and clinicians who specialize in trauma, notably P. Ogden et al. (2005) and Levine et al. (1997). Psychoanalysts have participated in this conversation from the very beginning of psychoanalysis, of course, but the contemporary interest in neuroscience can be traced at least to the late 80s, when Arnold Modell (1993), impressed by Edelman's *Neuronal Darwinism* (1987), speculated that empirical studies someday would be able to show beneficial structural change to the brain as a result of psychoanalytic treatment. The recent work of psychoanalytic researchers such as Schore and Fonagy et al. supports this hope. We find this way of thinking about body-mind to be deeply psychoanalytic. It is consistent with Freud's (1895) original ambitions, with Ferenczi's (1933) insights on the effect of trauma on the psyche, with Loewald's (1960/2000) description of a neutrality based on love and respect for the individual and for individual development, and with Winnicott's (1960/1965) emphasis that there is no way to think about the developing child's psyche without also thinking about his *somatic* condition and development.

One of the challenges of this integrative effort is that the conversation involves divergent theories of mind and the languages in which those theories are expressed. It is a potential clash of metaphors. For some psychoanalysts, the neurophysiological data that reveals more detail of how the brain is structured and how it functions may not yet convincingly demonstrate the emergence of a model of the mind. Meanwhile, other analytic writers are more persuaded and have argued that the data from the neurosciences demonstrates that psychoanalysis has been right all along.

As we approach the question of comparing and integrating the disparate clinical approaches of psychoanalysis and traumatology, we encounter a significant gap. Whether this is bridgeable remains to be seen. That it might be bridged is of value because each discipline offers beneficial insights to the other. One manifestation of this gap is the problem of language. How can we create a space large enough to encompass these different languages and their overlapping areas of interest? We suggest that there is value in using data from neurophysiological work to refine clinical interventions. This is in the interest of broadening the continuum of effective work to include, at the same time, the duality of the concrete and the symbolic. By concrete, we mean that which is neurophysiologically determined. In the domain of the symbolic, the definition has expanded. Once, it described precisely that which can be put into words. Now, we understand it to include the area of implicit relational knowing, which by definition does not "rely on translation of these procedures into reflective (symbolized) knowing" (Lyons-Ruth, 1998, p. 283).

Another gap that needs attention is the problem of the reach or scope of the clinician's attention. Because the traumatologists can neglect the transference/countertransference dimension of the clinical encounter, important aspects of clinical process, particularly that which is encoded as procedural knowledge that is enacted, can pass by unacknowledged and hence remain unanalyzed. And because psychoanalysis, the "talking cure," has focused so much on the word, on making meaning, we believe that a psychoanalytic approach can minimize certain crucial aspects of the clinical situation, most particularly what is carried in and expressed through bodily states, the patient's and our own, that cannot yet be put into words.

We believe that the insights derived from attachment studies, affect research, and the breakthroughs in neuroscience can form a kind of conceptual braid: They are mutually interimplicated. For example, the Boston Process of Change Study Group, in its investigation of how noninterpretive mechanisms lead to change and the question of what changes, look to cognitive developmental studies, neuropsychological data, and attachment studies to "refashion a psychoanalytic metatheory that is consistent both with the new research base and with a more fluid, mutual, and constructivist view of relational change in adulthood" (Lyons-Ruth, 2005, p. 579). Lyons-Ruth contends that "enactive knowing develops and changes by processes that are intrinsic to this system of representation and that do not rely on translation of procedures into reflective (symbolized) knowledge" (p. 579).

Clearly, not everything that contributes to changes in attachment style can be made explicit to a patient, nor ought that to be a goal. However, we suggest that this work includes a more expanded awareness for the therapist of what has often been taken for granted: tone of voice, pacing, gaze, and the therapist's use of her body. By making what has been implicit more explicit to ourselves as we think about what we do and how we do it, we can use these aspects of ourselves more judiciously.

Understanding the client's procedural knowing is expanded by the conceptual braid of neuroscience, attachment, and affect theory. The recent attachment research on the infant/caregiver dyad has indicated that the dominance of the right hemisphere of the brain in the first 12 months of extrauterine life enables only an implicit or procedural registration of affective experience (e.g., Schore, 2003a, 2003b). Fonagy et al. (2002) have argued that it is the caregivers' crucially important task to help the developing child to regulate his affective state when his immature nervous system cannot do this independently. The caregiver in a sense lends her mature nervous system to assist the child to develop the capacity for self-regulation, through which the child becomes able to develop a coherent narrative of his affective experience.

The research on the brain has shown us what this means biologically, physically, and structurally: that it is the right hemisphere dominance in development during this crucial phase that determines that it is the implicit or procedural register of experience that is possible for the infant. Schore (2003a) has compiled empirical evidence of damage to brain structure that is the result of the toxic biological environment brought about by abuse and neglect, which seems to confirm what clinicians have known for a long time: that there is indeed a cause-and-effect relationship between early experience and personality development.

We assume that we are familiar with the unfortunate results when caregivers cannot help the child develop the capacity effectively to regulate his affective state. We have inferred that severe personality disturbances are the sequelae of early experience of dysregulation and misattunement on the part of caregivers. For example, when discussing the intergenerational transmission of trauma, Main and Hess (1990) point out how the caregiver's inability to develop a coherent narrative for herself will drastically impinge on her capacity to help the dependent child to do so.

The "disorganized attachment" is the result of incoherent procedural messages predominant prior to the development of the capacity for declarative communication and this results in a neuronal structure distinctively different from an infant's who manifests a secure attachment. The inability to maintain a coherent narrative will also manifest in a disorganized or otherwise stressful attachment style. The neuroscience studies of the biological and physical effects of this affective/attachment environment show us that a measurable paucity of certain neuronal connections is associated with this attachment experience, along with a preponderance of stress-related hormones present in the brain and bloodstream.

Conversely, when the primary caregiving environment has been one where the caregiver can maintain a coherent, declarative narrative, she is more likely to be able to assist the developing child in the differentiation of her affective experience and the creation of a coherent and declarative narrative of her own. "[M]ental coherence can be revealed within autobiographical narratives that 'make sense' of past experiences and their impact on present functioning as well as allowing the mind to create a sense of hope for the future. An individual moves from being the passive victim of trauma to the active author of the ongoing story of his or her life" (Siegel, 2003, pp. 52–53), which establishes coherence. To regard as "resistance" what may be structural, biological features of the nervous system of some of our patients may produce an iatrogenic reinforcement of the very difficulties that have made treatment necessary.

This conceptual braid guides our effort to develop technical approaches that will make psychoanalytically oriented treatment more useful to people with trauma histories. Specifically, this is a group of clients who are prone to dysregulation, who tend to become hyperaroused and flooded with flashbacks, or hypoaroused and frozen. Often these clients rely on dissociation from intolerable self-states. A more traditional, word-oriented technique, based on a repression model of the mind, often has an effect that is more disorganizing than with patients who have a more flexible array of defenses available. We've found that both our interpretations of the transference, sometimes in relation to enactment phenomena, or our pursuit of a detailed inquiry of the narrative of the traumatogenic event(s) does not yield improvement, but rather unwittingly exacerbates dissociation by triggering the overwhelming situation that required, and continues to require, the dissociative response from the patient in order to survive. Often a patient will become hyperaroused, which can lead to a kind of psychic flooding, or hypoarousal, resulting in a retreat into a depressed withdrawal, in order to counteract the overstimulation brought on by the attention to the narrative.

The technical suggestions we are thinking about ought not to be conceived of in a linear way in relation to psychoanalysis. This is not a preparation for the "real" work. It may be more helpful to think of an arc of a pendulum swinging between what we'd recognize as a relational psychoanalytic approach and one informed by the data recently available from the neurosciences.

Perhaps the central organizing principle for the clinician is the shift of attention from meaning making to tracking the client's bodily sensation. Keeping in mind an understanding of brain anatomy and process, we suggest attending to the ways that we can help the patient stay in the area of felt sense. This involves maintaining the involvement with the instinctual or the reptilian brain and the limbic system, which is that part of the brain that processes nonverbal, affective experience.

This subcortically stored material, including but not limited to uncompleted fight/flight responses to threat, is often located motorically. It is not that the highly activated fight/flight response is in itself the problem; it is that it is uncompleted. Neuroscience data permits us now to understand that because the impulse is uncompleted, the limbic system continues to function as if the threat were still present. The nervous system has not been signaled that the danger is past, thus, the patient lives in a state of constant vulnerability to becoming highly activated by stressful situations and themes because the nervous system continues to respond as if there is danger everywhere. To enable the uncompleted impulse to move toward completion, we seek ways to slow down and focus the work, because the subcortical brain operates more slowly than the neocortex.

We conceptualize our thinking-through questions of technique with five major organizing principles, which we'll illustrate in detail with clinical material:

1) Psycho-Education and Resourcing: We think of resourcing as beneficial for both the client and the therapist. We note that when we are more resourced, we are not so anxious and so are able to stay more present. By maintaining our differentiated state by not being caught in the overactivated state of the patient, we can provide the necessary support for the patient's going on being, while protecting ourselves from being pulled into the collapsed repetition of the traumatic situation. Continued exposure to the horror of what many traumatized patients describe can make us vulnerable to the possibility of vicarious traumatization. Furthermore, our maintaining a state of differentiation preserves the psychic freedom to access a whole range of our emotions, including our own hopefulness and joy.

   The more resourced the patient is, the better equipped she will be to negotiate the inevitable pull into the traumatic material. Providing information about how the nervous system is structured and functions often reduces a patient's feelings of shame and badness. Finally, there is a comprehensible, reasonable explanation for many of the patient's difficulties in functioning.
2) Directiveness: We will be describing a therapist who is far more directive and active than in traditional psychoanalysis. Our aim is to enable the client to access material from a different part of the brain, and this concept guides our interventions. Because free association can be too activating for patients with a trauma history, the therapist cultivates the art of skillful interruption.

Although we do want to hear the whole story, we do not wish the patient to tell it in a way that will be dysregulating. The therapist may be attending to the potential arousing effect of the telling and may also wish to employ the technique of pendulation to support the patient's self-regulation: The therapist gently directs a patient toward a more resourced, safe, capable sense of herself when we see, through careful tracking of the patient state, that she is approaching being caught up in the trauma in such a way that she will be required to use defensive strategies, such as dissociation, which do not permit any discharge of the now-blocked fight/flight response.

3) Use of Language: We are directive in a way that works, that is inviting, and, perhaps most importantly, that gives the locus of control to the patient. Inspired by Milton Erickson's techniques, we may even ask the patient's permission to ask a question. Our use of language is aimed toward facilitating the patient's coherency.

4) Resources: Much of our directiveness will be in the service of helping the patient to develop a greater sense of having psychic resources. These can be conceptualized in roughly three categories: a) internal resources, such as the integrative capacities a patient may have, what ego functions are reliable, and how quickly they can restabilize themselves after becoming activated by traumatic material; b) interpersonal resources, that is, the relationship between the therapist and the patient, how reliable a working alliance might be, for instance, or the possibility for trust; and c) external resources, that is, actual things or activities in the patient's life that the patient reliably and safely enjoys, or resources in imagination, like a superhero who comes to the rescue at stressful moments. The therapist may be called upon to be quite active, supporting and strengthening all categories of these resources.

A careful assessment of what resources are available to the patient is crucial. In those cases where there is little sense of having resources, the therapist's creativity is called upon in helping the patient to build up a felt sense of safety that we then can refer to when pendulating between the traumatic material and a more resourced sense of self. If, for example, it is not possible to feel safe anywhere, or not possible to trust anyone, the point is not to validate that there is no possibility of safety or trust. By checking in a detailed way with the client's felt sense over time, she might come to experience a gently expanding sense of relative safety.

The process of attuned pendulation toward and away from activating traumatic material will often lead to the completion of the blocked fight/flight response. Involuntary muscle movements, signals that the blocked response is beginning to be expressed, are indications that this process is under way. This often scares the patient. She may want to control her movements. It is the therapist's job to support the patient through this loss of bodily control. At these times, explaining that this is the nervous system's way of completing the blocked impulse, and that this is how the nervous system regulates itself, can be extremely useful to the patient.

5) Transference and Transference Enactment: Beginning to work with the transference is done in a "nonpersonalized" way, or, as Winnicott (1960/1965) put it, as if we are the "environmental" mother, who can evolve as the patient's integrative capacity grows. We must be very careful to remember that the transference, or attachment style, is the only option for connecting. It is simply what relating *is* at present. Often, those who have survived a traumatic history are far more attuned to the affective states of others than their own. This awareness changes our theoretical and technical point of view. Rather than attempting to bring the quality of the transference to the attention of the patient, we see it as more effective to help the patient, in greater detail and for longer periods of time, to attend to her somatic experience as she relates to another, in the interest of promoting more self-regulation. We suggest that this is consistent with how Winnicott's "environment mother" provides for the infant. Thinking transference in terms of ourselves as the "object" of transference wishes requires the patient to think of us in that way, which is an impingement. It is a crowding of the patient and inhibits her access to her own felt sense in the present. Thinking transference in this "nonpersonalized" way leads directly to reconsidering enactment.

Schore (2003a) defines enactment in a very specific way that is worth consideration. This definition is based on research on brain development, indicating that the right hemisphere develops very quickly and practically exclusively during the first 8 to 12 months of extrauterine life, during which period the neuronal pathways for processing affective experience and attachment are created. Thus, the primary caregiving relationship actually determines significant aspects of the brain's structure.

Enactment is ubiquitous, then, because it is determined by brain structure, the neurological connections established during the crucial period of the primary caregiving relationship. We suggest that enactments are governed by the attachment styles of both members of the analytic dyad. We agree that we are always participating in enactments, but we think of participating in a different way: We do not try to interpret, or to rely on a verbal communication to attempt to bring to the patient's awareness those experiences that are not encoded verbally. Prior to words being useful to a patient, our aim is to help the patient become more aware of her bodily experience, her felt sense in the here and now, as well as the way it shifts and modulates in response to internal and external stimuli.

We, as analysts, step out of a personalized view as a separate center of subjectivity, moving out of the "we" into curiosity about the patient's felt sense or bodily experience in the present. We understand the enactment as a way to reestablish the attachment that feels like what it is to be connected to an important other. Using the insights derived from the neurophysiological data, we suggest this is a way more effectively to put into operation the analyst's task of holding the particular self-states of both therapist and patient that are in the foreground at any given moment.

Clinical Illustrations

So far, we have detailed the theoretical reasoning that led to the formation of five organizing principles for thinking about clinical technique. Now we describe four events in the course of a treatment conducted by Christopher Eldredge to show how these technical suggestions might actually look in the clinical situation. It must be kept in mind that the pacing of these sessions is crucial. Long silences are frequent, as the therapist has learned to trust that the nervous system needs to take its own time to settle and regulate.

The first clinical moment we'd like to discuss focuses on the self-resources of both the client and the therapist, and the engagement with the patient's prefrontal cortex mode of experiencing in order to resolve a collapse into the complementarity of the perpetrator/victim relational configuration. This resolution also demonstrates the therapist's reliance on the "environmental transference." This is an example of a familiar, uncanny experience: the repetition of the enactment of the traumatic situation. In this clinical moment, from an early stage of the treatment with "S," the therapist feels pulled into the role of perpetrator with the client. He is aware of a bodily sense of tightness as he hears the client tell him she "knows" he is angry with her and that he is likely to verbally attack her at any moment. It is apparent to the therapist that she is experiencing some form of hyperarousal as well as a freeze response, most notably evident by her dilated pupils, shortened breathing, clenched jaw. Before he feels that he can help her find surer footing, the therapist feels it is necessary to attend to his own experience of dysregulation. He first physically moves his body to a more expanded position that allows him to breathe more easily and return to the clinical situation with more balance. Then, as he works with the client's dysregulation, he eventually is able to help the client regain access to her social engagement skills, as well as her ability to more accurately assess a social encounter. Guiding a shift from a mode of experiencing dominated by the trauma, where the limbic system is the part of the brain most engaged, to a mode that includes access to her prefrontal cortex, where greater differentiation of affect is possible, is the therapeutic goal.

S: I know you're really mad at me. I'm five minutes late and this is the third time this has happened and you're really fed up with me.

T: I hear that you're worried that I'm really mad at you, but I'm also noticing that you seem really upset and a bit frozen. Do you feel that way?

S: Yes, I do. I have so many things to do today that I'm overwhelmed. And I'm worried that I'm getting a cold and I may get sick just when I need to be at my best for a team presentation at work.

T: How are you experiencing your body right now?

S: I'm tense, I'm tired and I also feel kind of numb.

T: Is there a place in your body where you don't feel numb or is it a more general feeling?

S: I guess it's kind of general but it's more noticeable in my arms and legs.

T: Is there a place where you are aware of more feeling?

S: Well, not really. Maybe a bit in my feet.

T: You can feel your feet on the floor?

S: Somewhat.

T: Would it be all right with you if I asked you to stay with that experience of feeling the contact of your feet with the floor for a moment?

S: Yes, that's O.K.

T: O.K. ...

(S. seems to relax a bit, her shoulders lower, her face looks less frozen, and she sits back in the chair.)

S: I felt so spaced out when I got here.

(The therapist senses some room to check with S.'s actual experience of him in the present.)

T: Would it be all right with you if I asked you to look at me directly?
S: O.K. …

(Gradually she raises her head and looks into the therapist's eyes.)

T: Is your actual experience in the moment that I am angry at you for being late?

(At first there is no response. As S. looks at the therapist, her eyes become red, and after a moment she speaks.)

S: Well, actually you don't really seem mad to me.

Rather than interpret the transference enactment, the therapist has maintained attention on the bodily experience of the pair, first on his own, and after achieving a more regulated sense of himself, on the client's. With the guidance of the therapist's questions about her bodily experience, the client is able to regulate herself more effectively, which leads her to be able to encounter the therapist in the present, rather than in the context of the traumatic situation. Here, the therapist's intention is to support the client's capacities for self-regulation so that confronting the traumatic material can be useful, rather than leading to a retraumatizing repetition.

The second clinical moment illustrates the value of including psycho-education at appropriate moments. This vignette also demonstrates the use of pendulation from a feeling of being securely resourced to the edge of a trauma vortex, working with overcoupled beliefs, and the use of invitational language to support the client's sense of being in control. The work also involves attention to the disorganized and hostile/dependent forms of attachment. Additionally, this is an example of the use of countertransference disclosure regarding the dilemma confronting the pair.

This clinical moment begins with the therapist's awareness of the client's highly agitated state when she enters the room. He can anticipate from previous experience with her that she is likely to begin crying in a way that will make it very difficult for her to speak once she has regained her composure. When this has happened on previous occasions, she has said that she knows it was a mistake for her to come to the session. In an attempt to slow down what feels like the inevitable collapse of the working alliance, the therapist clearly sets out this dilemma:

T: I sense that given how upset you appear to be that if I sit here and let you express what you are feeling with no comment, that you'll begin to cry very hard, become hoarse, and then say that you shouldn't have come. On the other hand, if I ask if we can slow down the experience that you are having, that you will tell me that you feel I am trying to silence you the way your father always did. It seems that what has gotten put together for you is the belief that you have only two choices when it comes to self-expression.

   Either you say what's on your mind, which often includes expression of strong emotion that will eventually feel injurious to you, that is, you'll be hoarse or the person to whom you'll be speaking will become punitive, or you have to be calm and "nice"—not causing any overt distress to yourself or others. But that tack will leave you feeling completely erased.

S: That's true.

T: So how would you like to proceed given that dilemma?

S: (after a pause) It feels like a bit of a relief to know that neither of those choices is really very satisfying. No wonder I feel so helpless. I'm not sure what to do, but I'm glad you asked me.

The third clinical illustration demonstrates how to stabilize the client who has dropped into a highly dissociated state, while also showing how the use of resources can help to mobilize the client's blocked fight response in relation to her aggressive and terrorizing father. The therapist keeps working in a nonpersonalized transference by keeping the focus on tracking the client's experience of her body, encouraging her to slow down her physical movements so that her nervous system can experience the full benefit of her completed fight responses. As this occurs, and she has a more up-to-date experience of herself, the client is more able to experience her social engagement ability in relation to the therapist, who is no longer experienced as a "giant." Also, as the therapist encourages her to pendulate between her present experience of strength and her terrified, younger self-state, the client not only experiences her current ability to defend herself, but she also gains the ability to have compassion for the little girl in this flashback who was all alone with no one to protect her.

   The vignette begins at the moment the client enters the therapist's office, flustered by being 20 minutes late.

S: I know you're furious with me for being late.

(S. is very agitated, talking rapidly, and rocking in her chair.)

T: It can happen that people are late sometimes.

S: No, you're really mad at me. I'm sorry.

T: I know that you're upset, thinking that you kept me waiting. Could we slow things down a little bit?

S: I can't hear what you are saying. I see your mouth moving but I can't hear what you're saying. It's foggy.

(The therapist realizes that the client is in a highly dissociated state and attempts to work with this collapse.)

T: As you notice the fog, what are you aware of in your body?

S: I'm small and it's still foggy.

(The therapist seeks to help S. connect to a resource that will address her collapsed, dissociated experience by attempting to shift her focus to something that she has previously reported as a resource that helps her to feel strong and present.)

T: In this moment you're feeling so much distress, what is it like to remember your friend, Sonia, and how much time the two of you spent laughing at the silliest things?

(S. smiles at first, then lowers her head.)

S: I'm always making mistakes and then I get yelled at. Nothing will ever change. I can't ever get it right.

(She moans and begins rocking.)

T: You don't make mistakes with Sonia.

S: Yes, but Sonia's different.

(S. begins to make fists as she says this.)

T: I know you aren't always comfortable hearing me mention things that I notice about your physical expressions, but I can't help noticing that you're making fists as you say that Sonia is different.

(S. pounds the armrests on the chair.)

S: Sonia doesn't judge me or yell at me.
T: Who does?
S: My father, he thinks he knows everything.

(S. is clearly returning from a collapsed, dissociated place with a lot of energy in her body.)

T: It looks as if your hands and arms want to move in some way. Is that true?

(She squeezes her fists more tightly.)

S: I'd like to punch him and get him out of my face!
T: How would it be to experience your fists and arms as sources of strength as you defend yourself from your father?

(She starts to punch vigorously into the air.)

T: Would you be willing to slow the action down a bit to give your nervous system the chance to deeply experience your competent fighting responses?
S: I'm scared. What if it doesn't work?
T: Just try to stay with your physical experience for a moment. Right now, you're here with me in the safety of this office.
S: I see his ugly, red face close to mine, yelling.
T: As you see that image, what do you notice in your body?
S: I feel my fists get tighter. I want him to shut up and get away from me.
T: Let your fists and your arms move if they want to.

(She slowly begins to push forward with her fists. As she speeds up, the therapist asks her to see if she can keep the movement slow and deliberate so her muscles and nervous system get the benefit of deeply experiencing the completion of her powerful and competent fighting movements to defend herself.)

T: How is that for you, to take charge of the situation in this way?
S: (smiling) It's weird, but it feels kind of good ... different, I guess. I'm not used to feeling this way.
T: What way?
S: In control and solid ... and ...

T: And?

S: Well, I guess, kind of strong …. But I'm a pretty weak and flaky person.

T: What do you notice if you allow yourself to alternate from your direct experience of being strong right now to your story of being a weak, flaky person and then back to your experience of strength in this moment?

S: Well, my thoughts about being weak seem less real because they don't match what I'm feeling right now.

T: As you stay with your current experience of being strong, does anything else become apparent to you?

S: (laughing) Yes, I seem bigger and you seem smaller. I mean, not smaller, but you don't seem like a giant. And I'm not scared about you being angry at me. In fact, you don't seem angry. This experience is so different from the way I felt when I came in.

T: Your present experience seems more up to date. You're not being transported back in time in a flashback to when you were a little girl being screamed at by her father.

S: That's true. I feel sad for that girl.

T: She didn't have anyone to protect her then, but you were fighting for her just now.

S: I want to. (She puts her arms around herself.)

The last clinical illustration involves working with involuntary muscle movement and work in the procedural memory. This extended piece of process also shows how the restoration of self-regulation leads to the capacity to regain therapeutic traction.

This vignette demonstrates how attention to and the use of involuntary muscle movement, described by Porges (2001) in his elaboration of the polyvagal theory of the autonomic nervous system, can facilitate a gradual emergence from a frozen collapse into a kind of fluidity that will allow the patient to use movement to access disconnected parts of herself. Once some kind of resource development and stabilization has been established, the therapist can assist the patient to move from the experience of obsessively thinking about an array of negative outcomes that trap her into escalating experiences of helplessness.

She can breathe more deeply and regularly as she moves out of dissociation and attendant levels of hyperarousal. She regains the ability to move her body more fluidly, and she becomes more able to associate to disturbing material in ways that allow her to see the possible connections between this material and her inability to write freely. As she finds the words that help her to feel more regulated, she continues to follow the involuntary movement of her writing hand. In this place of thirdness, or the transitional space of curiosity and possibility, the client can use the therapist as a resource to help her connect the dissociated parts of her frightening experiences that have heretofore only made themselves known in unverbalized, procedural ways. Crucial to this sense of resolution will be the completion of the response of disgust, so often an important component of the relational trauma and betrayal where the victim's inherent, authentic sense of self has been poisoned.

This vignette illustrates what Benjamin (1999) describes as "affective, symbolic play which allows two partners to construct a dialogue [that] positions the third in terms of the music or dance that two partners follow .... [I]t is as if we were sight-reading an unknown score. We make it up as we go, yet it feels as though we are oriented to something outside. If feels discovered as well as invented" (p. 206).

S: I'm so afraid, I'm freaking out. If I don't get that report done, I'll be fired. I can't do it.

(She grasps her sides and begins to moan as she rocks back and forth.)

T: Is there any place in your body where you feel a bit more relaxed?
S: No.
T: Do you have feeling in your body, right now?
S: No, I'm mostly numb.
T: Mostly numb. Is there any place where you have feeling in your body?
S: My back, I can feel my back on the chair.

(Attending to her back is the point of entry to a more resourced physical experience of herself.)

T: Good. Just take a moment to notice the feeling of your back against the chair.

(As she does, she takes a deep breath and exhales. S. remains still for a while, then spontaneously grasps an imaginary pen and speaks.)

S: I can't write. Something very bad will happen if I do. I don't know what it is, but it is very scary. I see hands around me and I know that I'm about to be murdered.

T: As you notice how afraid you are, is there any place in your body where you feel a bit less frightened?

S: No, I'm writing now, well, not really writing, I'm signing something. I'm signing a consent form that will allow me to walk into a burning building.

(S. is slowly moving her imaginary pen.)

T: I'm wondering if there is a way to slow this down. Perhaps there is a way to see about getting the fire out in the building before proceeding. What do you think?

S: No, this is inevitable, all that is required now is my signature.

At this point, it is clear to the therapist that his attempts to steer S. into a safer direction aren't working. He realizes that his mounting anxiety is reinforcing her experience of helplessness and feeling alone. He removes his attention from S. and focuses on his own body experience, to attend to his own anxiety, and eventually to feel more centered. He silently says, "I trust my ability to balance myself, and I trust my ability to make contact with S. when I am more centered." He notices that he feels more relaxed and he can breathe more easily. Shortly after this exchange with himself, something quite unexpected happens. S. puts down her imaginary pen.

S. starts to move her hand back and forth in the air. She isn't looking at the therapist. First, the movement is a gentle oscillation back and forth with her writing hand. Before long, she starts to move her other hand in a similar way.

T: I notice that you're moving your hands.

S: Yes, I'm feeling freer. I'm little and happy. I see myself reaching for a sink to wash my hands. It's fun. I'm splashing in the water. I'm excited because I'm going to a birthday party. What a great day, a party to go to. Then my mother slaps my hands and tells me I'm taking too much time to get ready. I'm shocked. I was just being happy. I didn't even spill any water on the floor. Why did she do that? I see her rough hands drying mine off.

T: Your mother couldn't be with your excitement then.

(S.'s face turns sad and anxious as she continues to make splashing motions, reaching up to the sink.)

S: Now I see other hands. I'm in bed with my father, who is laughing with me, but then he touches me in a way that makes me feel uncomfortable … touching me the wrong way. I feel happy to be with him but then scared and ashamed that he's touching me like that. Now, I'm back at the birthday party. I don't care about being there. I just sit in a chair. One of the mothers thinks that I might be shy and tries to get me to join in with the other kids, but I don't. I don't care about it at all. My mother finished off any fun. I just wait to go home. It is as if my fun self has been killed off. Just like in the bed. I was laughing until my father touched me the wrong way, and then fun was killed off. I just turned to stone.

T: Something is fun, like splashing in the sink and laughing with your father in bed, and then the fun is killed off.

S: Yes, that's right, that's exactly how it happened. Then I'm a stone. I don't care about anything fun. It doesn't matter. Other nice people try to come to engage me, but now I'm gray, I just see those nice people through a fog. I see their faces, but I can't really hear them. I don't do anything spontaneous. I just do my homework. People leave me alone when I'm at my desk doing my homework.

T: Do you like being at your desk, doing your homework?

S: Not really, but no one bothers me because that's what I'm supposed to be doing.

T: Do you remember doing anything else as a young person that was spontaneous that you actually enjoyed for which there were no negative consequences?

(S. makes a spontaneous hand movement. Her hand springs up and down.)

S: Yes. I used to be a springboard diver. I had a coach who was nice and my parents were never there. He was nice to me. While it was exciting, it could also be very scary. Particularly, three-meter springboard diving. You're high up, and you're doing a complicated dive. The first couple of times you need another pair of eyes watching until your body remembers what to do and when to do it. If your coach doesn't spot you correctly by calling you out of that dive at just the right second, you can have a bad accident and really hurt yourself.

T: You have to trust the person in charge of your safety.

S: Yes, you have to keep track of where the water is as you spin or you're lost. I'm spinning. I can see the water in the sink. Then I see the hands on me in the bed. I lose myself in the dive. I can't find my way and there isn't a good person spotting me. I lose my orientation to the water and crash. I'm finished. No coach. Just corrupt people. I hit the water and go under. No one to pull me out.

T: No one is watching out for you. It's very sad.

S: (taking a deep breath) Yes, it's sad. I haven't thought about those things for a long time. And I never connected any of it to the birthday party, to the bed with my father and my diving coach. I'm thinking about it. I feel nauseous. It's really awful. No wonder I don't think about these things coherently, it is really atrocious. No wonder I would want to sign a death warrant for myself. There is no way to win.

T: What do you notice in your body as you say, "There is no way to win"?

S: I feel some relief because it is true. There wasn't any way to stay open in such a dangerous environment. I feel sad. I was smart enough to get through an awful life with scary people. No wonder I become anxious about writing. Look at what would come out of my pencil if I had known all this. I probably would have been even more thoroughly obliterated if I had been able to say any of these things. I guess I did enjoy a kind of damage control, my limiting their concerted effort to killing off my joy and trust.

T: What is it like to say all this? What do you notice in your body as you put these images and thoughts together?

S: I've been ashamed of hiding for so long, when it turns out to be the very thing that may have saved my life. I also feel that you were a good spotter while I was up there in the middle of that high, difficult dive. You didn't get in my way, but somehow I knew you were there if I needed a spot. You were watching, but you let me wander where I needed to go, flow with the water, from the sink, to the diving board, to the bed, then out of the pool to safe ground. It's a lot. Yes, it's sad, but I don't feel crazy or ashamed. I'm amazed. I don't know where all those images and thoughts came from. I just followed my hand. I feel great relief. I know what I've just said is related to my anxiety about writing, but in this moment, I don't even care about that. I feel relieved to know what is bothering me and to feel a lot of shame leave. I'm feeling relieved. I'm tired, but I feel good.

Conclusion

We've presented a way of working that seeks to keep in play that which is more concrete, realistically recognizing the limits imposed by the structure and functioning of the nervous system, with what traditionally has been regarded as the symbolic, but now includes the domain of enactive relational knowing. The more literal, concrete interventions inform both the therapist's sense of thirdness and the patient's, which expands each partner's capacities to experience greater subjective complexity. In work that focuses on sensate experience, patients gain some freedom to allow for the completion of blocked responses to trauma. Working this way aims to include these historical events in a more flexible and resilient self-experience in the present, rather than triggering a dissociative response that obliterates dialogue between different experiences of self. We understand dialogic to be a process where each mode is preserved, and each can catalyze the other in an ongoing process. The enactive relational mode and its cognitive, symbolic counterpart are each accessed in therapeutic work that remains focused on sensate experience, holding a place for what cannot be put into words, must not be put into words, even while expanding the terrain of experience that can be symbolized.

References

Beebe, B., & Lachman, F. (1994). Representation and internalization in infancy: Three principles of salience. *Psychoanal. Psychol., 11*, 127–165.

Beebe, B., & Lachman, F. (2002). *Infant research and adult treatment: Co-constructing interactions.* Hillsdale, NJ: The Analytic Press.

Benjamin, J. (1988). *Bonds of love.* New York: Pantheon.

Benjamin, J. (1999). Recognition and destruction: An outline of intersubjectivity. In S. Mitchell & L. Aron (Eds.), *Relational psychoanalysis: The emergence of a tradition.* Hillsdale, NJ: The Analytic Press.

Bromberg, P. (1998). *Standing in the spaces: Essays on clinical process, trauma and dissociation.* Hillsdale, NJ: The Analytic Press.

Bucci, W. (1997). *Psychoanalysis and Cognitive Science: A multiple code theory.* New York: Guilford.

Davies, J., & Frawley, M. G. (1994). *Treating the adult survivor of childhood sexual abuse.* New York: Basic Books.

Edelman, G. (1987). *Neural Darwinism.* New York: Basic Books.

Ferenczi, S. (1933). Confusion of tongues between adults and children. In *Final contributions to the problems and methods of psycho-analysis.* M. Balint (Ed.) New York: Bruner/Mazel, 1980.

Fonagy, P., Target, M., Gergely, G., & Jurist, E. (2002). *Affect regulation, mentalization, and the development of the self.* New York: Other Press.

Fosshage, J. (2005). The explicit and implicit domain in psychoanalytic change. *Psychoanalytic Inquiry, 24*, 516–539.

Freud, S. (1895). Project for a scientific psychology. In *Standard edition* (Vol. 1, pp. 245–397). London: Hogarth Press, 1960.

Levine, P., & Frederick, A. (1997). *Waking the tiger: Healing trauma*. Berkeley, CA: North Atlantic Books.

Loewald, H. (1960/2000). On the therapeutic action of psychoanalysis. In Lear, J. (Ed.), *The essential Loewald: Collected papers and monographs*. Hagerstown, MD: University Publishing Group.

Lyons-Ruth, K. (1998). Implicit relational knowing: Its role in development and psychoanalytic treatment. *Infant Mental Health J., 19*, 282–289.

Lyons-Ruth, K. (2005). The two-person unconscious: Intersubjective dialogue, enactive relational representation, and the emergence of new forms of relational organizations. In L. Aron & A. Harris (Eds.), *Relational psychoanalysis, Vol. 2, Innovation and expansion*. Hillsdale, NJ: The Analytic Press.

Main, M., & Hess, E. (1990). Parents' unresolved traumatic experiences are relationed to infant disorganized status. Is frightened and/or frightening parental behavior the linking mechanism? In M. Greenberg, D. Cicchetti, & M. Cummings (Eds.), *Attachment in the preschool years* (pp. 161–182). Chicago: University of Chicago Press.

Modell, A. (1993). *The private self*. Cambridge, MA: Harvard University Press.

Ogden, P., Pain, C., Minton, K., & Fisher, J. (2005, Fall). Including the body in mainstream psychotherapy for traumatized individuals. *Psychologist-Psychoanalyst*.

Ogden, T. (1994). The analytic third: Working with intersubjective clinical facts. *Internat. J. Psycho-Anal., 75*, 3–19.

Porges, S. (2001). The polyvagal theory: Phylogenetic substrates of a social nervous system. *Internat. J. Psychophys., 42*, 123–146.

Saakvitne, K. W. (2002). Therapists at risk: Hazards and safeguards of psychotherapy practice. In L. Van de Creek (Ed.), *Innovations in clinical practice: A source book* (Vol. 20, pp. 325–342). Sarasota, FL: Professional Resource Press.

Schore, A. (2003a). *Affect dysregulation and disorders of the self*. New York: Norton.

Schore, A. (2003b). *Affect regulation and the repair of the self*. New York: Norton.

Siegel, D. (1999). *The developing mind*. New York: Guilford.

Siegel, D. (2003). In interpersonal neurobiology of psychotherapy: The developing mind and the resolution of trauma. In M. Solomon & D. Siegel (Eds.), *Healing trauma: Attachment, mind, body and brain*. New York: Norton.

Stern, D. (1985). *The interpersonal world of the infant: A view from psychoanalysis and developmental psychology*. New York: Basic Books.

Stern, D. (1998). The process of therapeutic change involving implicit knowledge: Some implications of developmental observations for adult psychotherapy. *Infant Mental Health J., 19*, 300–308.

Stern, D. B. (1997). *Unformulated experience: From dissociation to imagination in psychoanalysis.* Hillsdale, NJ: The Analytic Press.

Stolorow, R., & Atwood, G. (1992). *Contexts of being: The intersubjective foundations of psychological life.* Hillsdale, NJ: The Analytic Press.

Tomkins, S. (1962). *Affect, Imagery, Consciousness.* New York: Springer.

Tronick, E. (1989). Emotions and emotional communication in infants. *Amer. Psychol., 44*, 112–119.

van der Kolk, B. A., McFarlane, A. C., & Weisaeth, L. (Eds.). (1996). *Traumatic stress: The effects of overwhelming experience on mind, body, and society.* New York: Guilford.

Winnicott, D. W. (1960/1965). The theory of the parent-infant relationship. In *The maturational processes and the facilitating environment* (pp. 37–55). Madison, CT: International Universities Press.

5

The Coconstruction of "Psychoanalytical Choreography" and the Dancing Self

Working With an Anorectic Patient

Maria Paola Pacifici

> I am persuaded that movement is by itself expressive beyond any intention.
>
> I dance because I get from it a profound pleasure. ... I figure out dance as if it were a constant transformation of life itself.
>
> **Merce Cunningham**

Dance and Creativity as an Expression of the Self

Picture a minimalist stage and a white sheet at the background, evoking images of purity and contrasts. The gracefulness of the choreography and the humanness of the dancers' presence on the stage completely capture the observer.

The dancers are wearing coveralls with dates on them. These represent their birth dates and some meaningful events of their lives. Silently, the dance is deployed right behind and inside those figures, one movement after the other in the creativity of gesture. All this is visual, but other things may be imagined; for example, there may be other dates as well, places of the mind where something changed forever and where new bodily alphabets were learned and assimilated to live and "swim" in the future.

What happens in an observer watching a contemporary dance performance? What does the observer feel inside the body? Which emotions are transmitted from the dancers to the audience? What is the function of it all? We, applying Laban's (1950) method, might ask where inside the body does movement originate? What qualities does it possess? Where is it directed, and where in the space does it lead us? Which are the body and mind states to which movement is connected?

That choreographic image is contained in a dance performance of "Another Evening" brought to the stage some years ago by the contemporary choreographer Bill T. Jones. That performance triggered in the spectators conflicting emotions, ranging from fear of the past to a strange nostalgia for the future, from immobility and astonishment to an overwhelming desire to move.

Fragments of autobiographic movements were repeated in gestures intended to make it completed, to bring the whole movement under the skin of the audience, to jolt the audience and make them move. The dates on the dancers' bodies were thus transformed into words, warnings, memories.

Jones tells of Estelle, a mother who taught her son to shout unrelentingly his own name while they crossed a river (the river to adulthood); otherwise his soul would not make its way along the water. If the voice of a mother is distractedly muted, the son's soul may dissolve along the way. Perhaps this is the intimate message of Jones's choreography, as seen from the son's perspective.

Some dancers, despite their mothers' having been unable to guide them across the river to adult life, nevertheless accomplished the passage and engaged in a solo performance, in an attempt to interweave forgotten or never known gestures and limits. This solo thus becomes a prayer, a persuasion, and a transformation.

The dancers, with the power of their communications by gesture, succeed in bringing the audience "inside" the choreography, to feel the same nostalgia for a peaceful future. Thus, the dancers' movements become a strong intellectual power of good, suggesting the possibility of alternatives to the ungraceful, hurried lifestyles so often imposed on individuals by contemporary society.

Drawing from the dance experience—from both that felt on our own skin and that tasted while we sit comfortably in a theater— allows us to place the body and its meanings, unveiled by the movement, at the center of our own reflection on ourselves, both alone and in relation with others.

I believe that the art of movement can guide us in uncovering our own perceptual talents and help us to refine our knowledge of personal bodily states, especially in those of us who, as psychotherapists, wish to place the body and its meanings at the forefront of the analytic stage.

Attention to bodily experience, in the light of its links with psychic mechanisms in affective relations, is now well accepted. We must focus not only on our patients' body experiences, but also on our own, as it is through these experience that we might understand our patients. The body thus becomes the main theater of affect processing.

> It's not only patients who may react in their bodies, analysts too must be extremely attentive to their own bodies. That is, much of what we pick up from our patients we may first feel in our bodies, and perhaps most immediately in our breathing. Our bodies are the primary arena for the psychophysiological processing of affect. (Aron, 1998, p. 28)

The body's involvement in dance bespeaks pleasurable sensory components. The body, intrinsically both subject and object, becomes an active and skillful actor and, at the same time, an audience. Hence, dance represents an encounter between our somatic and psychic dimensions.

Dancers uses their bodies to communicate, to play, to express pleasure, desire, sufferance, vitality, curiosity for the beauty of life, and confidence in its rhythmicity. They use their bodies to grasp the continuity in the perception of time and acquire confidence in spatial orientation, competence, and reciprocity. All this they must achieve most particularly with respect to persons not accustomed to dance, because the dancers must express themselves through a "mute" art. Hence they necessarily have to refine an alternative communicative language that highlights its complex and fascinating nonverbal dimension.

As Merce Cunningham (Cunningham & Lesschaeve, 1988) stated, during the dance lesson, a dancer has to combat to let the movement enter the body and get along completely. I borrow this idea to under-line that sometimes, during an analytic session, we also have to work hard "with the body" so that our mind and that of the patient are attuned to such a point that the autobiographical meanings of the patient's history and the psychic function of both of us completely suffuse each another. The subjective experience thus becomes recip-rocal, a universe of creativity and clarity, in a kind of initial body-mind "improvisation" that marks the beginning of the analytic process. As Rotenberg (1988) stated, creativity is a major transfor-mational force in everybody's life. The psychoanalytic process, like many arts—music, the dramatic arts, dance—swings between a well-defined setting and improvisation; Ringstrom (2001), drawing a parallel between classical and improvisational theater, supports the idea that the former represents a metaphor of more technical issues, like method or theory, whereas the latter deals with the ongoing psy-choanalytic process as it develops. The same thinking could apply to dance, conventional steps being necessary for dance to occur and improvisation as the expression of creativity and authenticity, the patient's inner drives that are antidotal to the crushing and perva-sive inauthenticity of the patient's inner life and his life with respect to others.

Movement also may become a selfobject (Kohut, 1983) function, as a source of creativity, expressed through or triggered by move-ment itself. We can observe this function when a patient who is pro-ceeding toward a repair and transformational experience during the analytic process approaches a creative activity of any kind, whether dance or writing or painting. We may say that selfobjects are psycho-logical support systems; places, activities, arts, and persons may all provide vital selfobject functions.

In this sense, contemporary dance, more than classical dance, may become a selfobject experience. In contemporary dance, danc-ers train their bodies, the tools of their art, "not to accomplish the ethereal, effortless facade of ballet, but to discover the relationship between the weight of their bodies and gravity" (Press, 2002, p. 84), and to discover the art of improvisation so as to be connected with their inner world.

The choreographer Dan Wagoner has aptly illustrated the ability of movement to provide a selfobject function, claiming that he was absolutely absorbed with movement, loving and trusting it. All of his dances began with movement, and the basic problem or idea was always a movement problem. As he made choices, he danced them over and over, added on and explored in as many directions as possible, believing that movement will lead him somewhere interesting (quoted in Kreemer, 1987).

The Body and Self-Experience

The psyche is not confined in the body; rather, the two are in a reciprocal and continuous relation. Hence, transformation occurs in both. This continuity characterizes also the corporeal dialog between analyst and patient. At every moment of the analytic relationship there is a continuous search for the harmony (or disharmony) between the body and mind of both analyst and patient. This search cannot be made only through words without the body or only outside the body. It is most productive through nonverbal and spatial means. The possibility of knowing and exploring the analytic space and of moving around within it, shifting from chaos to fluidity, allows us to experience internal and external spatiality, which are most important for the very growth of an individual.

In Plato's (ca. 360 B.C.) *Phaedrus,* the internal and the external of the body are envisaged as a whole: "Socrates: Beloved Pan, and all ye other gods who haunt this place, give me beauty in the inward soul; and may the outward and inward man be at one."

This desire for integration of the internal and the external may be traced back to a stage of human life in which such unity was perceived by the infant as real. In fact, the child's earliest formal perceptions of the world are rudimental sensory experiences. The earliest self-experience focuses exclusively on bodily experiences that the infant and, subsequently, the child undergo during the first caring relations with others. Differentiation from the other and the subsequent sense of self originate from early bodily, sensorimotor, and proprioceptive sensations. D. W. Winnicott (1953) developed a model that attaches increasing value to the dimensions of *play,* art, and creativity in the unfolding of an authentic self.

Dancers translate into form and movement those mental images that go beyond sensory abilities, and the audience recalls those images in their unconscious, converting them in their own spatial-temporal dimensions. Art thus becomes "a common spiritual experience, one of an absolutely specific nature" (Kris, 1952, p. 32). Form becomes simultaneously an object situated outside the self and an object contained within the most intimate self.

The artistic dance experience may also constitute a reparative development and elicit the expression of hidden or devitalized, though nevertheless present, self-states, which comprise every human being's psychic potential. Martha Graham (1991), the famous dancer and revolutionary choreographer whose impact on contemporary dance is legendary, proposed that, through the relationship engendered from and within dance movement with others, people complete themselves by becoming dancers. Without a relation with one's most authentic self and with the self of another person there may be no understanding of why we move in space or even why we exist in this world.

Graham conceived the idea of a "new body," that is, a body that is aware of its inner energy, that consists in drives and desires, breathing, gravity, and sensuousness.

Dance induces an affective response in both performer and spectator; in fact, the latter is an active agent in attributing and organizing (even at an unconscious level) his or her own personal meaning of the communication, occurring through the movement. Infant research analyst Daniel N. Stern (2000) claims that music and dance convey "vitality affects," subjectively perceived changes of inner emotional states, and that such affects enter the intersubjective domain through "affect attunement" initially in the mother-infant dyad and subsequently in all social interactions.

A parallel may be traced in the intersubjective field, wherein the movement stemming from analyst and patient interaction emerges. During the psychoanalytic process, authentic awareness of reciprocal bodily selves occurs:

> Not the same as speech, bodily communication nonetheless is clinically critical in the flesh of not only patients but their analysts too. Enactment, conversely, constructs bodies. Bodies do not make minds, nor minds bodies; rather they are intersubjectively emergent, a density of origin with fascinating clinical ramifications. (Dimen, 1998, p. 68)

Like a dancer, who uses all the senses to transform movement into art and whose art is built on a listening habit, listening with one's entire self (Graham, 1991), an analyst must sensitize all the senses to perceptual channels to receive the other, in particular, the channels of the other's complex bodily dimension.

In contemporary improvisational dance ateliers, early teaching focuses on bodily tuning with others' movements, whether in couples or in a group. In fact, *kinesthetic empathy* in dance therapy is the basic inner core of dance in general, and of nonverbal communication more specifically. Such empathy expresses itself as an experience of empathic attunement to the other's movements and constitutes an experience of imagination. In improvisation choreographic ateliers, the feeling of belonging to a group, sharing the same affinities and sensibilities, often springs spontaneously among participants moving side by side, regardless of their histories and even their names. In fact, to "dance empathically" there is no need for such "superfluous" information; it is each person's gestural style that creates a bridge between one's own self and the self of another.

We may think of kinesthetic empathy (but cenesthetic as well—in medicine cenesthesia is used to describe the perception of one's own hollow organs) as the ability to imagine ourselves in another's movement. Kinesthetic empathy is comparable to the empathic attitude in psychoanalysis, which is represented by empathy, the ability to feel oneself in the other's inner world, that is, Kohut's (1959/1978) "vicarious introspection."

A cocreation is elicited by an expert leader within choreographic atelier groups, integrating the contributions of each individual dancer through empathic observation of the other's movement. To refine such ability, which all humans possess thanks to the relationship with their first caregiver, the group leader encourages the refinement of movement "transmission," which occurs by guessing the even minimal movements of the dancers (for example, those of a finger or a forearm movement) standing at each side of a dancer.

In this direction, dance represents a privileged area, a place to create an intersubjective field between dancers and among them and those who watch them. Dance is a human activity favoring transient intersubjective contacts, real or imaginary (Stern, 2004).

There is no need to express verbally what the body has already said in its own language. The authenticity of gesture is a precious quality of human relations. All too often, translating the body's language into words fragments and undermines a significant and rich process, which stands out as such and needs no useless specifications. Stern, elegantly working through in great detail what is happening in the present moment when two minds meet each other in a shared experience, stresses the value of dance as an opportunity to learn about the nonverbal dimension of human experience.

Dance, the Creative Process, and Psychoanalysis

Those who want to understand the creative process of dance and its cathartic effect as an art would do well to assist in the construction of a contemporary dance choreography. During such a creative process we may observe both the labor and inquietude of the creative artist, as well as the choreographic cocreation process, when the leader inevitably takes into account and integrates the improvised movement of the other dancers. Here the class becomes an arena of intersubjective corporeity. In this context, the depth of the creative experience may modify also the body images of the dancer for his self and for the other.

The parallel with the analytic process and the analytic relationship is evident. What Stephen Mitchell (1988) wrote about it is illuminating:

> If one is invited to a dance, one either attends in some fashion or does not attend in some fashion.... I do not propose going to the dance and complaining about the music, but enjoying the dance as offered, together with questioning the singularity of the style. How did it come about that the analysand learned no other steps? Why does the analysand believe that this is the only desirable dance there is? Most analysands need to feel that their own dance style is appreciated in order to be open to expanding their repertoire. (p. 212)

The reconstruction of one's own gestural style through, for instance, the practice of dance movement therapy (DMT) could constitute a stimulating experience for learning about nonverbal language and somatic functioning and their application to the analytic experience. After all, that experience allows us to pursue authentic knowledge of ourselves, from our history to our mental functioning. DMT is an experiential, body-expressive therapy developed during the mid-60s that considers the body as inseparable from the mind and embeds it in a relational matrix; the DMT recognizes a therapeutic and cathartic value to dance and reconstructs a history of gesture development, achieving "a corrective bodily experience."

Likewise, searching for authentic movement is possible in the process of DMT. Like the analyst's witnessing function during the analytic process, Mary Starks Whitehouse's (1958) Authentic

Movement (AM) discipline, one of the techniques used in DMT, witnesses the other's movement: "the core of the movement experience is the feeling of moving and being moved" (p. 43). AM is based on the relation between a witness who observes the movement and a *mover*, who, with eyes closed, feels the witness's presence. The witness focuses attention not only on what the *mover* is doing, but also on his own inner experience in interacting with who is moving in the space.

A grasp of the full range of nonverbal behavior makes it starkly clear that we are never "just talking," that we are always influencing one another through subtle and obvious aspects of nonverbal behavior as well as through what we express in words and language (La Barre, 2001, p. 6).

To be moved represents a form of AM arising from the unconscious, what Jung (1931) called "active imagination," that is, imagining that a visual image, dreamed or originating in fantasy, is connected to its corresponding physical action through the performance of movement. In fact, imagination and imitation have neural activity correlates that lie in regions near those activated when movement is actually performed. These neurons are called "mirror neurons" (Rizzolatti, Fogassi, & Gallese, 2001) and are attributed to an empathy function (Carr et al., 2003). This research line explains how and how much each of us is involved in the action of the other in the very moment of its occurrence—thanks to the activity of mirror neurons—during movement processing, just as if we were actually performing the action.

Joan Chodorow (1986), an eminent dance therapist and Jungian analytical psychologist, underlined that

> [a]s early as in 1916, Jung suggested that expressive body movement is one of numerous ways to give form to the unconscious. In a description of active imagination, he wrote that it could be done in any number of ways: "according to individual taste and talent ... dramatic, dialectic, visual, acoustic or in the form of dancing, painting, drawing or modeling." (p. 89)

The difference between AM and the other DMT techniques and the bodily dimension in the analytic process is the presence, in the latter, of the witness alternately as analyst and as observer of movement.

Gesture expressiveness and the value of silence are characteristic qualities of human beings and inexhaustible sources of important cues for the comprehension of a patient's and our subjective worlds.

We are intrigued with what comes from "inside" with respect to movement; as "talking cure" therapists, we should not forget that subjective experience, comprising bodily experience, is not a self-standing dimension, but a continuous research tool probing ourselves in the same instant as we deal with our patients' subjective experiences.

Our patients' words "touch" our bodies and induce physiological changes. Being aware of these changes is basic to our learning to stand with our patients and move along with them. In the analytic setting, it is important to observe constantly and methodically the movements between patient and therapist to improve the outcome and to learn how to "stand" with them and "move" along with them. Just as it is only by direct experience that we can gain confidence with the analytic work, it is only through direct experience that one may become deeply familiar with bodily experience.

Of course, as we observe our patients moving in our offices, we cannot always capture all the elements of their bodily experience; but we have to bear in mind that the nonverbal dimension is illuminating at least as much as the verbal one. After all, verbal language is a relatively recent acquisition, both ontogenetically and phylogenetically.

Becoming a Psychoanalyst: The Need to Include Training "of and on the Body"

My past work on the body in dance and in DMT (Coccanari, Pacifici, & Bollea, 1997) has deeply inspired me in my analytic work with patients. Drawing from my own experience, I always ask myself, when working with patients, and in particular with those with an eating disorder, what stems from both our bodies and how does this influence my thought?

What exactly can we observe when words are not enough? Beyond words are the positions of the body in relation to its parts; movement coordination and fluidity; the relation between two levels of expressiveness, verbal and nonverbal; the presence or lack of harmony between affect and movement; the symbolic contents of gestures themselves and of movements in relation with the other; the associations that the patient makes with movements and the associations made by me with my own movements; and so on.

It is not always possible to respond fully to these questions, but merely seeking a response frequently helps me to attune with my own body states and those of my patients.

My thoughts originate also from my adherence to contemporary psychoanalytic conceptions and trends, which tend to consider the analyst's mind not as a blank screen but, rather, like an intricate texture, full of her own personal history, her analyses, her experience with former patients, her theoretical framework and professional training, even in domains different from those strictly psychoanalytical.

I believe strongly in the need to add a "training of the body and on the body," side by side with the traditional courses, to broaden candidates' capabilities for body listening. For anyone endeavoring to be an analyst, body training offers an additional possibility to "dance" through the various experiences, integrating training in mind and body.

However, to speak about the body "without the body," that is, just talking about it without moving or dancing, is sometimes a hard task. In fact, refining our language to translate into words those experiences obtained through the body is a goal to pursue in both the theory and the practice of our clinical work. This effort is worth making, for we need an analytic tool that goes beyond the mind and addresses instead comprehensive unit, a "mindbody." Especially in view of the integration among the various disciplines concerned with getting to know the human being, such a tool is an absolute requirement.

The bodily experience of patients with eating disorders, for example, is palpable in the analyst's office more than is the case for patients with other types of mental disorders. From the "minimalist" myth of the anorectic patient's body, to the body of the obese patient that expands in space, the analyst's perception of her own body changes according to the possibility of being moved by bodily metaphors. One is moved when one shifts passively from one posture to another; but, in the English language, to be moved by something (or to be touched—touching is also related to knowledge of what is being touched) means also to feel an emotion secondarily to an event or a series of events (a process). Again, if one is to be touched, some movement must take place. We must conclude that dance, movement, body knowledge, and emotions are inextricably related to one another.

The importance of the somatic experience, rediscovered by contemporary psychoanalysis, has elicited interest in the body as a subject of experience. As many contemporary psychoanalysts agree, when the body and its functioning enter the analyst's office, as it does, for example, with the so-called psychosomatic disorders, it is the body, with its somatic memory, that keeps the score (van der Kolk, 1994). Clearly, we should be trained to reconstruct a "somatic biography" of the patient that could highlight the complexity of the patient's psyche in its relation with the other.

We may in fact consider the human self as consisting of a multitude of self-states, which brings to mind what Philip Bromberg (1998) has written on the multiplicity of self:

> Each self-state is a peace of a functional whole, informed by a process of internal negotiation with the realities, values, affects, and perspectives of the others. (pp. 272–273)

Through movement, everyone may experience a "dimension," a self-state, a "dancing self," without necessarily having to be a dancer. "The 'dancing self,'" writes Carol Press (2002), "is a metaphor for an individual who feels vitally alive and creatively engaged in the world" (p. 15). In fact, the dancing self may be represented as a harmonious "stream of consciousness," mostly somatic, proceeding through images, in a continuous mental dialogue with one's own self and with the other. The dancing self is also a potentiality that is expressed in affective relations through its own movement style.

We usually do not remember the exact movements of the dancers, but, rather, feel some kind of emotional trace evoked by the gesture—a flow, an image, a small movement, the essence or the scent of a danced movement—that awakened a napping dancing self. In the same way, sometimes, we do not remember the exact words of a patient, but we do recall the essence of the patient's mindbody in that particular moment.

Clinical Illustration: The Body Image in a Patient With Anorexia

Nonverbal language anticipates speech. It transmits thoughts earlier than their formulation in words (Trevarthen, 1998). In particular, the nonverbal revelations of body image are of particular importance in our achieving a better understanding of patients with eating disorders.

In anorexia nervosa, for example, the body witnesses, better than in other conditions, the profoundly relational aspect of bodily experience.

In anorexia, the overlap between the psychic and the somatic selves is incomplete, damaged. Yet, during the analytic process, this same denied and split body may become a means of profound communication and intense bonding and a cornerstone of the attunement that develops within the analytic relationship. Reconnecting the disharmonious movements and giving them meaning in the reconstruction of a unified psychosomatic entity requires the analyst's consistent attention, which should fluctuate between "knowledge of the body" and "the body's knowledge." Of particular interest is the intense and unique relationship that these patients have with their bodies—their gestural language, posture, muscular organization, gaze, the way they move their hands—that is, their body image.

I first met Evelyn, a patient with anorexia nervosa, when she was hospitalized in a psychiatric ward. Subsequently, I followed her about psychoanalytically, in private practice, for many years.

The transparency and dryness of Evelyn's body (she weighed only about 62 lbs. at that time), unbelievably light compared with the heavy substantialness of a material body, is what struck me during our first encounter. Emaciation was so severe that it seemed as though I could see inside her, yet it was a fierce body, an anatomical geography of shrunken and overlapping organ structures that could only barely support one another. I felt physically pushed into a space of immobility where breathing was difficult and even "dangerous."

> [A]lthough at one level conversation is turn-taking in a verbal back-and-forth, there is also a continuous relatedness of movement contributing to the feelings and words that arise." (La Barre, 2001, p. 15)

Evelyn was then 26 years old. The onset of her eating disorder could be traced back to the age of 12, when she was overweight, but she became anorectic thereafter.

The possibility of a dialog was narrow. No tears, no fluids, Evelyn's mouth was shut to the world and to others, in an undisputed gesture of refusal and unhappiness. Her life without food and almost without water was inexorably dried out. The word appeared to be substituted by silence. Nonetheless, this emaciated body communicated strongly and proclaimed the possibility of living.

My intrusion, my mere physical presence, scared Evelyn's body, much acted upon but perhaps never thought about. We shook hands when we met, and her small, slender hand appeared to be engulfed in mine. This gesture, and the long staring at each other, silently and in mutual curiosity, marked the beginning of a long therapeutic history, a kind of affiliation, as Evelyn's only possible chance for transformation. Yet ours was not a mute encounter between two material bodies. Then and in subsequent encounters I became flooded by artistic images, perhaps in an effort to breathe inside a deadly cloud of deathly anguish, reciprocal and unspoken. Images of color pastels, flimsy bodies, and pleading faces, like those painted by the 20th-century Austrian painter Egon Schiele, enfolded me.

Some colleagues urged me to quit; they held the therapeutic goal to be impossible because of the clinical severity of the patient's condition. Instead, the possibility of catching a glimpse of the beauty and grace of a breach of relation between us lured me as a gift of imagination. Between the visual impact of a dying body and the invisible dimension of a chance to survive, there remained a margin of discovery and curiosity, which I approached with some concern but without any hesitation.

When I first encountered Evelyn's body, I felt as though I were a heavy, but powerless giant, and all my corporeal substance seemed to become a hindrance. As usually happens with this kind of patient, the initial impact is totally body centered. The element of the body is very strong not only for the analyst but for the patient: The analyst has to integrate the deprived body of the patient at both a "visual" and a relational level. Similarly, the patient often "checks out" the analyst's body to "decide" whether that body is to become an ally or is hostile, even from an aesthetic perspective. I believe that both the analyst and the patient are affected by their bodies reciprocally, not only at the beginning of the analysis, but also throughout the entire course of the therapy.

At other times, beside Evelyn's body I seemed to float through initially cryptic and unintelligible bodily states, which, over time, allowed me to find a pathway among Evelyn's different self-states. I was thus enabled to become involved in Evelyn's treatment. Even when the analyst decides to treat a specific patient, however, the main problem is the patient's lack of internal motivation for the treatment. Consequently, this omnipresent resistance makes the therapeutic alliance more complicated and full of obstacles. To get in touch with the patient, the analyst must be flexible and respect the patient's initial lack of motivation as well as the patient's underlying resistances.

I sought to use an empathic style with Evelyn, which consisted of giving value to the syntonic contact with her "bodymind complexity." Thus, I immediately considered her as an autonomous subject and I offered her a space where she could feel protected from the requests of others. I helped her to recognize that her "no food solution" was a real danger to life. Like many other anorectic patients, Evelyn showed off her body as if it were a "foreign body," but at the same time she displayed an attachment to it by appreciating some parts of her body, such as her bones, her hands, or her hair.

Slowly, my body's smoothness, unlike Evelyn's rigidity, woodenness, and dehydration (her body moving like a puppet without strings, with no vitality affects), became for her an object of curiosity and a safe place to find symbolic solace and realize an encounter with a significant other.

By smoothness I mean a quality of the body that is fleshy, endowed with movement style, flexible, capable of establishing relations. When compared with Evelyn's body, my own was yielding and my normal body-build seemed to overemphasize my physical shape and my femininity.

Evelyn's body testified to her completely deranged body image; the challenge lay in coconstructing a new body that could derive desire and pleasure from life.

Body image is profoundly distorted in people with eating disorders, and this distortion is the most typical aspect of the problem. Construction of a body image may very well start even before birth, from a mixture of the parents' fantasied representations of their child's characteristics as the parents-to-be await their child's appearance. As David Krueger (2002) has written:

> The body image is the cumulative set of images, fantasies, and meanings about the body and its parts and functions; it's an integral component of self-image and the basis of self representation. In the last two decades, neurophysiological research has produced salient data on the development of the body image and the differentiation of the mental self as a bridge between mind and body. (p. 31)

Eating disorders are disturbances of the self that stem from a chronic perturbance of the mother-child interaction.

Although Evelyn repeatedly and constantly refused food and me as the other, I sought access. Starting with words and movements associated with the different affective states, I tried to find a symbolic food to share with her.

Food can be a particularly irresistible substitute selfobject, a first bridge between self and selfobject, providing soothing relief. Food is considered loyal and trustworthy, whereas people are not. Hence, food and rituals related to it are defended most passionately, as if they were human selfobject bonds (Bromberg, 2001). I had to arouse her curiosity and transform it into a vital alternative to her mechanical rituals and obsessions with food.

I thought about small beneficial gestures like those offered in a ritual dance, with ever-repeating patterns, that sooner or later will find the other available for dancing. Our complex dialogue, sometimes comprised of repetitive, very brief conversations, was already started.

> In conversation, even the specially constructed psychoanalytical conversation, we are moving together with another, initiating sound and motion, and responding to what we see, feel, and hear, all at once. Physical interactive patterns are quickly established that have an effect on what we think and feel. (La Barre, 2001, p. 16)

When Evelyn was 16, her father died suddenly from acute myocardial infarction. That occasion marked the worsening of her eating disorder. Bereavement left her empty and threw her into anorexia. For a long time the analysis focused on working through mourning.

Eating disorders frequently have their onset after a loss, or their symptoms intensify shortly after such an event. The symptoms may represent the end result of attempts at reinforcing the self through food restriction, a reaction to the fear of abandonment, the fear of falling into apathy and weakness. This is what happened to Evelyn, who, for a long time, was able to keep her father's loss buried under denial, covered by her anorectic symptoms.

Evelyn's mother is an inconsistent woman, showing some concrete thinking but also a psychotic aura, which worsened after the loss of her husband. Evelyn is bound to her through a syncytial relationship, which remained unaltered for a long period during the analysis. Even when Evelyn became aware that this relationship detracted from her identity and self-individuation, she could not relinquish the fusion with her mother.

Evelyn has an older brother toward whom she has ambivalent feelings. He is married and has children and is the only member of the family endowed with some vitality.

During Evelyn's long hospitalization I slowly and patiently gained her trust by accepting her state and promising to help her anyway to reduce the fear of losing control over feeding and weight. Thus we constructed a bridge between my beliefs and her fears. Evelyn accepted our relationship, but for years subjected it to the control of a paranoid lens, inherited from and shared with her mother.

Evelyn was subsequently released from the hospital and commenced private sessions with me. However, after some years we had to interrupt our sessions for two years when I had to move to another country. During this period we kept in contact by telephone and mail. When returned home, we finally found a comfortable and stable setting, which we have been maintaining since 2002.

Since Evelyn has to make a long journey to reach my office, we decided to modify our setting. We reduced by half the number of weekly sessions and doubled the length of time for each session. Evelyn has always declined the coach, so we have our sessions face to face.

Interestingly, one of my dreams was the guide for a part of my analytic work. In this dream we were gathering olives together under a very fruitful tree. We moved together, dancing and using affectively laden gestures and movements. Nature and countryside were the elements that linked Evelyn to her father and her memories of closeness to him; these were buried in the thick layer of bereavement and loss, which prevented her from recalling him alive. In my work with her, I tried to use the emotional hue of the dream, when we were under the olive tree, being together in the analytic office.

I tried to empathize with each of Evelyn's various self-states. Tasting and sharing her passion for nature, I made it an element to be explored, to move us from the exhausting associations with food and calories to a dimension of witnessing and discovery, in high and low tides of a meaningful biography.

At times, Evelyn brought me food as a gift—eggs, mozzarellas, sweet pastries—all meaningful to her and welcomed by me. I tried always to find a meaning for her offerings. She told me once, "Now, you taste and then you tell me." Only after much time had passed did Evelyn open her mouth to accept the same food. She was pleased that I would taste and "try," and when I did her trust in me swelled like fresh bread and we could "dance."

Some years earlier she had told me, "I feel like an oyster, mmmh … no, like mussel, because an oyster would be too much for me." (In Italian, the word *mussel* also described particularly unattractive girls.) "It's enough for me," she continued, "to stay within a mussel's shell, in the dark, so that nobody can eat me, since a mussel with a closed shell is a dead mussel." My associations were to her claustrophobic movement within a narrow and confined space, to a devitalized and almost dead body that shrinks and twists and does not express itself and cannot think of itself as "pearl," to her anguish to awaken or else be devoured by dependence, and to the vital need of our bond. All this led us to speak of space and death—of the space to live and move freely, of her passion for abstinence and discomfort. We both breathed at the end of that session in a new way, with a soothing and reassuring rhythm.

It took a good deal of time for her treasured, calming, and reassuring, but inanimate and inert, selfobject (the weighing machine) slowly to diminish in importance in favor of another selfobject—our affective, human, and reliable relationship. The selfobject experiences that she was discovering also had developmental continuity. Kohut (1983) wrote:

> A friend puts his arms around us or understandingly touches our shoulder, and we regain composure and strength; he is a mature selfobject for us now. (p. 397)

Evelyn's body transformation still suffers from about 25 years' deprivation. She still has no menses and has formed no romantic attachment so far. But, despite everything, she is still alive, she works, she is about to buy her own home, she weighs almost 94 lbs. now. She wants to live and has recaptured movement. She "dances" and moves her body around in an incredibly harmonious way. Her desire for life, thanks to the corrective somatic experience, is consolidated.

During the coconstruction of her somatic biography, which took place during our analysis, something very interesting happened. Evelyn started talking about her memories of being a "fat child," and I realized that I was barely able to imagine and believe that she had once been a fat girl.

Once she told me in a impetus of joy, "I could bring you some photos of myself, to show you how I really was!"

She did not remember her dreams at that time, but she brought me a much more meaningful "gift": the child Evelyn. Sitting close to each other, looking silently at the pictures, we were overwhelmed by a feeling of astonishment. Evelyn started to talk about her childhood and the history of her body, starting when she was 5 years old: "clumsy," "heavy," and "slow." She felt different from the agile children around her. Seeing herself in a picture where she was 14 years old, she described herself as "fat and sad."

I felt as if I were invited to participate in a dance where we had to deconstruct and then coconstruct the puzzle of her somatic biography. I put together the photos, the feelings, and her life account throughout many sessions, and slowly her somatic biography emerged.

Evelyn's movement and postures, which were initially rigidly controlled—her torso stiff and her abdomen swallowed by immobile hips, her shallow breathing and contracted diaphragm revealing a body that never moved as a whole and accepted aching bones in an armchair as natural—gradually became balanced and symmetrical.

In our mutual survival pact, we each had to accept something of one another in the complex negotiation prompted by food and concluding with our being reciprocally "moved" (in every sense). Evelyn accepted some gestures of my "dance" and my fluid movement in our shared intersubjective space; I, accepting a part of her relinquishment, could feel on my skin the unrelinquishable "value" of her deprivation.

Discussion

It is important to keep in mind and accept that, although people with eating disorders may present some basic symptoms—for instance, the necessity to be thin, amenorrhoea, rituals in eating, and so on—they can very often ameliorate many aspects of their selves and improve many different areas of their lives. But in some cases we have to consider anorexia as like a very complex existential condition, and perhaps we need to accept that the transformation is sometimes not "completed."

Characteristic of anorexia—and perhaps at the core of the problem—is the relinquishment of the desire for, and loss of faith in the reliability of, a human relationship. The need for a significant human relationship is evident in the effort to relate in some way with a human being, but it remains sequestered, hidden. Such patients become elusive and lack substance in relating with the other.

When trying to clarify and remedy the resistance to changing the attachment to symptoms in anorexia and bulimia, we must bear in mind the paradoxical aspects of pleasure. The self-healing attempts of anorectic and bulimic girls are a painful intervention, but they contain a substantial amount of pleasure and enjoyment in both bulimic crisis and anorectic fasting. The eating-disordered patient's self-healing project is like a lonely climb in which the maximum sat-isfaction is having obtained the end result without the assistance of the other.

Even in patients with an eating disorder, though, the perception of the somatic self and of body image may be enhanced by having some somatic experiences, linked to affective states, put into words. This phenomenon occurs both in the psychoanalytical process and in dance therapy (perhaps with significantly more immediacy in the latter). You may start working with the patient from the bodily experience or from the affective state; the results will be similar. You might start with somatic symptom metaphors, or trace back an affective state to bodily awareness. Through the use of empathy, you can reply to the patient, provided you keep in mind as many different aspects of the self as he can, both conscious and unconscious.

During the entire course of our work together, I have always kept in mind the sane and genuine aspects of Evelyn's life.

Among contemporary psychoanalysts there is consensus that there is a need to devise a relational modality to render tolerable the bond between analyst and eating-disordered patient. We can struc-ture and strengthen that bond by adhering to the "analytic third" theoretical model (Ogden, 1994). That model may guide us and support us when our "moving inside" the relation is viewed by the patient as a threat to identity.

We should, of course, be cautious and careful (like a cat walking amidst crystalline objects), not to consider words alone as sufficient to avoid falling in the trap of pleasurable conversation and intellec-tualization, so often set by eating-disordered patients in analysis. Rather, we must try to shift words toward an affective dialog sup-ported by the authenticity of somatic language.

The treatment challenge is a "body-to-body" one that may become exhausting and even result in loss; for the patient with an eating disorder, the body comes to resemble a combat zone. The world of patients with eating disorders is a closely guarded sealed one and difficult to access. It is composed of exclusive and much idealized passions. If we use somatic imagination to approach the complex and elaborate bodily metaphors, through a personal and creative record and ensuring a private and inviolable therapeutic space, we may become for our patients a real *"peace object"* (Bollea, E., 1998, personal communication).

The image of Bill T. Jones's dance returns to mind, along with the voice of Estelle, the woman he spoke of. This time she is Evelyn's mother. I feel all her weakness and resignation. I hear the voice of a mother who failed to help her daughter "cross the river" in the complex process of separation and self-individuation.

In our analytic work, Evelyn and I tried to find a "dancing self," to "move and dance" together. Starting from a desperate and unharmonious solo, she moved through novel bodily alphabets, invented a "new" body that could be aware and trusting of the other and that she could identify as her new, authentic self.

References

Aron, L. (1998). The clinical body and the reflexive mind. In L. Aron & F. S. Anderson (Eds.), *Relational perspectives on the body* (pp. 3–37). Hillsdale, NJ: The Analytic Press.

Bromberg, P. M. (1998). *Standing in the spaces*. Hillsdale, NJ: The Analytic Press.

Bromberg, P. M. (2001). Treating patients with symptoms and symptoms with patience: Reflections on shame, dissociation, and eating disorders. *Psychoanal. Dial.*, *11*, 891–912.

Carr, L., Iacoboni, M., Dubeau, M.C., Mazziotta, J.C., & Lenzi, G.L. (2003). Neural mechanisms of empathy in humans: A relay from neural systems for imitation to limbic areas. *Proceedings of the National Academy of Science of the United States of America*, *100*(9), 5497–5502.

Chodorow, J. (1986). The body as symbol: Dance/movement in analysis. In N. Schwartz-Salant & M. Stein (Eds.), *The body in analysis* (pp. 87–108). Wilmette, IL: Chiron.

Coccanari, M. A., Pacifici, M. P., & Bollea, E. (1997). Musica attiva. Un esperimento in un day hospital psichiatrico [Active music. An experience in a psychiatric day hospital]. *Minerva Psichiatrica, 38*, 45–52.

Cunningham, M. & Lesschaeve, J. (1985). *The dancer and the dance*. New York: Marion Boyars.

Dimen, M. (1998). Polyglot bodies. In L. Aron & F. S. Anderson (Eds.), *Relational perspectives on the body* (pp. 65–93). Hillsdale, NJ: The Analytic Press.

Graham, M. (1991). *Blood memory: An autobiography*. New York: Doubleday.

Jung, C. G. (1931). Foreword to *The secret of the golden flower: A Chinese book of life*, by Tung-Pin Lu (German translation by Richard Wilhelm). First published in English, 1931; new enlarged edition, 1962, Orlando, FL: Harcourt Brace, pp. xiii–xiv.

Kohut, H. (1959/1978). Introspection, empathy, and psychoanalysis. In P. H. Ornstein (Ed.), *The search for the self. Selected writings of Heinz Kohut 1950–1978*, Vol. 1–2 (pp. 205–232). New York: International Universities Press.

Kohut, H. (1971). *The analysis of the self.* New York: International Universities Press.

Kohut, H. (1983). Selected problems of self psychological theory. In J. Lichtenberg & S. Kaplan (Eds.), *Reflections on self psychology* (pp. 387–416). Hillsdale, NJ: The Analytic Press.

Kreemer, C. (Ed.). (1987). *Further steps: Fifteen choreographers on modern dance.* New York: Harper & Row.

Kris, E. (1952). *Psychoanalytic explorations in art.* New York: International Universities Press.

Krueger, D. W. (2002). Psychodynamic perspectives on body image. In T. F. Cash & T. Purzinsky (Eds.), *Body image: A handbook of theory, research and clinical practice* (pp. 30–37). New York: Guilford.

Laban, R. (1950). *Mastery of movement.* London: McDonald & Evans.

La Barre, F. (2001). *On moving and being moved: Nonverbal behavior in clinical practice.* Hillsdale, NJ: The Analytic Press.

Mitchell, S. A. (1988). *Relational concepts in psychoanalysis.* Cambridge, MA: Harvard University Press.

Ogden, T. H. (1994). The analytic third: Working with intersubjective clinical facts. In S. Mitchell & L. Aron (Eds.), *Relational psychoanalysis: The emergence of a tradition* (pp. 459–486). Hillsdale, NJ: The Analytic Press, 1999.

Plato (ca. 360 B.C.). *Phaedrus. Plato, Euthyphro, Apology, Crito, Phaedo (Great Books in Philosophy).* B. Jowett (Trans.). New York: Prometheus Books, 1988. Accessed October 3, 2006, from http://philosophy.eserver.org/plato/phaedrus.txt

Press, C. M. (2002). *The dancing self: Creativity, modern dance, self psychology and transformative education.* Cresskill, NJ: Hampton Press.

Ringstrom, P. A. (2001). Cultivating the improvisational in psychoanalytic treatment. *Psychoanal. Dial., 1*, 727–754.

Rizzolatti, G., Fogassi, L., & Gallese, V. (2001). Neurophysiological mechanisms underlying the understanding and imitation of action. *Nature Reviews in Neuroscience, 2*, 661–870.

Rotenberg, C. (1988). Selfobject theory and the artistic process. In A. Goldberg (Ed.), *Learning from Kohut: Progress in self psychology* (Vol. 4, pp. 193–213). Hillsdale, NJ: The Analytic Press.

Stern, D. N. (2000). *The interpersonal world of the infant: A view from psychoanalysis and developmental psychology.* New York: Basic Books.

Stern, D. N. (2004). *The present moment in psychotherapy and everyday life.* New York: Norton.

Trevarthen, C. (1998). Empatia e biologia. Psicologia, cultura, neuroscienze [Empathy and biology. Psychology, culture, neurosciences]. Milan: Raffaello Cortina.

van der Kolk, B. A. (1994). The body keeps the score: Memory and the evolving psychobiology of posttraumatic stress. *Harvard Rev. Psychiat., 1,* 253–265.

Whitehouse, M. S. (1958). The Tao of the body. Paper presented at the Analytical Psychology Club of Los Angeles in 1958. Previously published in D.H. Johnson (Ed.) *Bone, Breath and Gesture*, Berkeley, CA; North Atlantics Books, 1995.

Winnicott, D. W. (1953). *Playing and reality.* New York: Basic Books.

6

Yoga and Neuro-Psychoanalysis

Patricia L. Gerbarg

When the mind cannot control the mind, use the breath. It's easier.

Sri Sri Ravi Shankar

Introduction

Much of the literature on yoga and psychoanalysis focuses on similarities and differences between these healing traditions (Brar, 1970;
Chakraborty, 1970; Neki, 1967; Vaidyanathan & Kripal, 1999). What
would happen if we used yoga and psychoanalysis to complement
each other? How would such a partnership affect the progress of an
analysis and what adverse consequences might ensue? If we observe
that yoga facilitates psychoanalysis, how do we understand such
effects in light of current neuro-psychoanalytic concepts?

I will describe a practice called Sudarshan Kriya Yoga (SKY) and
its effects on a psychoanalytic treatment. SKY has been the subject
of controlled clinical trials as well as neurophysiological study. This
research provides evidence, along with clinical observations, to construct integrative models that may be of heuristic value. For reviews
of scientific literature on SKY, the neurophysiological basis for its

actions on stress response and emotion-regulatory systems, and its clinical applications, see Brown and Gerbarg (2005a, 2005b). Drawing upon peripheral models of emotion, polyvagal theory, and multiple coding theory, let us explore the interface between yoga and psychoanalytic approaches to the treatment of trauma.

Background Research Relevant to Yoga Breathing

Studies on mind-body interventions for stress-related disorders have been reviewed (Becker, 2000; Benson, 1996; Jacobs, 2001). Whereas older literature attributes therapeutic effects of yoga breathing to increased oxygenation, recent studies implicate increased parasympathetic activity and decreased sympathetic influence. The relationship between breath and emotion is bidirectional. Emotional states affect the rate, depth, and pattern of respiration. Conversely, the voluntary manipulation of breath patterns can account for as much as 40% of the variance of feeling states including anger, fear, joy, and sadness (Philippot, Gaetane, & Blairy, 2002). Yoga breathing is a form of peripheral feedback that can elicit emotional responses.

The voluntary control of breathing influences autonomic nervous system functions, heart rate variability (Lehrer, Sasaki, & Saito, 1999; Sovik, 2000), chemoreflex and baroreflex sensitivity, central nervous system (CNS) excitation, and neuroendocrine functions (Gangadhar, Janakiramaiah, Sudarshan, & Shety, 2000). Yoga breath practices produce different psychophysiological effects depending on duration of each phase of the respiratory cycle, tidal volume, number of repetitions, body postures, and use of the mouth, nostrils, and throat (Telles & Desiraju, 1992; Telles, Joseph, Venkatesh, & Desiraju, 1993). Variations of breath techniques are found in many traditions including Raja Yoga, Hatha Yoga, Iyengar Yoga, Zen, "Ha" breath of Hawaii, Qigong, Karate, Tibetan Meditation, and Aikido (Feuerstein, 1998). Eastern breath practices have been adapted to healing and fitness programs such as Mindfulness Meditation (Benson, 1996), Holotropic Breathing, and sports training.

Yoga can be beneficial for anxiety, depression, insomnia, obsessive-compulsive disorder, and post-traumatic stress disorder (PTSD) (Gordon, Staples, Blyta, & Bytyqi, 2004). Effective yoga programs combine yoga stretches or postures (*asanas*), breath practices (*pranayama*), meditation, and group discussions. Research and clinical experience indicate that SKY ameliorates stress, anxiety, depression, and PTSD.

Sudarshan Kriya Yoga

SKY, derived from the Eight Limbs of Yoga (Patanjali's Sutras, c. 200 B.C.), is taught in a 22-hour course by two nonprofit organizations, the Art of Living Foundation (AOLF) and the International Association for Human Values (IAHV). Training includes four forms of yoga breathing, gentle postures, group processes, yoga philosophy, stress management, guided meditation, and singing. Breath practices are taught in sequence: Victorious Breath (Ujjayi) or "Ocean Breath," sounding like the inside of a seashell (2–6 cpm); Bellows Breath (Bhastrika), using the arms to increase the force of inhalation and exhalation (30 cpm); "AUM" chant; and Clear Vision through Purifying Action (Sudarshan Kriya), advanced cyclical breathing. Many schools of yoga teach variations of the first three forms. Although cyclical breathing appears in other practices (Satyanarayana, Rajeswari, Jhansi Rani, Sri Krishna, & Krishna Rao, 1992), Sudarshan Kriya (SK) was created by Sri Sri Ravi Shankar and is only taught by AOLF and IAHV. Healing experiences and psychological changes tend to occur during SK.

Case of Post-Traumatic Stress Disorder, Attention Deficit Disorder, Learning Disabilities

Dan, a 28-year-old man, was referred for psychoanalysis by the psychologist who had treated him biweekly for 2 years. The patient had PTSD and attention deficit hyperactivity disorder (ADHD). His cognitive functions, attention, memory, affect, verbal communication, and social behavior were impaired. He was anxious, depressed, emotionally disconnected, and explosive.

Due to a birth defect, Dan spent the first 6 weeks of his life in a hospital, separated from his mother, undergoing painful medical procedures. This infantile period of medical trauma disrupted the early attachment to mother, deprived him of normal parental soothing, and exposed him to pain and helplessness. In the third year of analysis, he reported this dream:

"I am a very tiny lump in the middle of a field. These tall trees are standing all around me. It feels like they can do anything they want to me."

Dan became mischievous and troublesome. His mother, who began abusing alcohol when he was 7, berated and hit him abusively. When she tried to hug and kiss to make up, he angrily rejected her. These early traumas contributed to insecure attachment, mistrust, and inability to tolerate intimacy. His father worked long hours and was emotionally disconnected. Although Dan's IQ was well above average, due to learning disabilities, ADHD, and conduct disorder, he was misplaced into a program for the mentally retarded, compounding his sense of shame and defectiveness. Self-conscious about the scars from his surgery and socially inept, Dan was so anxious that he could barely talk to people. Despite being a very large man, he felt as helpless as a baby, as though anyone could hurt him (the way he had felt in the hospital and with his abusive mother). He used alcohol and drugs to numb his anxieties.

When Dan first came for analysis, his mind was so scattered that it was difficult to follow the meaning of his sentences. He could not remember what we talked about from one day to the next. It required several medications including Effexor (venlafaxine), Ritalin (methylphenidate), and S-adenosylmethionine (SAM-e) (Brown, Gerbarg, & Muskin, 2003) to improve mental focus, memory, and anxiety enough for him do psychoanalytic work. I also prescribed supplements to enhance neuronal energy, cellular repair, and memory including *Rhodiola rosea* (Brown & Gerbarg, 2004), B12, omega-3-fatty acids, and antioxidants.

The first 6 years of analysis focused on safety and trust, learning to communicate, and overcoming numerous life crises. He ended his marriage with an abusive woman. Early in analysis, negative maternal transference emerged as mistrust, anger, and fear were directed toward the analyst. Missing sessions and misusing medication, Dan tested our relationship to see if I would react angrily, strike him, or throw him away. He felt like his right upper body (the side nearest to me) was about to be hit, with an impulse to raise an arm to shield himself.

Dan often talked in a disconnected, altered state, inducing a parallel altered state in me, a semiconscious floating. His altered state stemmed from trauma, possibly memories outside of conscious awareness. Cimino and Correale (2005) propose that an analyst experiencing an altered state of consciousness is responding to a communication from the patient via projective identification. The disconnected drifting occurred when Dan did something "wrong," something he "forgot" to tell me. Disconnecting protected him from remembering, from having to tell me (the first rule), and from the pain of anticipated punishment. He also disconnected when something made him feel uncared for such as my starting the session a minute late or a fee increase. As Dan became aware of his sensitivity to rejection and as he was treated with kindness, he became less disconnected, more engaged. Positive feelings arose as he relaxed and opened up. Dan could not verbalize positive emotions, but they were evident in the gentle tones of his voice, his cooperativeness, and his kindness toward me.

After 7 years of psychoanalysis, Dan was leading a productive life and dating a woman of good character. His new partner's tendency to be critical was balanced by her kindness, understanding, and loving behaviors toward him. Nevertheless, Dan had one major complaint: He could not experience the emotion of love. His girlfriend wanted to get married, but Dan did not want to until he felt love. He described his heart as "encased in a metal box" through which he could feel only the slightest, briefest sensation of something he thought might be love. Dan's loving feelings appeared in the transference and in dreams, but he did not recognize them. As with many trauma survivors, he disconnected from loving feelings to protect himself from pain. Although his softness and attentiveness indicated the presence of love, he could not subjectively, physically, or consciously experience the feeling. We worked on his defenses against emotion, particularly his fear of being hurt if he felt love. There was progress, but not enough. Although his anxiety was far less intense, he still experienced it as

> a feeling of spinning or revving like a dentist's drill in my chest. Sometimes there is a bit of coldness or sometimes heat. Like everything in my chest is spinning, subtle, but not so subtle. Sometimes I get a little agita coming up from my stomach, like a little bit of "sourness" or like a little gas. [He burps.] Just thinking about the gas does it. When it is more intense it's more vibrational, like a motor running, more heavy, tight, humming, large, tight here [gestures over his entire sternum and upper epigastric area] with more pressure in the middle and more open out to the sides.

In the eighth year of analysis, I encouraged Dan to learn SKY. The first time he took the course, he felt "a little something in my chest," but it vanished. He took the course again 1 month later, feeling less anxious. During a group process, he spoke about things in the past that he had always been too ashamed to expose. The other participants were supportive. The next day during SK, Dan felt a strong emotion in his chest, a feeling of love. It lasted all day and when he awoke the next morning, it was with him. After the course, the love feeling faded, but Dan pursued it by taking many SKY courses—basic, advanced, and meditation. Through yoga, he learned to engender feelings of love. One year after the first SKY course, he married his fiancée. Once Dan became connected to his feelings with conscious awareness and physical sensations, loving emotions evolved into experiences of connection, gratitude, acceptance, forgiveness, and empathy. Over the next 3 years, by repeatedly inducing loving feelings during yoga, he became able to evoke positive emotions outside of yoga by thinking of certain emotion-words. Dan described his experience of *"the loving feeling in my chest"*:

> It starts when I bring in gratitude and connection. I feel more blood, like imagining the muscle of the heart, not the pumping, just known in a subtle way. There's an expansion in my whole chest cavity. I feel much more alive and connected with all that there is ... receptively connected with what might come to me, more open. A very big feeling of brightness in my chest emanates, a sun everywhere. I just feel receptive. I feel loved, good, relaxed, connected. I feel it from here to here [from the top of the sternum down over the epigastrium], a solidness there. Like the imagined heart really there, like I'm connected to it. I feel physically light.

One can almost envision visceral sensations, emotions, and symbolizations in a mutually reinforcing cycle. As Dan continued daily yoga, his memory and cognitive functions improved such that he was able to grasp emotional nuances, observe himself more clearly, and attain new insights. Yoga reduced his anxiety, a major cause of his difficulty communicating. He tolerated stress without losing control and let go of anger more easily. How did SKY improve Dan's cognitive functions and enable him to experience love and empathic connectedness with others? Peripheral models of emotion provide a framework for understanding these effects.

Neurophysiological Models

Peripheral Models of Emotion—Yoga Breathing
as Peripheral Feedback

Afferent autonomic and somatomotor feedback from the body is key to peripheral models of emotion and their extension into motivational behavior, decision-making, emotional and social behavior, and self-awareness (Damasio, 1994, 1999). Bud Craig (2003) defines interoception as the perception of "feelings" (pain, temperature, sensual touch, muscular and visceral sensations, vasomotor activity, and air hunger) that reflect the physiological state of the body and that have their primary representation in the dorsal posterior insula and may have meta-representation, mainly in the right anterior insula, a possible substrate for emotional awareness. This converges with Damasio's "somatic marker" hypothesis that brain regions involved in mapping and regulation of internal states (homeostasis) contribute to representational images of the body state and provide a basis for awareness of feelings states (Critchley, 2005).

The lungs and airways contain mechanoreceptors, stretch sensors (Yu, 2005), that fire in response to lung inflation and deflation, sending thousands of signals that encode information at multiple nodal points on the way to vagal afferents, providing information for the afferent homeostatic system described by Craig and Damasio. *By voluntarily changing the pattern of breath, one can alter the firing of lung sensors, thereby changing visceral somatosensory input carried by vagal afferents. We hypothesize this to be the first step in the chain of events set in motion by yoga breathing that ultimately leads to widespread changes in emotional and cognitive processing by shifting the balance of input to the insula and related areas involved in the representation of bodily feeling states, and in the reactions and behaviors linked to those feeling states.* Yoga breathing also stimulates sensory afferents from pharynx, larynx, chest wall, diaphragm, baroreceptors, and chemoreceptors (shifts in pO_2 and pCO_2).

Neural Networks, Autonomic Regulation, and Polyvagal Theory

Anxiety, depression, and PTSD are associated with overactivity or erratic activity of the sympathetic nervous system (SNS) and underactivity of the parasympathetic nervous system (PNS) (Berntson, Sarter, & Cacioppo, 2003; Thayer & Brosschat, 2005). Yoga breathing normalizes SNS activity and increases PNS tone. Thayer and Brosschat propose that within the central autonomic network, higher centers such as the medial prefrontal cortex (mPFC) inhibit lower centers such as the amygdala. In depression and PTSD, a hypoactive mPFC fails to control a hyperactive amygdala. Disturbances

in the dynamics between PFC, amygdala, and thalamus may contribute to fear-related symptoms as in PTSD. Respiratory sinus
arrhythmia (RSA) refers to the normal heart rate increase during
inspiration and decreasing during expiration. Heart rate variability
(HRV) is a spectral analysis of the variations in heart rate. RSA and
HRV are used to measure SNS and PNS activity. Low PNS activity
(low HRV) and hypoactivity of the PFC are associated with poor
affective information processing and deficits in working memory
and executive function. HRV and RSA indicate autonomic effects
on emotional regulation and expression, psychological adaptation,
empathic response, and attachment (Beauchaine, 2001; Porges, 2001).

Polyvagal theory proposes that in mammals, an old "vegetative"
reptilian unmyelinated vagal system, carrying somatic information
rapidly to the limbic system (Porges, 1995, 2001), regulates reflex
visceral functions (e.g., heart rate, bronchial diameter, gastrointestinal activity), while a new "smart" myelinated vagal system sends
somatic information to the thalamus and through thalamocorti-
cal projections to areas of cerebral cortex. The smart vagal system
probably plays a role in social behavior (emotion, facial expression,
attachment, attention, and communication). Sensory feedback from
visceral organs goes directly to brainstem vegetative and smart vagal
nuclei, and this activity is modulated by oxytocin (Carter, 1998). The
balance between the vegetative and smart vagal systems can shift.
For example, a sudden attack can trigger a surge of vegetative vagal
system activity, causing a person to freeze or engage in automatic
defensive behaviors, often with impaired cognition or awareness, as
though cortical thinking networks have been turned off. Conversely,
deep relaxation of yoga can shut down the vegetative system and
engender states ranging from calm alertness to "edge of sleep."

Effects of SKY Components on Autonomic Afferents and Emotional/Cognitive Processing

Component I. Ujjayi breathing at a slow rate (2 to 6 cpm) with expiration longer than inspiration is physically and emotionally calming.
Slow yoga breathing (including Ujjayi) increases RSA, HRV, PNS
activity (Cappo & Holmes, 1984), arterial baroreflex sensitivity, and
oxygenation. Contraction of laryngeal muscles with partial closure
of the glottis increases airway resistance, intrathoracic pressure,

baroreceptor stimulation, HRV, RSA (Calabrese, Perrault, Dinh, Eberhard, & Benchetrit, 2000), and stimulation of somatosensory afferents in the pharynx, chest wall, and diaphragm. Airway resistance enables breath control to prolong respiration. Breath-holds also increase PNS activity (Telles & Desiraju, 1992).

Component II. Bhastrika leads to SNS activation and CNS excitation, followed by emotional calming with mental alertness.

Component III. Chanting "AUM" may increase vagal tone and decreases SNS activation.

Component IV. Sudarshan Kriya consists of sets of cyclical breathing (no pause between inhalation and exhalation) at three rates (slow, medium, and fast). The slow breath cycles of SK are 8 to 12 cpm. Breathing 8 to 10 cpm decreases parasympathetic withdrawal in response to threat and may reduce anxiety.

Neurophysiological Studies

Sudarshan Kriya and Vagal Nerve Stimulation

Unilateral vagal nerve stimulation (VNS) is used to treat epilepsy and treatment-resistant depression. Although both SKY and VNS activate vagal afferents and thalamus (Schachter & Saper, 1998), they differ in several respects. VNS is limited to the left vagus nerve and produces few autonomic effects. In contrast, SKY stimulates both vagus nerves and has significant autonomic effects. VNS uses electrical stimulation (fixed frequency and amplitude). SKY creates variegated stimuli from millions of receptors and visceral afferents. These probably influence different fiber groups within the vagus nerves (S.W. Porges, personal communication, 2003) and may account for the rapidity and diversity of SKY effects.

EEG Coherence and Synchrony

In a pilot study of 10 SKY practitioners with different levels of experience, Stephen Larsen and colleagues continuously recorded EKG, HRV, EEG (19 cortical sites), and respirometry during 5-minute baseline, 70 minutes of SKY, and 20-minute post-SKY rest. In general, EEGs of beginners, who had completed their first SKY course

1 week prior to the study, showed small pockets of synchrony, but little "whole brain synchrony" (McKnight & Fehmi, 2001). *Synchrony* involves the degree of similarity in the amplitude, frequency, and phase of wave forms when comparing EEG recordings over one region of the brain with recordings over another region. Coherence analysis of the degree of synchrony is used to assess communication between distant brain regions. During rapid breath cycles, EEG disorganization increased and synchrony decreased. During rests after each set of breath cycles, synchrony increased. In practitioners who had done SKY for at least 18 months, baseline synchrony was higher and less subject to disruption during breath practice. In the most advanced subjects (4 years or more), alpha bands remained stable over central and peripheral areas, with very high degrees of continuous "whole brain synchrony" across all 19 channels during breath practices and rest periods. These findings are consistent with pilot studies showing increased EEG coherence with SKY (Bhatia, Kumar, Kumar, Pandey, & Kochupillai, 2003; Shnayder, Agarkova, Lyulyakina, Naumova, & Shnayder, 2006).

Neuroendocrine Effects: Oxytocin

Oxytocin (OX), the "cuddle" hormone, reduces the stress response to social separation and promotes social bonding (Nelson & Panksepp, 1998). It is associated with PNS functions and regulation of the hypothalamic-pituitary-adrenal axis (Carter, 1998). Stimulation of vagal afferents increases plasma OX (Stock & Uvnas-Moberg, 1988). We propose that OX release via vagal and other somatosensory stimulation enhances feelings of closeness, bonding, and well-being experienced by many people during SKY.

Nonverbal Visceral Messaging to Trauma-Related Schemas—Multiple Code Theory

Psychoanalysts face the challenge of using a primarily verbal technique to access trauma-related material that has not been verbally encoded and that may not be represented symbolically. Within multiple code theory, Wilma Bucci (2001, 2003) describes subsymbolic elements, actions, and sensory and visceral reactions that form the "affective core" of emotion schemas. Pathological schemas with defensive dissociation are resistant to change and may be blocked from linkage to verbal coding. Structural change, reconstruction of emotion schemas, must include subsymbolic bodily and sensory components. Bucci proposes that the referential process begins with activation of these schemas by free association, interpretation, and other means. She notes that schemas must be retrieved and verbalized before new material can be inserted, distorted elements revised, and links to affect changed.

The heroic efforts of analysts to divine the meanings of nonverbal communications, associations, and dreams may fail to penetrate defenses surrounding islands of trauma-related material that limit recovery of patients who have otherwise made substantial progress in analysis. Rather than continuing to push the verbal rock uphill, we could complement psychoanalytic treatment with mind-body approaches. Why not speak to nonverbal schemas in the "language" they understand by sending messages from the autonomic viscerosensory system, their place of origin? Yoga, painstakingly developed over 8,000 years, uses the body's exquisite interoceptive system of communication through peripheral and central neural networks. Skillfully tapping into this visceral Internet has the potential for rapid, nontraumatic access to crucial unconscious material with links to emotional and somatic components of trauma-based schemas. The case I present illustrates how such access could engender healing somatosensory experiences, leading to structural change and analytic progress.

The Interface Between Neuro-Psychoanalysis and Yoga: Psychoanalytic Process

1. Bringing Unconscious Contents From Trauma-Related Emotion Schemas Into Consciousness

By reducing Dan's anxiety and defensive reactions, Ujjayi breathing may have facilitated access to (unconscious) trauma-related schemas. Ujjayi with prolonged expiration quiets the mind and may decrease the rate of firing in the amygdala. Nerve cells in the central nucleus of the amygdala fire less during quiet breathing with prolonged expiration (Zhang, Harper, & Frysinger, 1986). Shifts in the functioning of fear circuits involving the amygdala, mPFC, and thalamus could occur in response to increased vagal afferent input as well as the "holding environment" of the psychoanalysis and the SKY group. When Dan talked about himself and received group support, his fear of being emotionally hurt diminished (partially extinguished). Significant emotional changes occurred during SK with improvements in emotion, cognition, and memory over the subsequent 3 years.

During SK, Dan experienced something new, "a strong sensation of love in my chest." Vagal afferent input, patterned by yoga breathing, could influence the insula, cingulate cortex, PFC, and visceral efferents, resulting in new subjective somatic (interoceptive) and emotional experiences with conscious awareness and verbalization of emotions. What had been a dysfunctional system moved toward somatic, emotional, and cognitive integration.

2. Enhancing Cognitive-Emotional Integration

It is postulated that the physiological challenge of SKY temporarily disrupts established brain wave patterns and synapses in areas containing trauma-related schemas. This may occur through disentrainment of electrical activity, fluctuations in autonomic input, changes in activity within structures involved in emotional regulation, coding and memory (limbic, thalamic, and prefrontal), shifts in pO_2 and pCO_2, and neurohormonal release (oxytocin, prolactin). This neurological "shake-up" may provide opportunities for new linkages and configurations to form. Under conditions of safety and relaxation, new input (experiences, concepts, emotions) with positive affective valence may gain access to previously closed areas (containing trauma schemas), promoting permanent structural change and recovery.

The daily practice of SKY appears to increase coherence and high-amplitude synchrony. Increases in high-amplitude gamma synchrony were observed in long-term meditating Tibetan Buddhist monks (Lutz, Greischar, Rawlings, Richard, & Davidson, 2004). Coherence and synchrony are associated with improved perceptual processing, cognitive functioning, memory, long-term coding of information (Guderian & Duzel, 2005), and neuroplasticity. Enhanced coherence and synchrony over time could account for improvements in Dan's abilities to perceive, integrate, think, remember, and articulate his ideas during analysis augmented by yoga breathing and meditation. One could view "splitting" (as in borderline personality disorders) as an inability to integrate positive and negative emotion schemas (representations). Similarly, dissociation (as in PTSD) could reflect disruption of processes necessary for integration of components of emotion schemas. Disturbances of long-range synchrony may also contribute to "disconnection syndromes" (Hummel & Gerloff, 2005). If emotional disconnection and dissociation involve analogous problems in long-range synchrony and integration, then interventions (such as yoga breathing and meditation) that enhance coherence and synchrony may be efficacious.

In the study by Larsen and colleagues (2006) described above, participants recorded their subjective experiences. During Ujjayi, 8 felt calm, peaceful, or relaxed. During SK, 7 had intense feelings of love, joy, playfulness, and/or connectedness. One recounted a "transpersonal experience" in which he felt such intense love and compassion that tears streamed down his face for 20 minutes. Three people identified their experiences as "spiritual." After SKY, all but 1 subject (a novice) felt calm, with individual reports of extreme relaxation, mental quiet, happiness, and improved focus. The responses to SKY in this study are typical of those we have observed in hundreds of individuals. Some people emerge from SK with new insights regarding themselves and their relationships. Others report seeing deceased relatives and engaging in conversations that settle unresolved grief issues.

3. Increasing the Capacity to Tolerate Intense Affects

Inability to tolerate painful affects is a common obstacle in psychoanalysis. The patient must be able to bear affects in order to allow them to emerge into conscious awareness and become accessible to the analytic process. Yoga breathing was particularly helpful in developing Dan's capacity to tolerate painful affects without becoming anxious or overwhelmed. At the beginning of the analysis, painful affects such as fear, shame, humiliation, and rage would cause severe anxiety and avoidance in many forms including forgetting, blocking, spacing out, nonsensical daydreaming, preoccupation with irrelevant material, as well as acting out by missing sessions. Pain associated with tender emotions such as sadness, vulnerability, regret, attachment, love, compassion, and empathy was so unbearable that these were completely eclipsed and inaccessible.

Initially, yoga breathing enabled Dan to experience his feelings while sustaining a calm mental and physiological state. During yoga breathing, he could feel increasingly intense emotions and stay with them for long periods of time without needing to suppress or avoid them. After such yoga sessions, Dan would consciously evoke and reexperience the feelings during analytic sessions to work on them further. In this way, he not only described what had occurred, he delivered the experience directly into the analysis where we could connect the feelings with earlier experiences, increase his understanding and acceptance of the emotions, and alleviate residual negative components such as shame and guilt.

Dan subsequently took it one step further by allowing the emotions to occur during real-life situations, observing, reflecting, and appreciating what he was experiencing, and discussing it further in the analysis. For example, when a close member of his family was diagnosed with cancer, he spent a lot of time visiting and supporting the family rather than avoiding the painful situation. In the analysis, he reported feeling deep sadness, crying off and on during the visits. He reflected that although the feelings were terrible, he was comfortable with them and very grateful to be able to have them.

4. Complications, Parameters, and Pitfalls When the Analyst Is a Yoga Practitioner

Introducing yoga into Dan's analysis entailed numerous challenging parameters because we lived in a small town where there was only one yoga breathing class. My husband and I both participated in the class. Under these circumstances, I would not have considered suggesting yoga in the early or even middle phases of an analysis. However, after 8 years of analysis, my sense was that the analytic relationship could handle the parameters and that the potential benefits outweighed the challenges that might ensue.

The patient already knew my husband because we shared office space. He respected my husband's expertise as a psychopharmacologist, knowing that I had consulted him regarding the integration of his herbs and medications over the years. In addition, my husband had assisted in obtaining medical consultations for the patient and his family. We had discussed his feelings about my husband during the analysis.

The patient had observed my family at community events for decades, and his parents lived a few blocks from my house. He had attended school with one of my siblings. Just as training analysts and their trainees adapt to interactions outside the treatment situation, the psychoanalyst in a small town learns to work with less anonymity.

Dan and I discussed the fact that being in a yoga class would create opportunities for him to observe me even though his eyes would be closed during the practices. We agreed that during the classes he would situate himself on the side of the room farthest from me to minimize exposure to one another's breathing and physical responses. We would also avoid engaging in conversations other than conventional greetings. During the yoga classes, usually Dan sat with his back toward me. Even when he was facing me at times, he would avert his eyes to avoid watching things that he felt he should not see. He was extremely considerate of my privacy and of the professional boundary between us. On occasions when he overheard my conversations or noticed my activity, he would discuss his reactions in the next session.

5. Transference Issues With the Yoga Teacher

Although transference issues involving the yoga teacher may need to be addressed in analysis, in Dan's case they were not significant. Dan took numerous yoga courses with different instructors, and his reactions were appropriate to the teacher's personality and style. He could tell who was driven by ego, who was inspired, and who had depth of knowledge.

6. Fear of the Effects of Yoga on the Analyst

SKY was created by a Hindu yoga master and spiritual leader, a guru. Although at first, Dan seemed comfortable with the spiritual aspects of the practices, as time passed, he began to worry that I had come under the influence of the guru and that it would affect my judgment. On the one hand, he was aware of my scientific and clinical interest in yoga, but at the same time, he worried that if I became a spiritual devotee of the guru, I would lose my independent clinical judgment. We discussed these issues in the analyses. I interpreted his worries to be an expression of his fears that I would change in a way outside of his control and that I would no longer be able to take care of him. Over time, his fears abated as he saw no change in my analytic stance, my commitment to the analysis, and my objectivity in working with him.

7. Triangulation, Separation-Individuation, and Mind-Body Preferences

Dan's wife became uncomfortable with the role of the guru in SKY teaching. She and Dan began attending Jewish retreats in which silence, Jewish meditation, Jewish chanting, and group processes were offered. Conflicts arose regarding whether to attend SKY or Jewish programs. These issues were interpreted on several levels, depending on which issues were most active at any given time.

I interpreted Dan's creation of a triangle in which he was caught between the wishes of his wife and the preferences of his analyst. We explored his stirring up conflict with himself as the center of attention, as the innocent, passive bystander watching the other parties get all riled up over him, as he had done during childhood. What could make him feel more valued than to see his wife and analyst fighting over him? Also, he was mobilizing his wife's competitive tendencies to challenge and provoke the analyst without taking responsibility for his actions.

On another level, this was all part of his separation-individuation struggle. Like a toddler, he wanted to run off and do his own thing while being able to look over his shoulder and make sure his mother was waiting for him. Would I try to stop him, control him, force him to submit as his mother had done when she used to pin him to the floor, flailing and screaming? I did not get angry like his mother who hit him, squashed him, or yanked his hair. Instead, I encouraged him to talk about his experiences at the Jewish retreats and received these gifts with the same interest and attention as when he talked about his yoga classes. Dan realized that the yoga practices enabled him to attain more understanding and deeper experiences at the Jewish retreats. He decided to maintain his daily SKY practice and weekly group sessions, as well as attending Jewish retreats from time to time.

It was important that I maintained neutrality in respecting Dan's mind-body experiences outside of SKY rather than pressuring him to limit himself to the practice that I preferred. The analyst should adopt an open-minded attitude while the patient explores mind-body practices. Inquiring into the patient's perceptions and experiences yields rich material and supports the patient's development as issues of separation, autonomy, and identity arise. The analyst who engages in mind-body practices may choose to share knowledge of that to benefit the patient. At the same time, we must be careful not to allow our enthusiasm for a particular practice to create pressure on the patient or to preclude the patient from pursuing other paths that may be more helpful or suitable for him.

Incorporating Yoga Into a Responsible Therapeutic Plan

Yoga should be regarded as complementary to rather than as a substitute for medication, psychotherapy, or psychoanalysis. Practicing SKY over time can help patients reduce reliance on medications, and some may taper off medications altogether. SKY can lessen anxiety and the defensive avoidance of painful mental contents (blocking, forgetting, or suppression). Yoga develops the awareness of subtle physical sensations that may unlock emotional and cognitive processes. Therapeutic breakthroughs may be catalyzed, particularly in cases where trauma-related schemas have remained inaccessible to persistent psychoanalytic approaches. Many people who are being treated for depression, anxiety, and other disorders report that medication and psychoanalysis help but only to a point. Symptom relief does not necessarily result in joy and well-being. Yoga can enhance the capacity for more complete emotional experiences and connectedness. Analysts and psychotherapists who practice yoga also benefit from reduced anxiety and increased calmness, stress-resilience, and mental clarity. Although it is possible for a therapist to teach simple, basic yoga breath practices to a patient, I would recommend that psychoanalysts refer patients to an outside certified yoga instructor. The correct teaching of the more advanced, powerful yoga practices requires years of training. Furthermore, teaching yoga involves face-to-face demonstrations of physical techniques that would disrupt the analytic frame and divert the process into a didactic dialogue.

Clinical Issues: Referrals and Precautions

Most people are able to experience the SKY courses without difficulty. However, clinicians should be aware of the following precautions and contraindications: Pregnant women and patients with uncontrolled hypertension; migraine headaches; severe COPD; acute asthma symptoms; recent injuries of the neck, shoulders, or chest; or recent myocardial infarction should not do breath-holds, Bhastrika, or any rapid or forceful yoga breathing. Gentle basic Ujjayi (without breath-holds), alternate nostril breathing, and meditation are safe and soothing.

Yoga breathing is generally contraindicated in seizure disorders, although meditation can be beneficial. Bipolar patients may be triggered to become manic, particularly from Bhastrika and rapid cycle breathing. Bipolar II patients whose mood swings are under good control on medication may do yoga breathing under supervision if they avoid Bhastrika and rapid-cycle breath forms. However, if they become agitated or anxious, the yoga breathing should be discontinued. Yoga breathing can increase excretion of lithium, causing a drop in serum lithium levels. Bipolar patients being treated on lithium alone should not undertake yoga breath training. Patients on lithium in combination with other mood stabilizers who begin yoga practices should have lithium levels monitored and adjusted if necessary. Individuals with PTSD primarily due to recent trauma or trauma during adulthood (e.g., accidents, illness, war, or natural disasters) usually do well with SKY. Patients with chronic PTSD from childhood abuse can benefit from SKY if they do not have significant dissociative symptoms. The therapist should contact the teacher, prepare the patient, and help process trauma-related material that may emerge. Severe character-disordered patients may not be suitable for the group setting. Psychosis is a contraindication for yoga breathing. Some schizophrenic patients benefit from gentle basic Ujjayi, alternate nostril breathing, and gentle yoga postures.

How and When to Introduce Yoga as a Complementary Treatment in Psychoanalysis

Factors to consider in suggesting yoga during psychoanalysis include the patient's readiness to engage in a regular mind-body practice, the phase of the analysis, the analyst's knowledge of and involvement in available yoga programs, and the quality of local yoga instructors. Clinicians who learn about mind-body practices, particularly by taking classes themselves, are best equipped to make appropriate referrals, prepare patients, explore the meaning of the patients' experiences, and help overcome obstacles to maintaining daily practice over time. Although there are immediate gains, long-term benefits may not appear for 6 to 12 months.

One need not wait for a therapeutic impasse before suggesting yoga to a patient. After the opening phases of analysis, when trust has been established, the analyst may introduce the possibility of starting a mind-body practice to improve mood, energy, anxiety, insomnia, mental focus, pain, or other symptoms. However, the analyst should attend to transference issues and be prepared for the emergence of previously inaccessible contents. Encouraging patients to talk about their yoga experiences brings important material into the analysis and furthers the psychoanalytic process.

Conclusions

By studying the effects of yoga on how patients subjectively experience their emotions and by close observation of changes in emotion, cognition, memory, and behavior, we may find ways to use yoga as an adjunct in the treatment of post-traumatic stress and other disorders. Yoga breath practices also provide a noninvasive means for researchers to probe the activity of neural networks.

Changing the pattern of breath can alter the firing of lung sensors and visceral somatosensory input by vagal afferents, leading to changes in emotional and cognitive processing. We postulate that yoga breathing increases vagal activity and PNS input to areas of the brain involved in fear conditioning, emotional memory (schemas), fear extinction, emotional response, social bonding, and behavior. These areas include prefrontal cortex, insula, amygdala, thalamus, parietal cortex, and hypothalamus.

When the SNS is dominant, attention to threat is heightened with negative thinking. Yoga may restore parasympathetic-sympathetic balance. By reducing overactivity of the amygdala, slow yoga breathing may enable an underactive mPFC to better control emotional responses. The links between sensory impressions, schemas (representations), ideas, emotions, and somatic reactions forged during trauma may be weakened or broken during yoga breath practices, creating the opportunity for transformation. Yoga breathing may enhance neuroplasticity, setting the stage for learning, fear extinction, and mutative change. A case of PTSD was used to illustrate synergistic effects of yoga and psychoanalysis. Although many yoga practices have psychological benefits, my focus has been on Sudarshan Kriya Yoga, because I have found it to enhance the psychoanalytic treatment of trauma.

Sigmund Freud (1929/1930) was fascinated by the effects of yoga on states of consciousness and body awareness, but admitted that it was beyond his comprehension. In *Civilization and Its Discontents*, he wrote, "It is very difficult for me to work with these almost intangible qualities. Another friend of mine ... has assured me that through the practices of yoga, by withdrawing from the world, by fixing the attention on bodily functions and by peculiar methods of breathing, one can in fact evoke new sensations. ... He sees in them a physiological basis, as it were, of much of the wisdom of mysticism. ..."

References

Beauchaine, T. (2001). Vagal tone, development, and Gray's motivational theory: Toward an integrated model of autonomic nervous system functioning in psychopathology. *Developmental Psychopathology, 13(2)*, 183–214.

Becker, I. (2000). Uses of yoga in psychiatry and medicine. In P. R. Muskin (Ed.), *Complementary and alternative medicine and psychiatry* (Vol. 19, pp. 107–145). Washington, DC: American Psychiatric Press.

Benson, T. (1996). *Timeless healing: The power and biology of belief* (pp. 222–234). New York: Scribner.

Berntson, G. G., Sarter, M., & Cacioppo, J. T. (2003). Ascending visceral regulation of cortical affective information processing. *Eur. J. Neuroscience, 18*, 2103–2109.

Bhatia, M., Kumar, A., Kumar, N., Pandey, R. M., & Kochupillai, V. (2003). Electrophysiologic evaluation of Sudarshan Kriya: An EEG, BAER, P300 study. *Indian J. Physiol. Pharmacol., 47(2)*, 157–163.

Brar, H. S. (1970). Yoga and psychoanalysis. *Br. J. of Psychiatry, 116 (531)*, 201–206.

Brown, R. P., & Gerberg, P. L. (2004). *The rhodiola revolution*. Rodale.

Brown, R. P., & Gerberg, P. L. (2005a). Sudarshan Kriya Yoga breathing in the treatment of stress, anxiety, and depression. Part I: Neurophysiological model. *J. of Complementary and Alternative Med., 11(1)*, 189–201.

Brown, R. P., & Gerbarg, P. L. (2005b). Sudarshan Kriya Yoga breathing in the treatment of stress, anxiety, and depression. Part II: Clinical applications and guidelines. *J. of Complementary and Alternative Med., 11*(4), 711–717.

Brown, R. P., Gerbarg, P. L., & Muskin, P. R. (2003). Complementary and alternative treatments in psychiatry. In A. Tasman, J. Kay, & J. Lieberman (Eds.), *Psychiatry* (2nd ed., Vol. 2, pp. 2147–2183). West Sussex, UK: John Wiley & Sons.

Bucci, W. (2001). Pathways of emotional communication. *Psychoanalytic Inquiry, 20*, 40–70.

Bucci, W. (2003). Varieties of dissociative experiences: A multiple code account and a discussion of Bromberg's case of "William." *Psychoanalytic Psychol., 20*(3), 542–557.

Calabrese, P., Perrault, H., Dinh, T. P., Eberhard, A., & Benchetrit, G. (2000). Cardiorespiratory interactions during resistive load breathing. *Am. J. of Physiol. Regulatory Integrative Comp. Physiol., 279*, R2208–R2213.

Cappo, B. M., & Holmes, D. S. (1984). The utility of prolonged respiratory exhalation for reducing physiological and psychological arousal in non-threatening and threatening situations. *J. of Psychosomatic Res., 28*(4), 265–273.

Carter, C. S. (1998). Neuroendocrine perspectives on social attachment and love. *Psychoneuroendocrinology, 23*(8), 779–818.

Carter, J. J., & Byrne, G. G. (2006). PTSD Australian Vietnam veterans: Yoga adjunct treatment, two RCTs: MCYI and SKY. *Proceedings World Conference Expanding Paradigms: Science, Consciousness and Spirituality* (pp. 49–62). New Delhi: All India Institute of Medical Sciences.

Chakraborty, A. (1970). Yoga and psychoanalysis. [Letter]. *Br. J. of Psychiatry, 117* (539), 478.

Cimino, C., & Correale, A. (2005). Projective identification and consciousness alteration: A bridge between psychoanalysis and neuroscience? *Int. J. of Psychoanal., 86*(Pt. 1), 51–60.

Clark, M. E., & Hirschman, R. (1990). Effects of paced respiration on anxiety reduction in a clinical population. *Biofeedback Self-Regulation, 15*(3), 273–284.

Craig, A. D. (2003). Interoception: The sense of the physiological condition of the body. *Curr. Opinion Neurobiol., 13*(4), 500–505.

Critchley, H. D. (2005). Neural mechanisms of autonomic, affective, and cognitive integration. *J. of Comp. Neurology, 93*(1), 154–166.

Damasio, A. R. (1994). *Descartes' error: Emotion, reason and the human brain.* New York: Grosset/Putnam Books.

Damasio, R. R. (1999). *The feeling of what happens: Body and emotion in the making of consciousness.* New York: Harcourt Brace.

Das, P., Kemp, A. H., Liddell, B. J., Olivieri, G., Peduto, A., Gordon, E. et al. (2005). Pathways for fear perception: Modulation of amygdala activity by thalamo-cortical systems. *NeuroImage, 26*, 141–148.

Descilo, T., Vedamurthachar, A., Gerbarg, P. L., Nagaraja, D., Gangadhar, R., Damodoran, R. et al. (2006). Comparison of a yoga breath-based program and a client-centered exposure therapy for relief of PTSD and depression in survivors of tsunami disaster. *Proceedings World Conference Expanding Paradigms: Science Consciousness and Spirituality* (pp. 64–78). New Delhi: All India Institute of Medical Sciences.

Djareva, T., Ilkov, A., Varbanova, A., Nikiforova, A., & Mateev, G. (1986). Human growth hormone, cortisol, and acid base balance changes after hyperventilation and breath-holding. *International Journal of Sports Medicine, 7*, 311–315.

Feuerstein, G. (1998). *The yoga tradition: Its history, literature, philosophy, and practice.* Prescott, AZ: Hohm Press.

Freud, S. (1929/1930). *Civilization and its discontents. Standard edition of the complete psychological works of Sigmund Freud*, Translated by J. Strachey, A. Freud, A. Strachey, and A. Tyson (Vol. XXI, 1961, pp. 72–73). London: The Hogarth Press.

Gerbarg, P. L., & Brown, R. P. (2005). Yoga: A breath of relief for Hurricane Katrina refugees. *Current Psychiatry, 4*(10), 55–67.

Gordon, J. S., Staples, J. K., Blyta, A., & Bytyqi, M. (2004). Treatment of posttraumatic stress disorder in postwar Kosovo high school students using mind-body skills group: A pilot study. *J. of Traumatic Stress, 17*(2), 143–147.

Guderian, S., & Duzel, E. (2005). Induced theta oscillations mediate large-scale synchrony with mediotemporal areas during recollection in humans. *Hippocampus, 15*(7), 901–912.

Hummel, F., & Gerloff, C. (2005). Larger interregional synchrony is associated with greater behavioral success in a complex sensory integration task in humans. *Cereb. Cortex, 15*(5), 670–678.

Jacobs, G. D. (2001). Clinical applications of the relaxation response and mind-body interventions. *J. of Alternative and Complementary Med., 7*, Suppl. 1, S93–S101.

Janakiramaiah, N., Gangadhar, B. N., Naga Venkatesha Murthy, P. J., Harish, M. G., Subbakirishna, D. K., & Vedamurthachar, A. (2000). Antidepressant efficacy of Sudarshan Kriya Yoga (SKY) in melancholia: A randomized comparison with electroconvulsive therapy (ECT) and imipramine. *Journal of Affective Disorders, 57 (1–3)*, 255–259.

Janakiramaiah, N., Gangadhar, B. N., Naga Venkatesha Murthy, P. J., Harish, M. G., Taranath Shetty, K., Subbakrishna, D. K. (1998). Therapeutic efficacy of Sudarshan Kriya Yoga (SKY) in dysthymic disorder. *Nat. Inst. of Ment. Health and NeuroSciences J.*, 21–28.

Larsen, S., Yee, W., Gerbarg, P. L., Brown, R. P., Gunkelman, J., & Sherlin, L. (2006). Neurophysiological markers of Sudarshan Kriya Yoga practices: A pilot study. *Proceedings World Conference Expanding Paradigms: Science, Consciousness and Spirituality* (pp. 36–48). New Delhi: All India Institute of Medical Sciences.

LeDoux, J. E. (2000). Emotion circuits in the brain. *Annu. Rev. Neuroscience, 23*, 155–184.

Lehrer, P., Sasaki, Y., & Saito, Y. (1999). Zazen and cardiac variability. *Psychosomatic Med., 61*, 812–821.

Lutz, A., Greischar, L. L., Rawlings, N. B., Richard, M., & Davidson, R. J. (2004). Long-term meditators self-induce high-amplitude gamma synchrony during mental practice. *Proceedings National Academy of Science U.S.A., 101*(46), 16369–16373.

Marangell, L. B., Rush, A. J., George, M. S., Sackeim, H. A., Johnson, C. R., Husain, M. M. et al. (2002). Vagus nerve stimulation (VNS) for major depressive episodes: One year outcomes. *Biol. Psychiatry, 51*(4), 280–287.

McKnight, J. T., & Fehmi, L. G. (2001). Attention and neurofeedback synchrony training: Clinical results and their significance. *J. of Neurotherapy, 5*(1/2).

Naga Venkatesha Murthy, P. J., Janakiramaiah, N., Gangadhar, B. N., & Subbakrishna, D. K. (1998). P300 amplitude and antidepressant response to Sudarshan Kriya Yoga (SKY). *J.of Affective Disorders, 50*(1), 45–48.

Neki, J. S. (1967). Yoga and psychoanalysis. *Compr. Psychiatry, 8*(3), 160–167.

Nelson, E. E., & Panksepp, J. (1998). Brain substrates of infant-mother attachment: Contributions of opioids, oxytocin, and norepinephrine. *Neuroscience Biobehavior Rev., 22*(3), 437–452.

Philippot, P., Gaetane, C., & Blairy, S. (2002). Respiratory feedback in the generation of emotion. *Cognit. and Emotion, 16*(5), 605–607.

Porges, S. W. (1995). Orienting in a defensive world: Mammalian modifications of our evolutionary heritage. A polyvagal theory. *Psychophysiology, 32*, 301–318.

Porges, S. W. (2001). The polyvagal theory: Phylogenetic substrates of a social nervous system. *Int. J. of Psychophysiology, 42*(2), 123–146.

Sakakibara M., & Hayano, J. (1996). Effect of slowed respiration on cardiac parasympathetic response to threat. *Psychosomatic Med., 58*(1), 32–37.

Satyanarayana, M., Rajeswari, K. R., Jhansi Rani, N., Sri Krishna, Ch., & Krishna Rao, P. V. (1992). Effect of Santhi Kriya on certain psychophysiological parameters: A preliminary study. *Indian J. Physiol. Pharmacol., 36*(2), 88–92.

Schachter, S. C., & Saper, C. B. (1998). Vagus nerve stimulation. *Epilepsia*, *39*(7), 677–686.

Shannahoff-Khalsa, D. S., Ray, L. E., Levine, S., Gallen, C. C., Schwartz, B. J., & Sidorowick, J. J. (1999). Randomized controlled trial of yogic meditation techniques for patients with obsessive-compulsive disorder. *CNS Spectrum*, *4*(12), 34–47.

Shnayder, N. A., Agarkova, N. O., Lyulyakina, E. G., Naumova, E. B., & Shnayder, V. A. (2006). Bioelectrical brain activity in humans who practiced Sudarshan Kriya. *Proceedings World Conference Expanding Paradigms: Science, Consciousness and Spirituality*. New Delhi: All India Institute Medical Sciences.

Sovik, R. (2000). The science of breathing—The yogic view. *Prog. Brain Res.*, *122*, 491–505.

Stock, S., & Uvnas-Moberg, K. (1988). Increased plasma levels of oxytocin in response to afferent electrical stimulation of the sciatic and vagal nerves and in response to touch and pinch in anaesthetized rats. *Acta Physiologica Scandinavica*, *132*, 29–34.

Telles, S., & Desiraju, T. (1992). Heart rate alterations in different types of pranayamas. *Indian J. Physiol. Pharmacol.*, *36*(4), 287–288.

Telles, S., Joseph, C., Venkatesh, S., & Desiraju, T. (1993). Alterations of auditory middle latency evoked potentials during yogic consciously regulated breathing and attentive state of mind. *Int. J. Psychophysiology*, *14*(3), 189–198.

Thayer, J. F., & Brosschat, J. F. (2005). Psychosomatics and psychopathology: Looking up and down from the brain. *Psychoneuroendocrinology*, *10*, 1050–1058.

Vaidyanathan, T. G., & Kripal, J. J. (1999). *Vishnu on Freud's desk: A reader in psychoanalysis and Hinduism*. Oxford, UK: Oxford University Press.

Weintraub, A. (2004). *Yoga for depression*. New York: Broadway Books Random House.

Yu, J. (2005). Airway mechanosensors. *Respiratory Physiol. Neurobiol.*, *148*(3), 217–243.

Zhang, J. X., Harper, R. M., & Frysinger, R. C. (1986). Respiratory modulation of neuronal discharge in the central nucleus of the amygdala during sleep and waking states. *Experimental Neurology*, *91*(1), 193–207.

7

Sweet Are the Uses of Adversity

Psychic Integration Through Body-Centered Work

Graham Bass

> Sweet are the uses of adversity,
> Which, like the toad, ugly and venomous,
> Wears yet a precious jewel in his head;
> And this our life, exempt from public haunt,
> Finds tongues in trees, books in the running brooks,
> Sermons in stones, and good in everything.

William Shakespeare
As You Like It, **Act II, Scene I, lines 12–17**

One might be thought a callous therapist to assert along with Shakespeare's Duke Senior that there is "good in everything." Nevertheless, there is an apparent paradox inherent in body-centered energy work and in psychoanalysis, known to all patients and clinicians. The precious jewel of healing is often best found by engaging with that which seems most ugly and venomous, in fathoming the depths exempt from public haunt, those hidden places of the psyche adorned with "Keep out!" and "Proceed at your own peril" signs. In the sanctuary of our

offices, we orient ourselves toward listening to the sermons that issue
forth from the stones trapped in the body's tissues and to the stories
that the petrified wood of formerly green aliveness tells. As we do so,
we feel the stones and wood start to change beneath our hands.

There is mystery in this. The encounter between two conscious-
nesses, two bodies, confounds all efforts at complete understanding.
Space is created for that which is old and locked in place to release
and reorganize. Something new and unexpected comes into being.
We are changed forever.

In both psychoanalytic and body-centered work, my focus is those
elements of experience that are not part of the patient's conscious
memory and sense of self, yet which deeply shape his experience of
his world. As psychoanalysts, we are used to thinking about "not me"
experiences—disowned, dissociated, or unavailable self-experience
secondary to trauma or long-term relational necessity. One of the
most challenging aspects of our work is to "locate" these self-states,
to bring them into relationship. Often, we do this by becoming aware
of our own resonance with them. We perceive them on the sonar of
our own internal responses before we see them present in front of us.
Deep speaks unto deep.

As analysts, we do this via our associations, affective states, and
dawning awareness of enactments. As body-centered therapists,
permitted the possibility of two-way communication between our
physical beings, other channels are amplified and enlivened.

When the patient's disowned self-experience communicates itself
to my own body, and I bring my body into relationship with the
patient through intentioned therapeutic touch, the patient has an
opportunity to become aware, in a new way, of his own unknown
depths. Stolorow and Atwood (1991) have noted that "the very boundaries separating mind and body, like those between conscious and
unconscious, are understood as forming in an intersubjective system" (p. 193). The intersubjective system of the patient and therapist
has the same potential to allow new organization and awareness.

"The body is the unconscious mind!" says psychoneuroimmunolo-
gist Dr. Candace Pert (1997). "Mind doesn't dominate body, it *becomes*
body…. The body is the actual outward manifestation, in physical
space, of the mind" (p. 187). Further, "repressed trauma caused by
overwhelming emotion can be stored in a body part…. Memories are
stored not only in the brain, but … all the way out along pathways to
internal organs and the very surface of our skin" (pp. 141–143).

Unprocessed, unintegrated experience, such as physical or psychological trauma, can be held in the body, in muscle, visceral, neurologic, or other tissue; as well as in a body position. These holdings create disruptions and imbalances in the body's structure, movement, and flow of energy. The practitioner can zero in on where these energetic disharmonies and blockages are being held and facilitate their integration and release. This process can occur with little or no conscious advertence on the part of the patient, or with clearly and intensely felt emotional accompaniment, visual imagery, memories, and associations.

I believe the "blockage" is an artifact of the psyche-soma's attempt to resolve a problem it has faced. It did the best it could given the physical, energetic, psychological, and relational structures then in place. Like nuclear waste sunk to the bottom of the sea lest it make our world uninhabitable, that which we do not have the structure to bear must be sequestered someplace in the far reaches of our beings where it will not do harm. But that sequestering comes at a cost. My role as therapist is to assist the system to find a new solution, with the resources currently available, one that is more consistent with optimal physical, emotional, energetic, and relational freedom.

In addition to psychoanalysis, I've studied and practiced Therapeutic Touch, Polarity, Craniosacral Therapy, acupressure, chi gung, and other touch and nontouch modalities over the past 35 years. They have all been part of my own process of healing and inform my work. In this chapter, I will use Craniosacral Therapy as a model.

Craniosacral Therapy is a therapeutic modality developed by osteopath John Upledger in the 1970s.[1] With very light touch, the practitioner engages with and monitors the craniosacral system in which cerebrospinal fluid is secreted and reabsorbed in and around the brain, circulating through the brain and spinal cord and causing an expansion/contraction of approximately 6 to 12 cycles per minute. This slow pulse can be palpated through the cranium, the sacrum, and, by extension, every part of the body from toes to fingertips. Although it is not typically part of one's conscious experience, a practitioner learns to feel it.

The movements may be minuscule, imperceptible to untrained touch, but they are measurable by scientific instruments. And to the experienced practitioner, these tiny movements can feel vast, as if instead of microns, distances of inches or even feet are being moved through. In addition to the rate of the movement, one can sense its quality, its amplitude, and a myriad of subtle variations within the movement and between left side and right. These indicate where some old story is being held, waiting to be told. To an observer, watching the practitioner seemingly immobile with hand in contact with the patient's head or arm, the variety of phenomena he may report may seem almost magical, if not a product of wishful thinking.

Many years ago, studying to be a registered nurse, I listened for the first time to a patient's heart through a stethoscope. I began to tune in to some of the sounds of the beating heart beneath the instrument's bell. I heard the lub-dub of systole as the left ventricle contracted, sending blood through the arteries. I waited in the intermediary silence of diastole as the auricles expanded and filled with blood. I noted the rhythm, strength, rate, and other qualities of the sounds. I rejoiced in my newly attained skills. Then, one day, I went on rounds with a cardiologist, who listened to patients' hearts and commented on what he was hearing: "Ah, here's an aortic stenosis." In different patients, he reported a mitral regurgitation, a pericardial rub, and more than a dozen other pathological processes. I listened hard, of course, and tried to hear what he was hearing. But mostly what I heard was "lub-dub."

There is much one can learn about listening. The human body and energy field speak many languages. In addition to the craniosacral rhythm, I may tune in to the meridians and organ systems as elaborated in traditional Chinese medicine. The chakra system of Indian medicine or the auric fields of the body may be part of a given session. My orientation is to "listen" to what the patient's body structure and energy system are presenting. I trust that the patient will reveal what language we are to speak and what body part is speaking it—finger, knee, liver, heart, or other. The "deep structure" of each language is the same: that of the fundamental unity of mind and body. With deference to the patient's inner wisdom, which guides the movement toward health, I listen. My listening is most meaningful not for what it reveals to me, but because it creates a space for things to begin to shift and move, within my patient and between us.

Case 1: Jane

Jane comes for her craniosacral session complaining of chest tightness, coughing, and difficulty breathing. She feels almost asthmatic.

She is taking a hypnosis training course, which is helping her to become freer in using her voice therapeutically. However, the coughing of the past week is interfering with her practice of newly learned skills. We agree that our primary intention for the session is to address what is going on with her lungs, but that we will be open to following whatever route to that goal her own body shows us, even if there does not seem to be an obvious connection.

She lies supine, fully clothed, on the massage table that I use in the craniosacral work, and I stand at her feet, as is my custom. I take a minute or two to center and ground myself in my own body and energy, tuning in to my own "instrument" before engaging with her. I feel the ground beneath my feet and the through-line from the bottoms of my feet to the top of my head, as well as the extension of that line down into the Earth and upward. I take a baseline reading, as it were. I calibrate my own system, so that I may be optimally aware of what changes may be taking place within me in response to her. I then place my palms lightly on the dorsal surfaces of Jane's two feet and tune in to her body structure and energy system.

"The body is the unconscious mind." I do not distinguish between body and psyche. I empty myself of expectation and knowledge. Whatever I might "know" about "body/mind" from studies or past experience is irrelevant. Whatever she has come for, whatever the identified "problem" is, my intention is only to listen. I trust that what needs to make itself known in the session will do so. I endeavor to hold the space for that to happen.

My hands "meld" with her feet, and through her feet to her whole physical and energetic structure. I "listen" with my hands and with my whole being, as my physical and energetic structure begins to resonate with hers. I await the invitation to engage with her structure and energy field in whatever particular place of engagement will best serve her.

When I put my hands on a patient, there is very often a moment in which I become aware that I have no clue at all as to what is going on. There is too much information, or too little, it seems impossible to know where to start or where to go. I don't know what is going on with the system under my hands, much less how to participate in any therapeutic change.

I have come to recognize this experience of "not knowing" as the requisite doorway through which I must pass in order to participate in any meaningful experience of change. There are temptations that

would distract me from going through that door. One is the feeling
that I need to *know* more. I should read more books, do more training. But when I submit myself to being with my patient in that condition of not knowing, I begin to enter with her into what has also been
unknown to her. Unknown, "not me," terrifying, too much to bear.

When I accept that the compass of my rational mind does not work
effectively in this foreign territory, when I don't try to find my own
direction, but just listen, then indistinct shapes begin to reveal themselves in the darkness. Faint cries begin to be heard. And if I resist the
temptation to hastily grasp what comes near, if I am able to stay with
my patient in that place of unknowing, then shifts start to occur.

As I stand at Jane's feet, I find myself, not surprisingly, drawn into
her chest/lung area. But I also become aware that her left sacral area/
hip is drawing me even more strongly.

In some sessions, there is a visual awareness, as if the area in question is lit up. In others, I feel the analogous area in my own body, as
if a vibratory resonance cues me to where the current work is in the
patient's body. I may sense a blockage or disruption along an acu-
puncture meridian. And often there is, as today, a sensation of my
hands being physically drawn in to a specific place, which can be in
or on the body, or within the energy field surrounding the body. I
recognize this as an energetic invitation. I accept it.

Jane's left sacral/hip area feels associated with the problem in
her chest, as if this area needs to be engaged before the chest can
be worked with productively. I trust that impression and move to a
seated position on her left side. I place my left hand under her sacrum
and my right hand lightly in contact with the anterior surface of her
left hip. I listen.

I feel the tissue beneath my hands drawing me in deeper. There
is subtle movement, as if her tissue and my hands are engaged in
an intricate dance in which both are playing traditionally masculine
and feminine parts. My hands are holding the space for her tissues to
do what they could not do on their own, as a male ballet dancer holds
the female dancer as she moves into positions that she could not hold
without that support. And my hands are also following, allowing her
structure and energy to lead, showing me where to go and how best
to assist.

After some minutes, the tissue moves into a pattern that feels
repetitive, not alive in the way that it did a few moments earlier. It
begins to feel like the movement has now become a defense against

going deeper. I apply just enough resistance to prevent the tissue from continuing in that perseverative pattern. It remains held in a position of maximum tension for some seconds before finding a new way to move, another direction/dimension/pattern that has not previously been available as part of the known choreography.

This new dance continues for about 10 minutes, and I begin to feel an intense release of heat from the tissues. At the same time, Jane begins to show signs of an emotional response—her breathing quickens, and her face reveals some intense feeling. Although a session often moves to completion without any words spoken, I choose at this point to ask, "What are you feeling?"

Jane: I don't know. I'm not sure. I don't know what's happening. Uh, I think someone's near me … I'm afraid …

Graham: You don't know what's happening … you're afraid … you think someone's near you …

J: Yes. It's not clear at all.

As my hands have been engaged with her sacrum/hip over the past few minutes, I have become aware of a strong impression that the body between my hands has become much smaller, as if it were a little girl's body. I ask:

G: Is there an age associated with this feeling?

J: I don't know.
   [Silence for a minute or two]
   Maybe about 6 years old.
   [Silence for a few minutes]
   I used to have severe asthma attacks at about that age!

G: Would it be okay with you if I spoke with the 6-year-old?

J: I don't know. I guess so. I don't know if she'll speak with you.

G: That's okay. We'll leave that up to her. But is it okay with you if she uses your vocal apparatus, if she wants to and is able to?

J: Yes, I guess so.

G: Good. Thank you.
   So, 6-year-old. Will you speak with me?

J: Yes.

G: Good. Thank you. I'm Graham. What's your name?

J: Jane.

G: Good. Jane, what's happening right now?

J: I don't know. I'm scared.

G: You're feeling scared. Where are you?

J: In my room. In my bed. It's dark.
G: You're in your bed. It's dark. Are you alone?
J: Someone is here.
G: Someone is here. Do you know who it is?
J: No.
G: You don't know who it is. What are they doing?
J: I don't know. They're hurting me.

Jane has previously been aware of childhood incestuous abuse by a family member. Many of the details of this have been elaborated in previous sessions. But the connection between the abuse and her childhood asthma had not been made. As this session continues, the 6-year-old speaks of her terror about making any noise during the abuse and about later revealing what had taken place during the night. Her voice, during the abuse and following it during the light of day, had been silenced. Expression of her feelings had been choked back. And now, her work in learning to use her voice freely and expressively has challenged that old place of restriction, bringing forth for therapeutic engagement the original symptom, and the young self that holds that symptom.

During this entire piece of work, my hands engaged with Jane's hip area, I am tuned into her craniosacral rhythm. At the first sign of Jane's emotional response and during the entirety of our dialogue, this rhythm, normally present, has been completely stopped. This is a phenomenon that Dr. Upledger (2001) has discovered and named the "significance detector" (p. 12). It is as if the whole craniosacral system is "holding its breath" in the midst of some deeply significant process of accessing and releasing old trauma.

As we engage with her 6-year-old, and she is able to share with us some aspects of her experience with which she has been all alone, there is an additional release of heat from the tissues in her sacral area. And with that release, an expression of a strong emotion, terror.

Because Jane's rhythm remains stopped during her expression of terror, I trust that her current process is one of integration rather than retraumatization. There is a further release of heat from her sacrum, and a softening of the tissues. I feel the energy "blockage" that had first drawn me to this area dissolve, and her energy moves more freely. Our work in her left sacrum is finished for now. My hands are drawn to her upper chest and throat area.

I place my left palm in contact with her thoracic spine, and rest my right palm lightly in contact with her upper chest area just beneath her throat. I feel the connection between my two hands through her body. I open my awareness to what it feels like between my hands. Becoming aware of a feeling of tightness in my own chest, of a constriction in my throat area, I remain engaged. Jane's craniosacral rhythm stops. She becomes aware of intense anger rising in her. With my encouragement, she expresses the anger verbally, for the first time, loudly demanding that the person in the room with her "Get *away* from me! Get *off* of me!" Her whole body participates strongly in this expression—legs, hips, sacrum, chest. There is a strong release of heat from her throat, and the tissues soften. She reports feeling a new openness in her chest and throat.

Since then, over 1 year ago, Jane's chest and throat symptoms have not recurred.

Theoretical Considerations

As I invite Jane's 6-year-old into both verbal and nonverbal engagement, I am facilitating a "therapeutic dissociation." This, according to Davies (1996), can help "a particular dissociated aspect of experience ... to elaborate itself, and to reveal both its historical roots and its present-day interpersonal influence within the safe confines of the therapeutic relationship" (p. 567). Alternate self-states come with their own state-dependent memories, affect, physicality, and relational experience. Jane experiences her terror within a version of Jungian psychoanalyst Robert Bosnak's "double consciousness," a state that I believe is a prerequisite to therapeutic change. In working with a patient's dream of a bull, Bosnak (2003) characterizes double consciousness as "fully experiencing the state of awareness that corresponds to the subjectivity of the bull, while being entirely aware that the bull is other, not self" (pp. 685–686).

Bosnak facilitates entry into double consciousness by his particular style of dreamwork. I believe that the same phenomenon occurs by virtue of the physical contact between Jane and myself, which establishes a grounding in and reminder of the existence of the adult Jane who is lying on my table. Jane can fully feel the terror held in and arising from her sacral area, and she can also be aware that she is safe.[2] While we are explicitly involved with the experience of the 6-year-old, staying in relationship to her and tracking her experience through the movements of Jane's body and energy, we are also implicitly in relationship to the adult Jane whose voice is being used by the child. By my staying in relationship to both Janes simultaneously, we are creating a possibility for both Janes, 6-year-old and adult, to come into relationship with each other in a new way.

I believe that it is this double consciousness that allows the intensity of the original traumatizing experience to be felt, as it were, for the first time, in a context of integration rather than retraumatization. The 6-year-old's terror, which she did not have the physical, emotional, or relational structure to bear, much less integrate, can be felt and integrated with the help of the adult Jane and the therapeutic relationship. Bromberg, Stern, and others have characterized this process, within a psychoanalytic setting, in similar ways, using different language.[3]

If I were treating Jane psychoanalytically, and her 6-year-old self shouted to "the person in the room" with her, "Get *away* from me! Get *off* of me!" I would operate from the awareness that *I* may be the "person in the room with the 6-year-old." My interest would be in elaborating the 6-year-old's experience of *my* hurting her, of *my* being on top of her. I would pay attention to my experience of participation in enacting a contemporary version of that old trauma with the 6-year-old. It would be through the cocreated present enactment that we would have a chance at arriving at something new. This is in accordance with a current relational model, which has it that "defensively dissociated states first become available for expression via enactment.... The conflict that cannot be experienced within one mind is experienced between or across two minds" (Director, 2005, p. 580).

In body-centered work, however, my interest is in remaining with the original trauma of the 6-year-old, helping her to elaborate that experience, while maintaining Jane's double consciousness. This might be seen in psychoanalytic terms as a "deflection" of the transference.[4] It is a version of a Sullivanian "counter-projection,"[5] which keeps me out of the original trauma as perpetrator and allows me to remain explicitly as therapeutic ally.

Case 2: Ann

Ann and I are about 15 minutes into our session, and my hands are very lightly engaged with her throat, which has presented as holding something that is ready for processing and release. I begin to feel some constriction in my own throat. I give myself permission to feel that constriction and whatever else may come with it, as openly and deeply as I can. Her craniosacral rhythm is stopped, communicating to me that we are in a therapeutically significant process. The feeling in my throat intensifies and then begins to diminish as Ann becomes increasingly distressed: "You're *hurting* me! *Stop* it! You're *strangling* me!"

I say to her, "Take a moment to put your hands on my hand. Move my hand with yours, feel the amount of pressure that I'm actually applying." She does so and feels that I am barely touching. She expresses great surprise at the discrepancy between what she has been experiencing and what her experiment reveals. Ann's therapeutic double consciousness is established.

I then say, "You can feel the pressure I am applying to your throat is not physically hurtful or dangerous to you. Can you allow yourself now to go more deeply into that experience of strangling and pain that is being held in your throat?" She does so, and as we engage together with that held experience, it becomes more fully felt, by both of us. We participate in the intersubjective field, in all of its complexity.

That complexity includes some disconcerting elements. As the constriction in my own throat continues to diminish, I become aware of a fleeting impulse to press harder on her throat. I maintain my light pressure. I have my own double consciousness, analogous to hers, of that which can be/is strangler and abuser within myself, alongside the compassionate therapist. It may be as much a challenge for me to tolerate my self-experience of abuser as it is for her to tolerate her self-experience of being abused. But we both maintain our (double) consciousness of the reality of the light pressure being exerted and the therapeutic intent of the session.

The constriction I felt in my own throat has now faded completely, along with the abusive impulse, as she has allowed herself to feel more fully the intensity of what has been held in her throat.

As we meet this challenge, I lightly holding her throat and she paying attention to where the increasingly intense experience of being strangled takes her, she experiences fear and anger, and memories arise. As these memories and feelings that have been held sequestered in her tissues come into consciousness, there are signs of tissue release in her throat. She is finding a new way to be in relationship with them, not merely as traumatized dissociated victim now, but as agent and experiencer.

For months following this session, until the present time, her chronic throat problems are ameliorated.

Theoretical Considerations

I believe that my willingness to feel something of what Ann has been holding in her throat, but which was experienced by her as too much to feel, and therefore had to be disowned, has helped free her to begin to feel it.

Bosnak (1996) has coined the term "symbiotic communication" to characterize the phenomenon of the therapist feeling in his own body some aspect of the patient's subjectivity. When I am able to hold that experience and my own subjectivity at the same time, and distinguish between them, that is my therapeutic double consciousness.[6]

I sometimes imagine that I play the role of an auxiliary hard drive, added to allow more room for processing. As I take into my own physical/energetic/emotional structure some of the information that did not "fit" in the patient's structure, space is created for reorganization to occur. Then she can "take back" her energy/feelings, and as she does so, my own experience of it diminishes. This phenomenon is a version of "the conflict that cannot be experienced within one mind is experienced between or across two minds," (Director, 2005, p. 580). However, because there is a fundamental unity of mind and body, it is also being experienced between or across two bodies.

Perhaps such phenomena as projective identification in the psychoanalytic setting are related to this. Without the body connection/attunement/feedback, the time frame is generally prolonged. There is more "static," a difference analogous, perhaps, to a slow-speed dial-up Internet hook-up compared with a high-speed cable connection, where more information can be downloaded more quickly.

I see this shift in body tissue and in consciousness as taking place within a cocreated crucible of the intersubjective field of therapist and patient. This crucible is comprised of many elements. Among them are the following:

- The patient's capacity to risk allowing the part of her that holds the old experience to be known and come into relationship with the therapist
- The patient's capacity to tolerate, for the first time, feeling the emotional pain held in her body

- The therapist's capacity to feel some of that pain along with the patient
- The therapist's capacity to tolerate being "the abuser"

My therapeutic intention must be strong enough to withstand the powerful energies, now liberated, that begin to move in the course of the session, within myself, within the patient, and between the two of us. I must neither collapse into them nor withdraw from them. If the crucible holds, what gets formed in the creative heat and pressure is something new, not seen or known before.

In order for this to happen in the body-centered work as I experience it, the various interpersonal and intrapersonal self-state configurations and potential enactments, which would merely repeat a version of an old familiar dynamic, must be felt but not acted on. This presents different challenges in the temporally compressed frame of a body-centered session, compared with a psychoanalytic engagement where we have the "luxury" to experience, develop, and use these self-state configurations therapeutically over longer stretches of time. The reality of the physical contact between us allows us to avoid spending a great deal of time caught in a transferential experience of me as strangling her in some way, and allows me to be very clear about the countertransferential pull to actually strangle her.

Of course, what happens in the therapeutic encounter between us is codetermined by the uniqueness of her experience of trauma and by the uniqueness of what I bring to the table, including my own personal history and genealogy. We can look at our cocreated experience through many different lenses. On micro levels of somatosensory awareness, for instance, I am aware of the tensing of her throat muscles in response to the approach of my "innocent" hand. That tensing activates in me old patterns of response to early maternal deprivation. My impulse to strangle comes not only in empathic resonance with and response to the somatic memory that she holds in the tissues of her neck, but is also my own idiosyncratic and multiply determined response to the rejection of my body that her traumatized tissues communicate. I may not be the only person in Ann's life who responds to her micromuscular tensing and flinching with aggressive feelings or withdrawal. But others she encounters are often not conscious of what evokes these feelings in them, and her well-being and psychological healing and growth may not be their priority.

If I were Ann's psychoanalyst engaged in an enactment that entailed some version of my strangling her, I might not draw her attention to the way in which I was not "really" strangling her. Rather, I would want her to elaborate her experience of me strangling her, as I allowed myself to feel more fully my own complementary experience. It would be through a recognition of the enactment we were engaged in together, and through parsing the elements and genealogy of it, that I might hope for some therapeutic movement.

Working with touch, with actual hands on actual throat, brings in extra tools and requires some to be left unused. I do not verbalize my impulse to strangle Ann: too much vulnerability for either of us to be borne, too much risk of retraumatization, not the time or place to explore that particular dimension of the intersubjective field. Rather, my direct access to, and feedback with, alternate self-states, through the physical/energetic manifestations associated with them, can facilitate a return to the original trauma, bringing what has been dissociated into relationship and integration.

Conclusion

I experience the use of the body in body-centered therapy as analogous to Bromberg's (2000) use of dreams in psychoanalytic work. He says, in regard to the dream:

> One of its manifestations in psychoanalysis is to contain and hold, as a separate reality, unprocessed experience that is not safely containable at that moment within the "me" that defines the analytic relationship for the patient. In other words, the use of a dream in analysis might, in one respect, be thought of as a transitional experience that allows the potential linking of self-states that are hypnoidally disconnected, permitting the voices of other self-states to be heard and to find access to the dynamic structure that the patient defines as "me." (p. 694)

In body-centered therapy, the body itself, engaged with and stabilized by the touch of the therapist, serves as that kind of transitional experience, allowing the linking of disconnected self-states. The body as psyche's dream!

It may be because of the mind-body split inherent in our contemporary culture that the body can serve as a transitional experience in this way. To the extent that the body is experienced as "other," it can hold and represent those self-experiences that fall into that category of "other." And to the extent that the body becomes "re-membered" in the course of a given session, that which is held and represented in the body part being engaged with can also be "re-membered," taken back into relationship, now as self rather than other.

The body structure holds all the information necessary to replay elements of the original traumatic experience. These elements include audio, visual, somatosensory, and emotional dimensions. And as that information is accessed and brought to consciousness, very palpable and clearly sensed enduring physical changes take place in the body tissues. There may be movement, softening, opening, releasing of heat, feeling of cold, sensation of electricity, and other somatic experiences. The patient is often aware of strong emotional, sometimes abreactive, content, with memories.

I believe that were we able to monitor the patient's body in the course of doing psychoanalytic work with dissociative self-states, the same phenomena would be evident. Changes in self-state would be reflected in subtle and not-so-subtle physiological changes.

When I work in a craniosacral mode, physical contact of my hands with my patient is not the sine qua non of the work. Sometimes my hands are off the body, engaged in the energy field. And what I am sensing within the body can often be at a level of magnitude (or "microtude") that is beyond what is commonly thought to be accessible. I, and others, work with impressions not only on the musculoskeletal level, but also on the level of individual muscle fibers, neurons, cells, and even DNA.

Why, then, can I not do the same work seated a few feet away from the patient, as in a psychoanalytic consulting room? I think that the answer is that in many ways I can, and often do. I think that I, and probably all experienced psychoanalysts, are tuning into the "significance detector" of stopped craniosacral rhythm and other subtle cues as to the authenticity of the patient's engagement at any given moment. We act in response to those cues, usually out of awareness. There is always an interpenetration of energy fields of patient and psychoanalyst. We are *all* doing "body-centered energy work."

As I participate in that interpenetration, in psychoanalytic office and in craniosacral therapy practice, when I am fluid enough to relate to alternate self-states as they allow themselves to be known and embodied, within my patient and within myself, my engagement with them can lead to my patient's, and my own, eventual increased capacity for self-relatedness.[7]

As alternate self-states come into relationship, they often bring with them those aspects of traumatic experience or relationally unacceptable self-experience that were beyond bearing at an earlier time; survival was contingent upon their being cast out.

I invite to be known those subterranean aspects of my patient's psyche-soma, the "ugly and venomous" toads that have been exiled to inner darkness, whose nighttime cries may call forth their complement within myself. My patient and I must bear their visitation, for the "precious jewel" they hold is an immense amount of life energy that can be reclaimed and made available for creativity and loving. I have known no more powerful path to healing than this. Sweet indeed are the uses of adversity.

Notes

1. Upledger and Vredevoogd (1983) credit osteopath William G. Sutherland, in the early 1900s, as an early investigator of the craniosacral system. Other precursors and contributors to contemporary craniosacral therapy include Andrew Taylor Still, Rollin Becker, and Robert Fulford. In addition to Upledger's Craniosacral Therapy, other contemporary approaches to working with the craniosacral system include the Biodynamic Cranial Osteopathy of James Jealous, the Craniosacral Biodynamics of Franklyn Sills, and the Visionary Craniosacral work of Hugh Milne.
2. Bosnak (personal communication, 2006) notes that double consciousness consists of "two parallel experiences, not a mixture of experiences. It is not one foot in and one foot out, but rather two feet in and two feet out."
3. See Director's (2005, p. 581) summary of some of these formulations.
4. Havens (1993, p. 167) refers to Kernberg's (1968) use of "deflection" of the transference.
5. Havens (1993) notes that Sullivan often kept himself out of the transference as much as possible, refusing, as it were, to hold the patient's projections, and focusing instead on bringing his patient back to the original trauma. Havens termed this "counterprojection."
6. Bosnak (2003) notes the difficulty of maintaining a therapeutic double consciousness: "In the West we have been trained, from very little on, to approach subjectivity by way of total identification. We identify fully with 'our' subjectivity ..." (p. 686). However, in the intersubjective field that my patient and I participate in creating, I can "experience a subjectivity without having to exclusively identify with

it" (p. 686). I find that the body/touch dimension of the work helps greatly in this regard.

7. Analogously, Bromberg (2003) notes that "when the therapist or dreamworker is able to relate to each aspect of the patient's self through its own subjectivity, each part of the self becomes increasingly able to coexist with the rest, and in that sense is linked to the others. It is an experience of coherence, cohesiveness, and continuity, that comes about through human relatedness" (p. 704).

References

Bosnak, R. (1996). *Tracks in the wilderness of dreaming.* New York: Delacorte Press.

Bosnak, R. (2003). Embodied imagination. *Contemporary Psychoanal., 39*(4), 683–695.

Bromberg, P. (2000). Bringing in the dreamer. *Contemporary Psychoanal., 36*(4), 685–705.

Bromberg, P. (2003). On being one's dream. *Contemporary Psychoanal., 39*(4), 697–710.

Davies, J. M. (1996). Linking the "pre-analytic" with the postclassical: Integration, dissociation, and the multiplicity of unconscious process. *Contemporary Psychoanal., 32*(4), 553–576.

Director, L. (2005). Encounters with omnipotence in the psychoanalysis of substance users. *Psychoanalytic Dialogues, 15*(4), 567–586.

Havens, L. (1993). *Participant observation: The psychotherapy schools in action.* Northvale, NJ: Jason Aronson.

Kernberg, O. (1968). The treatment of patients with borderline personality organization. *Int. J. of Psychoanal., 49*, 600–619.

Pert, C. B. (1997). *Molecules of emotion.* London: Simon & Schuster UK.

Stolorow, R. D., & Atwood, G. E. (1991). The mind and the body. *Psychoanalytic Dialogues, 1*(2), 181–195.

Upledger, J. E. (2001). *Craniosacral therapy: Touchstone for natural healing.* Berkeley, CA: North Atlantic Books.

Upledger, J. E., & Vredevoogd, J. D. (1983). *Craniosacral therapy.* Seattle: Eastland Press.

8

Coming Into Being

Employing the Wisdom of the Body and Mind-Body Therapy

Helen M. Newman

> The longing to surrender is longing to let go of defensiveness ... for one's essence to be known and recognized ... a longing for the birth, or rebirth, of the true self.
>
> **Emmanuel Ghent**

In 1989, 8 years after establishing a private practice as a psychotherapist, I began a period of study and training in psychotherapy and psychoanalysis at the New York University Postdoctoral Program. It was a truly exciting time to be part of the NYU community: The relational perspective was coming into prominence, and the faculty included many distinguished clinicians, writers, and teachers. Varied viewpoints were represented, allowing for stimulating debate and exposure to multiple traditions of working with patients.

In 1993, I entered a polarity therapy training program, my intent being to learn more about bodywork. I had been a willing participant in a few body-oriented therapies and had found them to be a useful adjunct to my own psychological journey. But, also, my work with patients seemed to be lacking some unnamed dimension, and I was drawn to searching for it. The answer to the question of what might deepen the psychological process seemed to lie somewhere in the realm of the body.

I later attended the graduation ceremonies for each of these life-transforming programs in the same month of the same year—June 1998. I felt as though I had been inhabiting two different foreign countries, each with its own language and customs. And certainly my understanding of body therapy and the mind-body approach seemed at odds with the framework and protocols of psychoanalytic practice. Yet, I was subsequently to realize that links could be made between the therapeutic goals and aims underlying these two seemingly disparate realms, and their respective languages.

In the years after these graduations, as I continued the practice of psychotherapy and psychoanalysis, I also continued to grapple with the question of how to integrate an emphasis on the body within talk therapy. As more and more body-based therapies gained popularity (e.g., somatic experiencing, focusing, hakomi), I began exploring their theoretical concepts and teachings more closely. Eventually, I unwittingly began to bring a new and different awareness to my clinical style—one grounded in the teachings and principles of body therapy that I had absorbed. For example, even though I might not actually utilize techniques of polarity therapy with a patient, I would find myself using the *sensibility* of body therapy and energy healing as a source of guidance for both myself and my patients.

The effort to recognize and harness the body-centered experience within psychoanalytic psychotherapy remains an ongoing challenge for me, as it does for others in our field today (see Aron & Anderson, 1998). Although I often find this integration to be daunting on a practical level, I am now convinced that it offers a necessary, valuable, and fruitful therapeutic direction, facilitates patients' movement toward what feels genuine and alive, allows them to transform, and opens them more to their true selves (Ghent, 1990; Winnicott, 1958).

Why Polarity Therapy?

Polarity therapy is one of the modalities that employs the "wisdom" of the body to enable patients to gain awareness of their inner experience. As a psychotherapist, I was accustomed to working with patients who had difficulty accessing their inner experience, who were dissociated from certain feeling states, or who complained of being "stuck" in repetitive thoughts and actions. Many of them resisted shifting from mental "stories," or efforts to "figure out" what was wrong, to the more immediate experience of what was arising for them moment by moment. I was intrigued by the question of how they could "know" themselves in a more authentic and connected manner–less from mental "knowing" and more from organic, embodied "knowing." I felt certain that in order to connect more with the truth or "rightness" of an experience—even the effect of an interpretation or insight—one had to be centered "in" one's body. So how, specifically, to bring this "wisdom" of the body into the therapeutic relationship?

It was clear, back in the early 80s, that the large array of available body-oriented therapies followed a radically different style of working compared with traditional psychotherapy methods: hands on, less verbal, more direct and present-oriented, less transference-laden. Knowing my goal was eventually to integrate somatic understandings into a more broad-based psychological approach, I eventually decided on a formal program of study in polarity therapy. I had a few reasons for this choice. First, polarity therapy is one of the few bodywork disciplines rooted in a comprehensive theoretical foundation that is compatible with traditional psychotherapeutic approaches (in fact, a counseling component is part of it). Although it addresses physical complaints and illnesses, it also draws on aspects of psychological experience such as affect, attitudes, memory, and imagery. Second, polarity theory has roots in spiritual teachings and practices, thereby complementing my interest in meditation. Third, its gentle, hands-on system does not necessitate mechanical or intrusive manipulation of the body. And, last, it offers a provocative view of relational processes as constituting an energetic exchange between individuals.

What Is Polarity Therapy?

Polarity therapy, an energy-based system of bodywork, was founded by osteopath, naturopath, and chiropractor Randolph Stone (1986), who combined Eastern principles of healing with Western thinking to create his own science of "energy medicine." The universal concept of energy (e.g., "chi," "prana," "vital life force") refers to subtle pulsations or life energy currents that circulate within and around the body, constitute our aliveness and vitality, and underlie the creation of all mental and physical form. This life energy expresses itself in everyday experiences, emotional patterns, and relationships. Just as Freud (1940) and Jung (1969) recognized the role of energy and its distribution (i.e., certain bodily zones or complexes) in constellating particular experiences of self, Stone (1986) highlighted similar effects resulting from interference with the proper flow and alignment of life force throughout the body. Most important, he demonstrated that subtle life-energy currents, which follow the same electromagnetic principles found throughout nature, must be in fluent and harmonious *movement* if physical health and well-being are to occur.

A typical polarity session starts off with talking between patient and therapist (just like any psychotherapy session) before proceeding to the hands-on portion of the session. The initial period of communication is aimed at inquiring into the concerns, feelings, and experiences of the patient so that the therapist can determine both the psycho-emotional and the physical issues needing attention. These issues inform the direction of the hands-on part of the session. Eventually, knowledge of the patient broadens to incorporate object relationships and early history, including long-standing physical problems and illnesses.

During the bodywork itself, the patient lies fully clothed on a massage table, while the therapist gives attention to various places where energy is stagnant or constricted (rather than moving and alive). Emphasis is placed on five currents, or fields, of energy known as the five elements (ether, air, fire, water, and earth). These represent different but interrelating frequencies and densities of energy within the body, each one emanating from a still, neutral center, or field. The elemental fields are akin to what are known as "chakras" in yoga, in that each has particular locations in the body as well as forms reflexes to influence organs, muscle areas, and physiological functions such as digestion and circulation. In body therapy, each of the five elemental fields—in its balanced (open and flowing) versus imbalanced (constricted or weakened) form—also correlates with specific psychological characteristics, including attitudes, and emotional and behavioral tendencies. When all the elemental currents are in harmony, and moving without constriction, optimal mind-body awareness and health are restored.

Polarity theory maintains that energy becomes obstructed or "unbalanced" when habits of thought and emotion have been locked in the body in specific ways. Emotional wounding or chronic stress can result in tension and contraction of particular parts of one's body such that there is a blockage of energy flow through those regions (Anderson, 1998; Sarno, 1991). Habitual constrictions and imbalances eventually affect muscle groups and deeper structures of the body and lead to chronic pain, discomfort, and disease. Suppose, for example, a child who lives with a threatening authority figure responds to the threat of violence by holding her breath in fear and "swallowing" her anger. This habitual response pattern might eventually lead to bands of tension in her diaphragm, obstructing free circulation of energy between top and bottom halves of the body, and breaking up a sense of somatic "wholeness." As an adult, she could then suffer from an inability to contact her grief, a lack of vitality, or some disconnection between her thoughts and feelings. In any case, the original situation's emotional response will have led to a *physical* "holding" pattern within the body's structure, locked in place by unbalanced energy patterns at a subtler underlying level (Sills, 1991).

In polarity practice, the goal is to focus attention on these imbalances and treat them through various gentle techniques and energy reflexes. The therapist opens and releases blocked areas of the body (along with exploration of the client's concomitant emotional and behavioral experiences), in an effort to reestablish the flow and balance of life force. Greater ease and a healing relaxation follow. In addition, during and especially at the end of a polarity session, both therapist and patient have the opportunity to process whatever feelings, memories, images, and the like arose for the patient while attending to his bodily experience. As the patient occupies, and expands awareness of, his own body territory, corresponding shifts of consciousness occur (Wilber, 2001) and dissociative tendencies are often ameliorated. Thus, over time, increasing levels of awareness and self-regulation are brought to both the physiological and the psychological realms.

How to Utilize Principles of Polarity Therapy in the Psychoanalytic Relationship

Because mind and body constitute one interacting system, the body often serves as a map, mirroring various issues and conflicts playing out in the psychic realm (see, e.g., Ulanov, 2001). How do the teachings and techniques of polarity therapy inform as well as deepen psychoanalytic work? In what ways are the principles compatible or consistent with psychoanalytic understandings? How can the sensibility of a body-oriented approach be useful when one is working within a relationship that excludes touch? These are the questions I'd like to turn to next. In doing so, I will define certain specific principles that have influenced my thinking and try to show how they can serve as conceptual maps or metaphors for the psychoanalytic processes typically employed.

Elemental Patterns Create and Reflect a Sense of Self

Polarity therapy's five-element relationship is the doorway into our psychological as well as physical realities. Throughout a lifetime of development, various experiences, wounds, and relational events lead to contractions not only in our bodies (how we physically "armor" ourselves), but also in our psyches (how we emotionally "armor" ourselves). The elemental patterns map out these mind-body contractions of energy, reflecting habitual adaptive patterns. Through an interweaving of the elements, and the laying down of somatic and psychic structures over time, a sense of self is eventually created and maintained, and the entire process of health and disease is negotiated (Sills, 1991).

I often find it useful to understand the life of a patient in terms of the five elements (ether, air, fire, water, and earth energies). Thinking about a patient elementally involves trying to understand which elements are dominant, which are in a dynamic state of conflict, which are overly constrained, and which are weak and in need of support. This understanding, in turn, would suggest characteristics that are likely to be present in or missing from that person's cognitive, affective, and behavioral repertoire. For example, if a patient chronically picks fights with her spouse, or is displaying hostility toward me, or complains of feelings of helplessness or blocked competitive urges, I will probably think along the lines of a "fire" energy imbalance (anger is the dominant emotion of the fire element). My listening will then attune to whether other emotional and physical issues line up with this elemental analysis.

In general, when patients present physical complaints, symptoms, or illnesses, it often helps me to think of which element holds the problem (e.g., lower back problems suggest water or earth issues). When patients appear to be emotionally constricted in a particular elemental direction (e.g., earth), I might also wonder if they are having difficulties (or are cut off from) those parts of the body that house that element (neck and knees). Thinking elementally is like collecting "clues" to how body, mind, and emotions interact to form an interdependent matrix of functioning. These clues can then inform communication and intervention choices in a particular therapeutic moment.

For example, early illnesses and emotional traumas generally give rise to particular elemental patterns and the inhibition of certain kinds of self-expression. A person with a history of chronic asthma might have a weakness in her air element, and a person whose parent died during his childhood might have suffered a blow to his earth element. These elements, home of primary wounds, then remain as vulnerabilities at the core of the psyche-soma system, just as a "basic fault" (Balint, 1968) sets up a vulnerability in one's psychological organization. Identifying the vulnerabilities allows me to be particularly resonant to those elemental configurations and to the primitive, unconscious issues or experiences associated with them.

In addition, each element possesses its own quality of energy, or "emotional atmosphere," which can be grasped either with regard to the patient's own energy or as a feature of the interpersonal "field" between therapist and patient (Stolorow, Brandchaft, & Atwood, 1994). For example, we all recognize the energetic difference between a patient who is depressed and one whose energy is more "light" and alive. We also recognize that when people are "spacey" (i.e., denser energies of water or earth are not being contacted), they may appear less solid, more "ungrounded." Sometimes, it is possible to induce a particular quality of energy into the room, so that the patient is subtly exposed to its influence. For example, the therapist's more fluid and flowing movements or slower speech and breathing patterns may introduce an atmosphere of the water element when a patient is in a speedy, anxious mental state (air element).

Coming Into the Body Restores Psychosomatic Wholeness and "Being"

While elemental patterns reflect each person's idiosyncratic experience of self, every sense of self is, by definition, a *contracted, disunified* one—a departure from an original, more essential state of psyche-soma wholeness. In developmental terms, bodywork models illustrate how we start off life in a state of mind-body cohesion (the state of "being"), but then lose contact with our organismic being over time, as we move out into the social world and respond to life events, stressors, and inevitable social conditioning (the state of "becoming"). Whereas part of this loss takes the form of physical constrictions, and disconnection from certain energetic centers, much of it takes the form of constricting psychic structures (e.g., narcissistic defenses, false-self configurations, and internalized bad objects). These structures isolate us from the somatic realm and therefore from our original, more fluid state of "being." A variety of symptoms can ensue (see Wilber, 2001), along with a gradual "forgetting" of our original, true-self experience.

In polarity therapy, being and becoming are viewed as a dialectic within individual experience. One aim of the work is to help people experience and restore a more embodied sense of self through contacts that move them temporarily away from their immersion in repetitive, or even painful, patterns of "becoming" (e.g., compulsive behaviors, mental chatter, and archaic identities). Such techniques as cranial work, work with the ether element, and long, still, quiet, hands-on contacts often provide opportunities for people to center themselves in their own somatic beings, often a source of vitality, aliveness, and a more expanded experience of self.

Within psychoanalytic practice, Winnicott (1958) made the most cogent case for restoring psyche-soma cohesion and contact with being. He suggested that interference with movement from an embodied, organismic center can undermine formation of a life that feels real and set the stage for a false-self experience. Although writing in the context of the capacity to be alone, he argued:

> It is only when alone in the presence of someone that the infant can discover his own personal life. The pathological alternative is a false life.... When alone in this sense ... the infant can ... be in a state in which there is no orientation ... without being either a reactor to external impingement or an active person with a direction ... in the course of time, there arrives a sensation or impulse. In this setting, the sensation or impulse will feel real and be truly a personal experience. (p. 34)

Ghent (1990), who built on Winnicott's (1958) formulations, also addressed the subject of being, speaking of patients' yearnings to be known and recognized in their essence, or "wholeness." He underscored the need to dismantle the false self and to dissolve defenses as a route to the expansion and liberation of the self—a project that supports contact with being rather than becoming. Various spiritual writers echo this idea; although alienation from being is the source of suffering, the journey back to moments of being can seem like a coming home, a renewed intimacy with forgotten parts of the self (Almaas, 2004; Maitri, 2001). The spiritual components of body-oriented therapies are a topic I have explored elsewhere (see Newman, 2005).

In my clinical experience, I have found that support for being and true-self experience is greatly enhanced if the body is involved. Only if we (both therapist and patient) are in our bodies can we be fully present in our experiences. Only if we are present are we able to contact fully, and to receive, whatever is newly arising, particularly at the emotional level (Bromberg, 1998; Epstein, 2001). Furthermore, because the body houses the memories of preverbal experience and because attunement with bodily sensation provides "limbic resonance" (Gendlin, 1996; Levine, 1997), inviting the body to "speak" its messages (cf. Looker, 1998) proves invaluable.

Psychoanalytic work can help patients move toward an organic sense of wholeness, without the use of physical touch, but by "touching" into physical experience. Many ways of facilitating a body-centered awareness have already been documented (see Aron & Anderson, 1998), but I find the easiest, least intrusive approach to be that of gently and consistently inquiring into what a patient is experiencing in his or her body. That kind of question (or comment), which I learned from the counseling component of polarity training, encourages people to focus attention differently and more expansively, as they move from thoughts alone into a psyche-soma consciousness. The questions can be used at any moment in any therapy session to bring a patient into the present moment. To underscore their usefulness as doorways into somatic experience, here are some pertinent examples:

1. What are you experiencing (or feeling) in your body right now?
2. As you talk about that, I'm wondering what you're noticing in your body ....
3. Is there a place in the body where you can locate that feeling/emotion?
4. What happens for you as you contact that part of your body?
5. As you follow that sensation, let's see what else arises ....
6. Is there an image that captures what you're feeling in your body?

Attuning to patients' physical and energetic experiences provides the mirroring to help them come in contact with their own inner sensations and feelings. By coming "home" to the body, patients are able to re-sense what it is like to be present as a mind-body unity who is just being. This opens the way for them to have an experience that feels more personal, more true and more autonomous (Ghent, 1990; Winnicott, 1958). The return to a state of being, and sensing into that return over and over again, provides an alternative experience to the customary state of "getting lost" in the automatic habitual mental and behavioral patterns of becoming. This model, popularized in meditation practices (Epstein, 2001) as well as bodywork, is one I now embrace as a psychoanalyst to harness a body-therapy sensibility.

When Energies Are Locked Into the Maintenance of Form, We Are Predisposed to Disease and Discomfort

Perhaps the most influential and useful concepts I have taken from my polarity studies are the principles of involution and evolution. These form the bases for understanding not only the bodywork model of health and illness, but also the importance of supporting patients' inherent movement toward states of being. These are difficult concepts to explain, especially for readers unfamiliar with this tradition, so I invite you to bear with me in hopes that you will reap something of interest from this section.

Involution and evolution pertain to how currents of energy travel within the body. Normally, energy emanates from a neutral, still center in the body, which is called the "source," because it is the very wellspring of life and consciousness. As energy leaves this center, it moves outward into a positive field and finally takes expression in some form (this is the *involutionary* current). Then, the energy flows inward through a negative phase, returning to source (this is the *evolutionary* current). All energy moves in this polarity cycle of intelligence. It can be understood as a grand life pulsation (like breathing out and breathing in), or as an oscillation between a stable "ground" (like silence) giving form to a corresponding "figure" (like musical notes).

Problems in this flow, or pulsation, occur when energy has reached the completion of its form but then fails to return to source. As Sills (1991) notes:

Somehow energies become bound up or stuck in the forms that they are creating. Thus thoughts can become rigid beliefs, judgments held in desperate fashion ... emotions, instead of flowing freely and harmoniously, become trapped in indulgence, suppression and physical tension. The physical body itself holds on to patterns of stress, tension, toxicity and rigidity .... Energy becomes trapped in the maintenance of patterns which are crystallized, rigid, and counterproductive. Problems arise when we identify with the forms that are being created. (pp. 81–82)

In the process of physical disease, blocked energies, which have become trapped in their involutionary pathways, become more and more rigidified, disordered, dense, and sluggish. They have lost the "intelligence" of source. The movement back to health begins when energies are freed to begin their evolutionary return to their origin. In the bodywork model, reestablishing energetic currents in balance with this still, neutral center (where they resonate with the innate intelligence of the life source, or "being") is the expression of health.

This process applies equally well to depicting psychological and emotional states of "dis-order" or distress. When patients are *stuck* in constricting, often painful, involutionary patterns (e.g., the paranoid personality who clings to grandiose notions of self, the workaholic who has lost a healthy rhythm between work and rest, the depressive who cannot find any hopefulness about the future), they, too, suffer the inability to return to contact with their "source intelligence," but in this case, they are alienated from their own inner source of "being," or essence. In other words, patients become psycho-emotionally "out of balance" when they lose a harmonious, rhythmic flow between states of involution (becoming) and evolution (being). The free movement and expression of their life force is compromised. They attach to and identify with their symptoms, patterns, and structures (the figure or "forms") rather than contacting and resonating with their more whole, true selves (the ground). And patients have great difficulty letting go of these forms once they have become incorporated into a stable self-image. For this reason, supporting the evolutionary journey becomes a necessary therapeutic endeavor! However, we can view the analytic process as ideally an attempt to work from both ends simultaneously—helping people understand and disentangle from object relational patterns that bind them (involution) while, at the same time, providing support for a more centered, true-self experience (evolution). Here, adding the contribution of the body to the mix is fruitful and compelling.

A return to a more authentic experience of being brings patients the benefit of seeing that many of their adaptive, defensive patterns, although valuable, are self-states and identities that have eclipsed their more unified, true natures. As they learn ways to release crystallized, rigid forms, both physical and mental, the result is a greater possibility that patients will experience themselves and their personal qualities (i.e., "re-sources") as something more, and grander, than the particular patterns they have attached to. They can dis-identify from old forms not only by understanding their origins, but also by creating ways to give movement to those "stuck energies." Perhaps they will then be more able to "stand in the spaces" among many selves (Bromberg, 1998), or reclaim selves that were previously unavailable to them.

One depressed patient I worked with, for example, was strongly identified with her mind and prone to what she called "superego attacks." She eventually began to express, image, and then name the "dark, gloomy constellation of tyrannizing thoughts," which always came in to wreck her good moods, as "the blob." Her ability to recognize and then say to herself, "Oh, here's the blob again," helped her to "know" it in a more organic, experiential way, and then create some detachment from it. Later on, by giving the blob an actual melody on her guitar (she was a musician), and finding ways to move her body to express the form, color, and energies of the blob, she found that, although the blob did not disappear, it would move through her, or within her, without "becoming" her. Rather than feeling that she *was* the blob, she could perceive herself in her more whole and fluid state, realizing her true nature as being something more solid and inclusive. She also found that her music could reliably provide a pathway back to that solid center when she was inevitably caught in contracted states. As greater embodiment developed over time, her tendency toward dissociation and depression was tempered by a growing sense of presence and awareness of "being"—now a source of empathy and compassion.

Psychoanalysis and the Evolutionary Process
The evolutionary journey is aptly referred to as the "journey of being" because it restores contact with one's core, true-self experience, which, in turn, brings emotional vitality, integration, and health to the system. In psychoanalytic psychotherapy, providing support for the evolutionary journey is thereby a primary component of our work. This support can occur in many ways. It might be initiated when we first notice patients' articulation of conscious or unconscious

yearnings to find parts of themselves that they feel are missing. Or it may begin during moments when a patient touches a more "soulful" quality (see Woodman, 1993), which allows him to see beyond his limited, conditioned self, and contact can be made with the more spacious, essential nature that has been there all along (Almaas, 2004). Ghent (1990) illustrated this potential exceptionally well:

> The yearning that might be represented as a wish to dismantle the false self ... is a wish for transcendence ... the wish to be penetrated ... for one's essence to be known and recognized ... a longing for the birth, or rebirth, of the true self. (pp. 146, 212)

The evolutionary process is perhaps best facilitated by working intersubjectively (Stolorow et al., 1994), allowing—through the safety of the holding environment (e.g., Slochower, 1996) and the transference—each patient's essence to be known and recognized. In addition, the therapist's own qualities—the capacity to be "present," be empathic, be attuned, and listen—serve the same supportive and transformative function. As first noted by Bion (1970), the listening process can increase the likelihood that communication from the emergent, often inchoate realm of being will be offered as well as received. In a similar vein, working with embodiment and somatic awareness (Gendlin, 1996; Levine, 1997), now a common practice, can help patients reach and release deep places of emotional wounding or trauma. Bodily and nonverbal messages transform intersubjective experience by producing a "language" that is more immediate, more direct, more imagery laden, and less subject to the formulations of the conscious, logical mind (Aron & Anderson, 1998; Looker, 1998). From the support that the analytic relationship and these myriad approaches provide, the opportunity for a greater sense of mind-body cohesion can present itself.

Although benefiting greatly from the use of these various psychoanalytic formulations, I also attempt to remain mindful of the polarity relationship between involution and evolution. I realize that patients are experiencing the pulls of both forces, and I try to discover where they are with respect to each one. A number of related considerations and questions continue to guide my thinking. For example, how can we, as psychotherapists, invite contact with states of being most effectively for each patient? How can we recognize and capture fleeting "whispers" of authenticity, the potential opening into something new, emergent, nondetermined? What therapeutic interventions might facilitate greater contact with presence, aliveness, hope, and further open such realms as imagery, sensation, the body? And how can we best be with and investigate those "barriers" to awareness of true self that appear in the form of defenses, conditioned identities, hopelessness, shame, and fear of change? How can these rigidified and entrapping experiences of involution be held, understood, and worked with at the *same* time that we are embracing and encouraging a "letting go" into more liberating forms and identities?

No Matter What Form Energy Takes, Its Movement Is Due to Some Sort of Dynamic Polarity Relationship

One perspective on these questions is offered by a concept central to polarity therapy and rooted in the idea of "holding polarities." As mentioned earlier, energy patterns follow electromagnetic principles found throughout nature; they move between positive and negative fields ("poles") in a movement pulsation. When the energy is stuck or imbalanced, this movement is compromised, and the energy field no longer resonates with its source. However, by being with both dichotomous poles of any energetic current, and getting energy to move back and forth between them, a basic life pulsation is restored. On a somatic level, when a practitioner "holds" two contacts simultaneously (i.e., one hand on the pelvis and one hand on the upper chest), it allows the energy to "ping-pong" into a state of balance. A process of movement and integration is then initiated, allowing for something "new" to arise.

The polarity principle is a useful analogy, once again, for working at the psychodynamic level. The therapeutic relevance of "holding poles" is that we can be with (hold) whatever shows up as two opposing and seemingly contradictory aspects of experience—simultaneously. Examples that come to mind include dichotomies such as excitement and collapse, expansion and contraction (a biggie!), agitation and calm, hopelessness and hopefulness. Any of these can be elaborated with respect to both emotional and physical experience.

Usually, patients fall into the trap of setting such polarities into opposition, trying to disavow one pole in an effort to avoid conflict or remove an experience perceived to be the source of suffering and humiliation. Therefore, I encourage them to be present with both the preferred pole and the pole they are disavowing, so they can observe the inevitable dialectic these energies create and better accept the negatively perceived part. Sometimes, I invite a patient to feel into the "edge" where one side of the polarity (freedom and ease) meets up against its other side (tightness and constriction); we explore how she encounters that "edge" and where in the body it might be manifesting.

The idea of being with seemingly contradictory aspects of experience and "holding the opposites" is not new to psychoanalytic thinking. Jung (1969), for example, spoke frequently about polarities, proposing that the path to the self (wholeness) comes through integrating and transcending them. The Jungian principle of the "transcendent function" suggests that by integrating opposites, a new transcendent experience occurs. Similarly, Benjamin (2005), drawing on the concepts of "big energy" and "little energy," illustrates how, by being with both of these dichotomous, often dissonant experiences—that is, by following their interdependent movement pulsations—a new, third aspect of experience can be reached. "Thirdness" is the state, or mental function, in which oppositions are transformed, creating a "transcendent" opportunity for harmony.

Perhaps the most central polarity in all psychotherapeutic work is the overarching dichotomy between involution and evolution, as just discussed. Yet attendant to this dialectic is an important paradox. We live in both an object relations-driven reality (a matrix of conditioned identities rooted in interpersonal experiences) and a more fundamental, essential reality (the nonconditioned aspects of our true natures, or being). The very same conditioned identities that we need and cling to for our basic sense of self and safety can, at the same time, be major obstacles, or blinders, to contacting our true natures. And yet we cannot be on the journey to psyche-soma wholeness and health without them. For it is ultimately the recognition of the flow between these two opposing dimensions of experience, when held by therapist and patient together, that eventually yields a letting go, and a certain transformation.

Holding the Polarities: A Case Scenario

A clinical example of holding polarities comes from a patient who has a great deal of guilt about expanding in the world, being successful, following her desires. Whenever this expansion begins, there follows an energetic "collapse" that keeps her tied, in her object relational world, to her depressed mother and the safety of that connection. In our work together, we have explored the feelings of collapse and the self-statements that go with them, essentially self-attacks and shame concerning her smallness and her "loser" status. We have also investigated the sense of fullness and joy that comes with "being big" and expressing her power.

Despite her continued frustration with the "small person" who sabotages her movement into the world, she finally allowed a dialogue to begin between these two parts. First she uttered all the beliefs and feelings the "powerful" person held; afterward, I asked her to sense how that felt in her body. Next, she itemized the thoughts and feelings of the "little one," who did not want to be powerful; we spent time sitting with how she felt after that voice was expressed. Unexpectedly, a lot of sadness appeared. After inquiring into the sadness, she was able to contact yet another voice—that of a needy child who was almost in a state of panic. By allowing each "voice" to have its say, rather than trying to eliminate the despised small self, she began to recognize an important "voice of fear" that needed attention. Eventually, the little sabotaging self began to feel less desperate to be heard (thus less likely to take control).

By letting each pole have its voice, she became able to witness both parts in their oscillating appearance, therefore creating a more objective perspective. She is now able to recognize and contain the emergence of those self-states without overly identifying with either one (Bromberg, 1998). She is also able to appreciate that the "backlash" is simply a necessary contribution to a larger polarity movement. Therefore, she can have more compassion for herself, rather than "beating herself up," when her power and expansiveness are followed by emotions or actions that pull her off that center. We are still working on the ways she can find her way back to her own alive source of energy when the barriers to expansiveness arise.

How to Apply Methods of Polarity Bodywork to Psychoanalytic Psychotherapy

Body-oriented therapies, such as polarity therapy, rely on techniques of working with self-experience that appear to differ radically from conventional approaches of talk therapy. Some of the methods, however, do offer a means of supporting the aims of psychotherapy and psychoanalysis. From my own study of mind-body therapies (e.g., Gendlin, 1996; Kurtz, 1990; Levine, 1997; Sills, 1991; Stone, 1986), I have distilled a set of common practices that I find to be most applicable in deepening psychoanalytic inquiry. Four of these interrelated methods can be formulated as follows:

1. Tracking sensation and following the energy charge
2. Helping the patient to have an immediate experience in present time
3. Contacting what is new, emergent; tapping into states of "being"
4. Cultivating an allowing, witnessing attitude of inquiry

At the heart of these somatic approaches lies the valuable idea that the body has innate intelligence; to harness this intelligence, it is fruitful to help the patient *come into contact* with his or her body, *in present time,* and have a *direct experience and awareness* of whatever arises. The wisdom of the body can offer patients an alternative to "mental knowing," an alternative to the past and future orientations that block them from more organic and spontaneous experiences. Working in this way introduces a powerful form of attunement that embraces primitive emotional experience and the yearning for what needs to be recognized and completed.

Tracking Sensation and Following the Energy Charge in Present Time

The idea of tracking bodily sensations, both our own and that of our patients, is by no means a new idea. Many clinicians nowadays are attending to talk about the body, paying closer attention to nonverbal messages and breathing patterns, noting how patients are holding and moving their bodies, and inquiring into somatic experiences (e.g., Aron & Anderson, 1998). Even just observing the nonverbal habits of patients opens potential space for exploration. For example, one of my young, male patients has a habit, when sitting on the couch, of assuming a particular nonverbal posture: He places his arms around his stomach, in a gesture of "holding" or "hugging" his abdomen. My inquiries into this posture, and what it felt like for him, led to interesting associations about his stomach as a center of tension (the place where his nervousness and performance anxiety weaken him), his need for support, his inability to soothe himself, and so on. By feeling into his arms, he also contacted a heaviness that reminded him of an experience during the week when his arms had actually felt paralyzed. Discussion of the feeling of paralysis led, in turn, to an extremely poignant communication about a particular self-state that caused him distress. Clearly, this insight might never have emerged without the simple attention to an innocent nonverbal action.

In polarity practice, being attuned to bodily sensation also means following the energy charge. In the bodywork itself, following the energy means staying attuned to where the energy is arising and moving, and where it seems to want to go next. In the larger work of therapy, however, it means listening for, and tuning in to, where the energy seems most alive or where a charge seems to be emerging. One might observe an increase in breathing, a flush to the face, a more animated tone of voice, a shift in posture or movement while reporting a dream, a faster rhythm, a twitching of the legs, and so on. Inquiring into these shifts often leads the patient to contact with an experience that is more immediate and less predictable.

A clinical example of "following the energy charge" comes from a patient who reported a dream in which she found herself sitting at a restaurant table across from an ex-lover. In the content of the dream, he was standing up to leave, when he handed her a small pocketknife, perhaps a belonging he was returning to her. Then, they exchanged some words about not seeing each other anymore, and he left the restaurant. When she reported the part about the pocketknife, however, I sensed a rise in her energy along with a hand gesture enacting how her fist received and closed over the item. I asked her to zero in on how this experience of receiving the knife felt, in her body, at that moment, as she was holding and feeling the knife.

Concentrating on the gesture and the sensory experience, she exclaimed animatedly, "It's cool, sleek, metal. It feels great. I can feel the weight of it, and it gives me a feeling of power." Her huge enjoyment in holding the knife and the concomitant strengthening of her power led to more discussion and awareness concerning issues of empowerment in her life, including how the ending of her relationship might be returning power to her. While there were certainly other ways to reach these same insights, using a somatic experience as the portal to further inquiry not only grounded her in her body and in the present experience, but also supported a deeper, authentic felt awareness.

Another dream came from a male patient who is very attached to beliefs about himself as being a weak, scared person. When he is caught in his self-hatred about his fearfulness, he forgets that he also possesses a strong side, and he becomes very deflated. In the dream, he was trying to hold a door closed against a fierce intruder who looked like a big, hairy monster. He described his frantic attempts to keep the monster out by applying all his force on his side of the door while the monster was pushing back to get in. For most of the session, our discussion of the dream centered on the questions, "Who or what wants to get in? Who/what is he (the patient) trying to keep out?" Entertaining the possibility that he and the monster might actually be two warring parts of his own psyche, the patient soon circled around to his fallback identity, bemoaning his plight as the "weak guy" who cannot "stand up" against people successfully. I pointed out to him that since both characters in the dream were *him*, or parts of him, it was interesting that the energies he described seemed to be so palpably strong and aggressive. Could he bring back the imagery of that "force" and feel the energy in his body now? Could he feel and recognize this energy as part of himself? He was able to do this successfully, first being with the energy of the monster and then experiencing the embodied sense of his own energy as the one pushing on the door. By the end of the session, one pivotal question remained: "How can you be such a scared, weak person and yet demonstrate all that force and energy?" We are regularly able to use the energetic power of that dream as an anchor point, to return to the "body memory" of the experience when his self-hatred arises. In this way, he is reminded of what it feels like to "be in his strength."

Cultivating a Witnessing, Allowing Attitude

This method has to do with one last therapeutic approach that was reinforced for me by my polarity studies. Because patients tend to become caught in patterns of judgment and shame, and because fears and defenses often shut down or eclipse the gentle and inchoate surfacing of their true selves, it is useful to foster an attitude of allowance and acceptance. Open-ended inquiry into "what is here" or "what is emerging" creates a greater likelihood of contacting what *wants* to emerge (Kurtz, 1990). That is why returning people to their bodies, and bodily information, when they are "lost" in their narratives and repetitive stories can be therapeutic. It is also therapeutic to put interpretations and probing questions aside in favor of simply just being with whatever is arising (Bromberg, 1998; Epstein, 2001). Doing so makes a session, at times, a bit like a meditative journey rather than an attempt to "figure things out." Patients who continually judge and criticize their experience are aided greatly when they finally "get" what it is to just give their attention to something and allow it to be there without judging it or pushing it away. The therapist, of course, takes the lead in modeling this form of inquiry, but it is only when the patient succeeds in allowing the open flow of experience—whatever is emerging—without labeling or rejecting it, that contact with "presence" occurs and support for the evolutionary journey takes hold.

Concluding Comments

While doing the research for this chapter, I was struck by the vast significance of Stone's (1986) original premise that "energy underlies all form." This has become a quite popularized idea, as evident in the writings of the modern physicists (e.g., see Bohm, 2002), but I only now fully comprehend the therapeutic implications that follow from this simple statement. It is interesting to consider that our very thoughts and feelings, for example, are subtle energetic manifestations with energetic repercussions. They can, after all, stop us in our tracks, or they can elate us. They can move through us in a flash, or they can linger and crystallize into obsessional states. By extension, the entire psychotherapeutic enterprise can be understood, in part, as an energetic process, involving the moving, shifting, realigning, and releasing of interpersonal and intrapsychic energy forms to effect greater emotional freedom and equanimity.

The principles discussed in this chapter were offered to stimulate thinking about the effort to integrate perspectives on the body into our clinical work. This effort certainly remains a work in progress, and what I offer is in no way the final word on the subject. But I have tried to demonstrate that both body and mind provide doorways into rich worlds of experience, and that to appreciate how these worlds mirror and interweave with one another can have profound value. Because psyche and soma both manifest constricting structures and patterns, to move fluidly between these two realms, exploring ways to gently release the constrictions, is to engender greater freedom for the whole "being." As the body "lets go" and develops greater ease, so, too, does the mind, and vice versa. That is why it is common, in polarity sessions, for a patient to contact long-standing grief and cry deeply after a sustained energetic contact with her heart area has been made. And why it is common, in psychotherapy sessions, for a patient to report that his back pain has diminished after a deep immersion in unconscious emotions (Anderson, 1998; Ulanov, 2001).

The bodywork methods discussed above—tracking sensations, feeling the energy charge, being present in an allowing way, having an immediate experience—further illuminate the potential of the "unspoken dialogue" between analyst and patient. They suggest ways of employing somatic awareness to deepen therapeutic interactions and nurture a sense of embodiment. They suggest ways of helping us all to recapture a fuller, more organic, more "re-sourced" experience of self so that we can disengage more readily from painful identifications or outmoded ways of relating and realize the vast potential in "being" our resilient true selves (Almaas, 2004; Ghent, 1990). For although constricting, numbing, and closing down will inevitably occur in moments when we are fearful or self-protective, the intermittent openings—and the felt bodily experience of them over and over again—will eventually allow for greater containment of difficult emotions, a more solid, secure ground for self to stand on, and a more expanded capacity for presence and aliveness.

References

Almaas, A. H. (2004). *The inner journey home*. Boston: Shambhala.

Anderson, F. S. (1998). Psychic elaboration of musculoskeletal back pain: Ellen's story. In L. Aron & F. S. Anderson (Eds.), *Relational perspectives on the body* (pp. 287–322). Hillsdale, NJ: The Analytic Press.

Aron, L., & Anderson, F. S. (Eds.). (1998). *Relational perspectives on the body*. Hillsdale, NJ: The Analytic Press.

Balint, M. (1968). *The basic fault: Therapeutic aspects of regression*. Evanston, IL: Northwestern University Press.

Benjamin, J. (2005). From many into one: Attention energy, and the containing of multitudes. *Psychoanal. Dial., 15*, 185–201.

Berger, B. (1998). *Esoteric anatomy: The body as consciousness*. Berkeley, CA: North Atlantic Books.

Bion, W. R. (1970). *Attention and interpretation*. London: Tavistock.

Bohm, D. (2002). *Wholeness and the implicate order*. New York: Routledge.

Bromberg, P. (1998). *Standing in the spaces: Essays on clinical process, trauma, and dissociation*. Hillsdale, NJ: The Analytic Press.

Epstein, M. (2001). *Going on being: Buddhism and the way of change*. New York: Broadway Books.

Freud, S. (1940). An outline of psycho-analysis. *Standard Edition*, 23: 144–207. London: Hogarth Press, 1964.

Gendlin, E. T. (1996). *Focusing-oriented psychotherapy*. New York: Guilford.

Ghent, E. (1990). Masochism, submission, surrender: Masochism as perversion of surrender. *Contemp. Psychoanal.*, *26*, 108–136.

Jung, C. G. (1969). *The structure and dynamics of the unconscious: Collected works*. Princeton, NJ: Princeton University Press.

Kurtz, R. (1990). *Body-centered psychotherapy*. Mendocino, CA: Life Rhythm.

Levine, P. (1997). *Waking the tiger: Healing trauma*. Berkeley, CA: North Atlantic Books.

Looker, T. (1998). "Mama, why don't your feet touch the ground?": Staying with the body and the healing moment. In L. Aron & F. S. Anderson (Eds.), *Relational perspectives on the body* (pp. 237–262). Hillsdale, NJ: The Analytic Press.

Maitri, S. (2001). *The spiritual dimension of the Enneagram*. New York: Penguin Books.

Newman, H. (2005). Spiritual dimensions of body-oriented therapies. Presented at meeting of the Association for Spirituality and Psychotherapy, New York City, May 13–15, 2005.

Sarno, J. E. (1991). *Healing back pain: The mind-body connection*. New York: Warner Books.

Sills, F. (1991). *The polarity process*. Rockport, MA: Element Books.

Slochower, J. (1996). *Holding and psychoanalysis*. Hillsdale, NJ: The Analytic Press.

Stolorow, R., Brandchaft, B., & Atwood, G. (Eds.). (1994). *The intersubjective perspective*. Northvale, NJ: Aronson.

Stone, R. (1986). *Polarity therapy: The complete collected works, Vol. I*. Sebastopol, CA: CRCS.

Ulanov, A. (2001). *Attacked by poison ivy: A psychological understanding*. York Beach, ME: Nicolas-Hays.

Wilber, K. (2001). *No boundary*. Boston: Shambhala.

Winnicott, D. W. (1965). *The maturational processes and the facilitating environment* (pp. 29–36). New York: International Universities Press.

Woodman, M. (1993). *Conscious femininity*. Toronto: Inner City Books.

Part III.

Analysts Using Bodily Experience in the Treatment Relationship

9

Tipping Points Between Body, Culture, and Subjectivity

The Tension Between Passion and Custom

Steven H. Knoblauch

In a Friday session, Frannie describes her experience sitting in church and experiencing a deep sense of confirmation that she should choose a road of adventure, pursuing an opportunity to do important, needed work in a foreign country where she has developed relationships with church personnel and health care providers who have benefited from and would continue to benefit from her presence and contributions to their work of bringing badly needed services to the community there. This decision comes within the context of her having a lover abroad and the painful conflict she experiences over her ambivalence about divorcing her husband. That decision is occurring within a cultural history constituted as part of a religious Catholic family where pleasure and wrongness are too frequently conflated and which conflation totally obscures questions of agency and vitality. What kind of response does Frannie expect this statement will trigger from her analyst and with what significance to her own subjectivity? What does this decision have to do with her marital difficulties and how she experiences my responses to these? How might my personal history and marital status be affecting her or my subjective experience of this moment? How might each of these considerations be related to Frannie's experience of the impact of her passion and the different cultures through which she has been commuting?

Frannie describes how sitting in church, she is almost visited with a sense of confirmation, a sense that there is a right and a wrong surrender for her. As indicated in some of her significant dreams, Frannie and I have achieved this point of awareness in previous sessions. Frannie's dreams reflect a relentless conflict between staying and going. As an example, in one recent dream, her childhood friends are driving her to the airport to catch a plane to join her lover, but they continually frustrate her as they miss turns that lead to the airport. She worries that she would miss her plane and lose the opportunity to be with her beloved. The dreams begin to reveal more about her subjective sense of herself and her relationship with otherness. In another dream, she is having enjoyable sex with her husband, who asks her why she is having sex with him if she is going to leave him (a decision that she has not consciously made at the time of the dream). The scene then shifts to being in a car her husband is driving. Frannie is in the back seat having sex with herself. She is surprised to find she has a penis. In her associating to the dream, she speaks about the power she feels over her husband. She feels she must be the one who sets the direction and initiates action in all realms of their shared activity.

In a more recent dream, she describes a disturbing scene consisting of two of her best female friends from abroad killing a dog. She watches from a window in a car as she passes by. In her associating to this scene, she reflects that though she could imagine that Americans would view this event as barbarian, in her dream she understands and accepts the killing as a necessary and reasonable practice within the culture in which it occurs. She is still in the car, not part of this culture which she understands and whose organizing principles make sense to her, maybe even more sense than those that have shaped her life as an American, thus far. She explains how in the dream she is feeling that the behavior of her good friends is not cruel but compassionate. She then associates to a recent encounter with her husband in which she has told him that she will begin to arrange to leave him and end their marriage as she feels, under the circumstances of her unresolvable dilemma, this is the most compassionate direction to take. I wonder out loud whether Frannie believes I feel that leaving her husband is barbaric. I wonder if the car might be a safe space where she can reflect on events from a distance, as in our treatment space, but still not feel as connected to them as she in fact wants to feel. Could she still be having with me the experience of being constricted by my judgments of her, about which she is still in conflict as she struggles to find her own authenticity and agency? Her response is that these speculations seem right but she finds no release from her conflict coming from my verbalizing these possibilities.

Here, I begin to gain a sense of how Frannie's cross-cultural experience is impacting the subjective conflicts with which she struggles in her experience of her marriage and the monocultural traditions of family and religion in which she has been held in such a tight grip. Here, I begin to reflect on the differences and similarities between my cultural history and hers. I wonder in reverie in what ways Frannie's sense of me as a Euro-American and married (which she has previously indicated she believes because of a reference I make to the difficulties of sustaining an intimate tie) might color our interactions and her ongoing conflict. I will return to these considerations in the coming pages.

As the last dream fragment and association suggests, Frannie is moving to a resolution of her dilemma, at least as it concerns her marriage. But even with an apparent decision about her external affairs, her internal conflict persists. Frannie is a 30-something daughter of first-generation Italians. Her grandparents, whom she loved and idealized, imbued her with a strong sense of the importance of family cohesiveness and the importance of carrying forward "traditional" values. (This was an American lower middle-class socioeconomic space marked by a shared norm of distrust of change and otherness.) Frannie was a "good" Italian/Catholic girl. But, she had many secrets and feared the judgments of others lest they discover the ways in which she violated the teaching of Catholicism. In her early adulthood, Frannie had delightedly discovered that a good childhood friend from whom she had kept many secrets, particularly about her sexual experiences in adolescence, had, in fact, been doing the same with her. Their sharing their tales of norm violation gave each a sense of power, individuation, and mastery.

Frannie knows that she can't know for certain how much of her leaving for work and a new partner abroad might be a repeat of her childhood secret "bad girl" violations of the family and church norms that provided security and a sense of reliability and stability to her life. At the same time, she continues to experience those practices and beliefs of the past as annihilating of her capacity to creatively generate an expanding expression of her skills and passions as well as a deepening of the quality and range of her relational capacities. To surrender to the norms of her family, community, and church seems to be a malevolent version of surrender, a masochistic submission (Ghent, 1990). To surrender to the adventure, challenge, and passion of new professional opportunities and a different kind of partner, better educated and with a wider range of interests and activities, seems to be a different kind of surrender ... an act of autonomy, expressing mastery at navigating and negotiating internal conflict. (This is occurring within a socioeconomic space in which cross-cultural awareness is valued and characterized by norms of strong faith in constructive change and recognition of, and respect for, otherness, particularly as it might be characterized by different customs and practices.)

Despite the rational analysis we can bring to these options, giving a value of malevolence to one and benevolence to another form of surrender, Frannie finds herself a vacillating captive to a continuous sense of being overwhelmed by an unresolvable dilemma. She is powerfully drawn to each option with a foreboding sense of uncertainty and fear that she will do the *wrong* thing. Reflection and analysis of her struggles come quite easily to this articulate and well-educated professional, in sharp contrast to the collapse of options and internalized persecutory voices of family, community, and religion, voices that continue to capture her in stasis.

Sitting in the chair opposite me, her posture is typically relaxed as she positions her hips facing toward me in my chair. Usually, I sit with a matching posture. My hips are similarly positioned so that my body faces hers. Our postures seem in a configuration of "good enough" mutual mirroring. In these moments, Frannie's gaze is intensely on my face. This, again, also is typical of her presentation. She often seems to search my face for clues that I am understanding her experience, or that I may have some unanticipated response that could represent a new and additional understanding. It is important to add that my impression of these kinds of gaze meetings has been that Frannie's intense scanning of my face often feels like the kind of hypervigilence characteristic of a child who is expecting either a transgressive response or nonresponsiveness from the other.

Frannie's voice in subsequent moments becomes slightly, but noticeably, higher pitched than at other times. I have come to recognize this register in pitch as often accompanying the pain of the self-doubt in which she becomes totally absorbed, as the dilemma of her ambivalence becomes unbearable. In these moments, I am often feeling an ego-dystonic sense of being a particular kind of other in the transference, a ghost projection haunting Frannie's sense of her own subjective "truths." In reverie I wonder, "Am I a priest or nun from her childhood experience handing out punitive judgments over any violation of a strict code of conduct for living, which Frannie experiences as blocking any expression of her own creativity or vitality? Or could I be the grandparents or father, carrying such a set of religious beliefs for 'acceptable' social conduct, constantly surveying the activities and choices of this granddaughter/daughter, lest she stray into a damned way of life?" Choosing to work in a different country entails not just leaving her marriage. It means she will terminate treatment! Does Frannie feel damned by me for choosing to leave treatment? Am I damned angry at her for making such a choice? And what might be the basis for such a powerful affective response? Here I begin to experience the clash of different cultural norms, not only in Frannie's experience, but also in mine, as I grapple with my internalized expectations for clinical performance coming from my subjective sense of the psychoanalytic culture in which I am embedded, and my personal reactions to my struggling, courageous patient that suggest different meanings than my cultural context might privilege.

For Frannie to join her lover/fiancé abroad could be a dangerous and destructive enactment of the ways in which she secretly lived an alter life, a "delinquent" response to the family and religious practices of her childhood culture. Was this secret life of violation a false or true self expression? (Winnicott, 1960, pp. 148–150). On the other hand, could choosing a new life abroad also represent generativity and creativity leading to an expansion of forms of self expression and relatedness, previously constricted, if not annihilated, by an inner object world constructed out of early relationships of nonrecognition and fear-driven narcissistic psychic colonizations by parents and other authority figures, particularly driven by religious beliefs?

Entering the Dense Complexity of Micro-Moment Body Meanings

In moments similar to this one in which Frannie becomes paralyzed by her ambivalence, I have noted around Frannie's eyes and forehead a tightening of muscles and skin creasing, signaling the tension beneath. In these instances, Frannie seems uncertain of what to expect from this other ... me. Will I confirm or correct her? Or will I respond in a way that sustains an openness to both or additional options? This kind of response of openness to change and difference, which can seem analytically focused and therapeutically appropriate in many instances, can be (and I have come to recognize, has often been) experienced by Frannie as an annihilation of the meaning of the newness of what she has offered. It's as if not to raise some kind of critical inquiry could, in fact, be a willingness to be open to change, but also, and this is the pivotal point, could be a veil for disapproval, an inauthentic avoidance, a glossing over of the significance for her and possible others including myself, of this struggle. "You've got to be enraged at me for leaving you!" I sense my discomfort with being scanned and possibly experienced in these ways. In part, I feel as if I am being constructed as a violator of her voice and agency. But with equal significance, I am reminded of my own experiences growing up in a working-class cultural milieu where I developed a similar kind of expectation for punitive judgment from authority figures. Here, a clash for me is between my concordant identification with Frannie and internalized norms constructing a particular set of expectations for how I should understand and respond to trans- ference meanings shaped by the professional community to which I identify. I am wondering how these reflections are shaping the unfolding of our interactions and our subjective experiences of self and other. I am struggling with my desire to continue a good treat- ment with a bright, self-reflective patient, and a voice within me that vicariously identifies with the risk-taking, open person following her passion, firmly seated in the center of the power of her conviction to leave her husband, her country, and me.

But *here in this micro instant* as Frannie represents in words her move from ambivalence to decisiveness, *Frannie's body and the meaning it seems to carry have shifted.* She is leaning forward in her chair as if perched for action, maybe even confrontation. I don't feel that she is not relaxed, but her alert readiness while still relaxed in a different way than previously, now communicates to me a vital- ity compared to a sense of resignation or even avoidance that it has often seemed to carry previous to this moment. There is a different muscular configuration to her facial display. It impacts me as a wave of shifting feelings. She seems to be smiling, *but it is a sly smile, as if to suggest that she has found something somewhere, maybe within, maybe without, that I won't be able to undo … even unintentionally.* Here, her power to stand up to my power is palpable. The pitch of her voice as she announces the outcome of her church reflections is not in that range I described earlier, but rather slightly lower, enough to signal a kind of strength, different from what I usually encounter.

But it is not just the changes in the embodied dimensions of her self-presentation that are different and seem significant. These are, of course, intrinsic to the moment as I sense a shift in the tension in the air. The tension is not just an internal dilemma between right and wrong at this point. At least, such a dilemma is not in the foreground of experience for me, and I perceive Frannie to be similarly focused. Rather, the tension in the room is potentially a "crunch" that could occur between the two of us as I might be experienced transferentially as the grandparent/father, consciously or unconsciously carrying expectations and beliefs in custom and practice, a cultural net of habits constituted to "crush" her creative but "transgressive" thoughts and actions in the "crunch" between her passions and previously internalized values concerning custom. Although intrapsychic conflict can clearly be objectively identified here, the subjective distinction between internal and external collapses at this moment of crunch between passion and culture. It is not as if culture is internalized in a mind, or inscribed on a body. Butler writes, "Categories of true sex, discrete gender and specific sexuality have constituted the stable point of reference for a great deal of feminist theory and politics. … But is there a political shape to 'women,' as it were, that precedes and prefigures … their interests …? How is that identity shaped, and is it a political shaping that takes the very morphology and boundary of the sexed body as the ground, surface, or site of cultural inscription?" (Butler, 1990, pp. 128–129). It is as a blur where experiences of passion and culture cannot be subjectively or intersubjectively differentiated. Is Frannie, or am I, an agent of self-direction or caught unconsciously in a web of cultural imperatives constructed for how to think, feel, or act?

In this moment, I am quickly becoming aware of the shift that Frannie's embodied state is catalyzing in me. I am excited about this change. My excitement is, in part, the narcissistic pleasure I am taking in the recognition that I am achieving some awareness of what her body seems to be conveying, consistent with and central to the kind of conceptualization I and others have previously offered for the mutative potential of this kind of expanded therapeutic attention on the part of the analyst (Knoblauch, 2000, 2005; for additional discussion of the significance of attention to this implicit embodied level of dyadic exchange, see also Alfano, 2005; Anderson, 1998; Aron, 1998; Beebe, Knoblauch, Rustin, & Sorter, 2005; Dimen, 1998; Gentile, 2007; Gunsburg & Tylim, 1998; Harris, 1998; Jacobs, 1986, 1994, 2005; Kimble Wrye, 1996, 1998; La Barre, 2001, 2005; Lyons-Ruth, 1999; McLaughlin, 2005; Orbach, 1999, 2003, 2004, 2006; Shapiro, 1996; Sonntag, 2006; Stern, 2004). But my excitement is also precipitated by a keen sense of, at least, some of my own embodied experience, experience that is specific to how Frannie is impacting me at this critical point. This is an embodied nonsymbolic level of countertransference experience, which I can now, posthoc, transduce into the symbolization of word meanings in this written narrative.

I would describe these nonsymbolized dimensions of my experience in the following way. My level of internal activation has been increased, and I am sitting up a bit straighter and more ready to be receptive and responsive than has been my tendency. This is information for Frannie, in addition to whatever semantic meaning I might communicate with my words or not. To be more specific, as I am beginning to become aware of the shift, I realize that I have previously often matched her relaxed posture and that this matching can send, and may have been sending, a signal of collusion with her states of resignation and frustration with her stasis. (In other words, my body joined, in resignation and collapse, with her body through my unconscious matching of posture and the potential meanings that that embodied mutuality might have for each of our subjectivities.) My signal of collusion could be based on my own, until now, unreflected-upon narcissistic bias toward marriage to which I have made a commitment. On the other hand, could I be unconsciously "rooting" for my patient to escape the psychic confinement of the constricting cultural norms that grip her and which I have experienced in my own early history?

So now in this moment, I can feel how my eyes are open wider than usually. My eyebrows are raised. I am wondering if my face is not expressing a sense of recognition and even, maybe, surprise. I am about to speak. This could be critical to whether my surprise is experienced in the realm of shock and judgment, however subtle, that might trigger for Frannie an internal slide into a sense of being *wrong*. How to respond? Here, I am haunted similarly to my patient by the fear of doing the *wrong* thing, a powerful illustration of inter-subjective resonance on an unsymbolized dimension of exchange that can carry the same affective impact as a symbolized verbalization. Here to be *wrong* is to constitute an enactment coconstructed on subtle unspoken but embodied dimensions of experience, in which we are both defeated by our nonconscious acceptance of a culturally contextualized normative binary that, in fact, neither of us consciously believes. My countertransference dilemma is given further denseness by the confusion between being *wrong* within a set of expectations for conduct designed by religious and socioeconomic codes, and expectations coming from a set of professional codes of conduct. Here, for me, there is an intersection of potentially toxic binaries constituted by the multicultural dimensions of the contexts that grip my interaction with Frannie.

The Tipping Point

What happens next is not something that I was able to shape out of my reverie or any predetermining therapeutic guidelines. It is some-thing I am increasingly coming to recognize, always post hoc, as a central aspect of the kind of shift or *tipping point* that this moment I am describing becomes. Such clinical moments are characterized by subtle somatic or kinesthetic shifts occurring at a *micro-process* level of analysis compared to the more usually attended-to *structural* level of analysis. I pause in my narration of this brief micro-episode to emphasize how unpremeditated, unformulated, and improvised my participation is at this point in the encounter. But I also want to emphasize how central and catalytic what I am about to describe is to the kind of *tipping point* that constitutes therapeutic action involv-ing the complex nexus of custom and subjectivity.

To begin with a simple grasp of this otherwise multiply dimen-sioned point of action, I want to explain, briefly, my metaphoric use of the term *tipping point* in this narrative. Then, I want to carefully signal to you the reader, how I am drawing our attention to the kind of micro-rhythm that Frannie and I create at this point ... to the uniqueness of the characteristics of this micro-rhythm and its dif-ferent syncopations from previous shapes of micro-rhythms Frannie and I have constituted in this treatment. I focus on this in order to provide the micro-detail necessary to define this moment as the kind of *tipping point* that I am trying to highlight with this example. Such points constitute a dramatic capacity to catalyze a shift or reorganization of subjective experience. (Stern & Tronick, 1998, have called this kind of moment a *now moment*.) But of particular interest, and for creating a finer distinction for this chapter, is *the capacity of such tipping point moments to counteract and/or even reverse the effects of culturally customary beliefs and practices carried often unconsciously in the subjectivity of either patient or analyst, or both.* This clinical distinction is important because it provides a way for psychoanalysis to focus on embodied nonsymbolized communication dimensions that expand our descriptions of how a change event/process is effected. This kind of change is constituted by the kinds of psychodynamic forces traditionally considered, e.g., family patterning, traumatic experience, and the transference/countertransference field, but also contextualized, and therefore understood, as colored/shaped by the power of culturally normative expectations held by both patient and analyst, however local or more global these cultural effects may be. First, the metaphoric use of the term *tipping point:*

In her contribution to the symposium in honor of Emmanuel Ghent titled "Nonlinear Systems Theory and Psychoanalysis," Esther Thelen makes the point, "All theories are metaphoric, as they create a bridge between any phenomenon and its representations" (2005, p. 259). From this perspective and, in keeping with the approach to metaphoric use of theoretical terms that I first illustrated in chapter 6, "Mind Metaphors," in my book, *The Musical Edge of Therapeutic Dialogue* (Knoblauch, 2000), I want to briefly but carefully trace the use of the term *tipping point* in systems theory and its metaphoric value for psychoanalytic process and, in particular, the relation between culture and subjectivity.

In his contribution to the symposium noted above, Craig Piers defines a *system* as "a set of components or parts that interact to form an organized and coordinated whole. A *dynamic system* is a system that changes over time, rather than remaining fixed, or static" (2005, p. 230). Piers then defines a *nonlinear dynamic system* as "a system whose evolution is *discontinuous, nonproportional and unpredictable.* Breaking it down: this means that, under certain conditions, nonlinear systems change in sudden, abrupt, and discontinuous ways." Piers explains that what he means by nonproportional is "there is not always a clear and proportional link between cause and effect; small changes often have a profound effect" (p. 231). A nonlinear system is different from a linear system in this way because the evolution of a linear system can be plotted on a straight line and is continuous, proportional, and predictable. But small changes in a nonlinear system can cause it to self-organize or reorganize, causing state transitions that may seem nonproportional with regard to what seems to be the size of the cause and the power or size of the effect.

To explain this disproportionality, Piers introduces the term *sensitive dependence on initial conditions* as first used by Lorenz (1993) to mean that "small alterations in the current state cause subsequent states to differ greatly from the state that would have followed without the alteration" (2005, p. 239). Thus, slight changes can effect radically different long-term behavior and/or experience.

Seligman (2005), in the same symposium, addresses the clinical utility of such a conception of change. He suggests that the idea of sensitive dependence on initial conditions is a theory of *tipping points*. Seligman explains, "*There is a point in a nonlinear dynamic system at which change in a particular input will change the basic dynamic of the system*. The often cited example of the butterfly in Rio whose fluttering wings lead to a hurricane in Miami illustrates this concept. The butterfly's wings may provide just the extra microdose of air velocity to tip the weather pattern into the new storm system" (2005, p. 289). He then offers several clinical illustrations of the effects of a therapeutic "butterfly" moment on the interactive shape of a treatment and the "hurricane" pattern in the life of the patient in treatment.

I employ the metaphoric value of the term *tipping point* in my discussion of the interaction between Frannie and me to capture the subtle way that a micro-shift of nonsymbolized rhythmic patterning between us catalyzes, not just a change in the pattern we construct within our own intersubjective process, but also, and of critical importance, a shift or *tipping point* in Frannie's subjective organization of the system of customs that contextualize the meanings of such patterning. This shift or *tip* reorganizes the possibilities for different relational patterning and subjective experience, liberating Frannie to experience affective states differently than she might in the context of previously culturally constructed expectations.

And so, as Frannie describes her decision to leave her husband, arrived at in deep reverie occurring in a most powerful architectural (church) and symbolic context for the practices, rituals, and traditions against which her decision will fly, I shift my body in relation to the perceptible shift in her body and tone of voice. I am sensing something that I now narrate to you in the following words, which I want to emphasize were not in thought form in the moment I describe. Here is a symbolic description of what my body experience seemed to be speaking to me without words: "I am struck by the decisiveness of Frannie's decision ... that she is not seeming to look for my reaction to her thoughts as she usually does, but rather I feel her delivering an announcement with firmness and resolve for which discussion has passed. This feels different. She looks and sounds different and it makes me feel differently toward her to experience this clarity and resolve in her eyes, her body, and the tone and meaning of her words." I do not speak of the rhythm (in part vocal and in part body movement) of our exchange. I can't in the moment. I am still caught up in constituting it with my response. But in this narrative, I want to focus my analytic lens upon this brief moment of exchange to observe (post hoc) and describe the shape and feel of this moment in order to illustrate how it was different from a pattern that had previously become entrained between us and how the shift of this rhythm tipped the previous state of tensions between Frannie's passion and the customs that contextualized her judgments and emotions. This moment or *tipping point* marked the beginning of a new kind of entrained rhythm in her interactive experience with me and with others.

Now, let me slow down and rewind (so to speak) the previous moment Frannie and I constituted. Frannie's shift forward in her chair, accompanied by her sly smile and lower (and I now add slower) vocal utterances, felt (in retrospect) paradoxically as if she had subtly applied a brake to shift something in our pacing and cadencing. I say paradoxically because there was not so much a slowing down as a shifting, with both slowing in speech flow but a kind of acceleration in expressed vitality, a sense of growing strength in tone (lowered), pace (slowed down), and body (presenting directly with poise compared to the reduced tonus in the muscular effort and a sense of withdrawal in posture that was so familiar in the recent and typical rhythms of our exchange). These multimodal, nonsymbolized body dimensions of Frannie's presentation, at the same time accompanied by a semantic dimension of her speech, the symbolic meaning of which was of equal significance, catalyzed a significant shift in my rhythmic accompaniment to her shift. This shift occurred on dimensions of posture and activation (experienced as vitality). My posture and vitality shifted to meet hers. I cannot say how my face or gaze might have been experienced by Frannie. But I can say that within the brief micro-second of our shift from resignation and defeat, to vitalized triumph and liberation, as carried in the rhythms of our body dialogue, I sensed, in the slyness of Frannie's smile, a feeling and meaning of triumphant reversal of a power gradient. This power gradient had been constituted within repeated psychic annihilations for her in past experiences of *crunch* between passion and custom, a *crunch* and its reversal, which I am here attempting to trace in her experience of and with me, as well as in her past.

What does this body shifting in the consulting room have to do with subjectivity and, even more, the nexus of the bidirectional impact of Frannie's passion and culture? Frannie could have experienced me transferentially as critical and dismissive of her announcement to violate the codes of the tradition that had held her so tightly as she grew up, and still in her present psychic states. But (despite my concern for being *wrong* in the terms of, at least, two different cultural codes for practice and belief) I could tell that she was not experiencing me that way as she described the conditions of her reflections and then pronounced her decision. *I could sense this (even though I could not yet speak or think symbolically of what I sensed) by the shift in the timing of her gaze, from the extra micro-second hold of a hyperactive scan (a brief pause to which I typically would find myself responding with a verbal observation about her indecisiveness and her seeming to rely on me for some kind of confirmation or direction), to the longer and slower shifting formation of a "sly" smile, marking a shift in rhythm and meaning.* This rhythmic marker, constituting a forming into a facial display, a very particular kind of smile, created in me a sense of joy and liberation. The beliefs and practices that had haunted Frannie's sense of herself as *wrong* had been loosened, and Frannie seemed to know that she was engaging me in this liberation process. She seemed confident that I would not do or say the *wrong* thing. And the shift in the rhythm of our facial dialogue helped me to feel a similar shift from a concern for my being *wrong* to a feeling of vitalizing release and openness to the unknown of the liberating consequences of her sense of agency. Here in this micro-moment, a *tipping point* occurred in which the butterfly exchange of our smiles commenced a shift in our dyadic system that catalyzed a shift, if not a hurricane (to be consistent with the metaphor), in

Frannie's subjective experience of the systems of cultural meanings, sanctions, and prohibitions that contextualized our interaction.

What if I had not responded to Frannie's sly smile as I did? What if I had persevered in my concern for being *wrong* within the terms of my own psychoanalytic cultural beliefs and practices, for the possibility that I would retraumatize her either with "too much empathy" or with an enactment of punitive judgment? What if my desire, as well as my culturally shaped belief that Frannie's breaking off in mid-treatment constituted a *wrong* judgment, overpowered and inhibited my response? I have thought a great deal about this possibility. I think that a key factor in how I was experienced by Frannie and how we subsequently understood and worked with this moment, and the decision it embodied for her ongoing struggle, was not just what I would say next, but something that emerged unbidden and unformulated (Stern, 1997) in our body dialogue. I believe that if I had not responded spontaneously, out of an improvisatory stance, to the rhythm that formed into Frannie's sly smile with a syncopated rhythm forming into a smile, things might have gone very differently, at least in that moment, on that day. But having responded as I did to the shift in micro-body-rhythm to which Frannie's rhythms invited a new entrainment, we now constituted a new context in which she was able to shift to a firm sense of her capacity to act as an agent of her passions and retexture the conflicting cultural beliefs and practices she was navigating. And furthermore, my micro-recognition and response in rhythm with her shift constituted for me a rapid shift from doubt about my response to a sense of surrender (Ghent, 1990) to what we were constituting, coming from her response to my response.

I cannot "prove" that the timing and formation of my responsive smile was pivotal to the meanings coconstructed for the tensions between passion and custom, but I can report that Frannie and I have subsequently reflected upon this event, and (although our reflections most probably have been shaped by my own prejudices about clinical attention, which tend to give equal value to nonsymbolized body communication including the tone and rhythm of verbal utterances, in addition to the semantic/symbolic value of verbal as well as shared descriptions of nonverbal activity) we have found this organization of the meaning of events for creating a narrative a good fit for our reconstruction of that episode.

I want to emphasize here that this clinical episode is offered in order to illustrate a critical meaning that nonsymbolized body communication can have for therapeutic understanding. We have only begun to give consideration to the web of cultural influences (including race, ethnicity, gender, sexual preference, age, and socioeconomic status) that contextualize and shape subjective experience and dimensions of the intersubjective encounter. It is important to note that these forces do not eclipse traditional understandings of conflict and dissociation. Rather, a consideration of these forces offers the clinician a wider scope of attention to make sense of the suffering and longings of our patients. This conception is a widening of the system that constitutes the field in which nonlinear processes constitute and emerge from critical *tipping points* that can be recognized for their catalytic value to therapeutic change.

It is interesting to note that passion and custom are often difficult to reconcile. Freud's representation of these forces in one's intrapsychic life with the concepts of id and superego accurately depicted this challenge to psychic equilibrium (Freud, 1923). But Freud's emphasis was more on the constricting, annihilating internalizations that cultural expectations catalyze and not so much on the way that culture also can offer a kind of holding environment (mother country) of affirmation and security. This chapter is offered as part of a contemporary effort to further unpack the range of meanings and implications that cultural belief, practice, and custom can have on subjective experience, with particular emphasis on the regulation and expression of affect as it is either sanctioned or exiled by cultural norms.

Scarry (1985) has written about the political use of physical and psychic torture to impose annihilating effects of pain on the body, erasing the capacity to represent and reflect on experience. (Grand has addressed such annihilating effects in a powerful series of clinical descriptions in her book *The Reproduction of Evil: A Clinical and Cultural Perspective*, 2000.) Although this is an important consideration in a global climate in which the use and impact of torture has garnered increasing attention for its traumatizing impact on regulating and equilibrating capacities for individual experience and the ongoing shared sense of stability to collective experience, the clinical phenomenon taken up here is a product of a set of more subtle coercive effects than intentional physical or psychic torture. This distinction is as important to understanding the ways in which the body registers points of collapse or generative expansiveness for clinical attention in psychoanalysis, as is an understanding of the distinction made in the field of race relations, between overt acts of racism and the kinds of unconscious and often dissociated forms of institution-alized or customarily reinforced practices that have come to be rec-ognized for their annihilating impact on a sense of being human and being valued by others.

The kind of clinical phenomena taken up in this chapter, then, occur while thinking is still possible, though dissociation and con-flict are central issues in the work with this patient struggling over the effects of events that have constituted a shift in economic class and norms for conduct. These phenomena are shown to occur in response to the effects of cross-cultural differences on experiences of intimacy and commitment in personal and professional realms of the patient's experience (which I would argue can be as pivotal a kind of intersubjective space for traumatic impact as the strangling effects of a univocal culture conformity, or a space for transformation). It seems that as we are beginning to revisit the impact of culture on psychoanalytic practice, we need to expand our scope of attention to include the multicultural intersections occurring both within and between persons that add complexity to countertransferential as well as transferential experience.

Focusing on the particular implications of micro-body rhyth-mic activity as it is intersubjectively constituted provides a unique opportunity for understanding the metaphoric clinical utility of one of the key concepts coming from an understanding of nonlinear dynamic theory, the *tipping point*. One particular form of *tipping point* of clinical interest is that constituted in moments where previ-ously internalized cultural customs clash with existing self experi-ence, particularly one's embodied experience of passion. Bearing the tension of such conflict, often (but not always) dissociated, repre-sents a challenge to the attention of both patient and analyst. Cul-tural custom often works in subtle unreflected-upon ways for both members of the analytic pair. *Tipping points* constituting shifts in the subjective experience of different cultural systems of belief and practice can be equally subtle. Attention to both the nonsymbolized as well as symbolized dimensions of the clinical exchange focuses the clinician on cues to such influence.

In this chapter, the clinical illustration emphasizes how body rhythmic dimensions of the exchange can carry critical cues to trans-ferential and countertransferential experience for an understanding of the possibilities for the patient to either repeat constrictive affective experience, or to accomplish a liberating shift to an expanded sense of agency and range of affective expression. Clearly, though it does not have to be, this is a heroic tale. But to the central thesis of this chapter, this is a tale that clearly illustrates subtle opportunities for recognizing a particular form of *tipping point*, marking a shift in the power of custom to shape subjective experience. This shift is accomplished with clinical attention to emergent body rhythms as significant mutative contours of the clinical exchange that simultaneously serve as *tipping points* in the organization of cultural beliefs held, and customs practiced, by either patient or analyst that can dramatically and rapidly reorganize subjective experience for the patient in a present moment.

References

Alfano, C. F. (2005). Traversing the caesura: Transcendent attunement in Buddhist mediation and psychoanalysis. *Contemp. Psychoanal., 41*, 225–247.

Anderson, F. S. (1998). Psychic elaboration of musculoskeletal back pain: Ellen's story. In L. Aron & F. S. Anderson (Eds.), *Relational perspectives on the body* (pp. 287–322). Hillsdale, NJ: The Analytic Press.

Aron, L. (1998). The clinical body and the reflexive mind. In L. Aron & F. S. Anderson (Eds.), *Relational perspectives on the body* (pp. 3–37). Hillsdale, NJ: The Analytic Press.

Beebe, B., Knoblauch, S., Rustin, J., & Sorter, D. (2005) *Forms of intersubjectivity in infant research and adult treatment.* New York: Other Press.

Butler, J. (1990). *Gender trouble: Feminism and the subversion of identity.* New York: Routledge.

Dimen, M. (1998). Polyglot bodies: Thinking through the relational. In L. Aron & F. S. Anderson (Eds.), *Relational perspectives on the body* (pp. 65–93). Hillsdale: NJ: The Analytic Press.

Freud, S. (1923). The ego and the id. *Standard edition.* 19:3–66. London: Hogarth Press, 1953.

Gentile, K. (2007). *Creating bodies: Eating disorder as self-destructive survival.* Mahwah, NJ: The Analytic Press.

Ghent, E. (1990). Masochism, submission, surrender: Masochism as a perversion of surrender. In S. A. Mitchell & L. Aron (Eds.), *Relational psychoanalysis: The emergence of a tradition* (pp. 211–242). Hillsdale, NJ: The Analytic Press. 1999.

Grand, S. (2000) *The reproduction of evil: A clinical and cultural perspective.* Hillsdale, NJ: The Analytic Press.

Gunsberg, L. & Tylim, I. (1998). The body-mind: Psychopathology of its ownership. In L. Aron & F. S. Anderson (Eds.), *Relational perspectives on the body* (pp. 117–135). Hillsdale, NJ: The Analytic Press.

Harris, A. (1998). Psychic envelopes and sonorous baths: Siting the body in relational theory and clinical practice. In L. Aron & F. S. Anderson (Eds.), *Relational perspectives on the body* (pp. 39–64). Hillsdale, NJ: The Analytic Press.

Jacobs, T. J. (1986). On countertransference enactments. *J. Amer. Psychoanal. Assoc., 34,* 289–307.

Jacobs, T. J. (1994). Nonverbal communications: Some reflections on their role in the psychoanalytic process and psychoanalytic education. *J. Amer. Psychoanal. Assoc., 42,* 741–762.

Jacobs, T. J. (2005). Discussion of forms of intersubjectivity in infant research and adult treatment. In *Forms of intersubjectivity in infant research and adult treatment* (pp. 165–189). New York: Other Press.

Kimble Wrye, H. (1996). Bodily states of mind: Dialectics of psyche and soma in psychoanalysis. *Gender and Psychoanalysis, 1,* 283–296.

Kimble Wrye, H. (1998). The embodiment of desire: Relinking the body-mind within the analytic dyad. In L. Aron & F. S. Anderson (Eds.), *Relational perspectives on the body* (pp. 97–116). Hillsdale, NJ: The Analytic Press.

Knoblauch, S. H. (2000). *The musical edge of therapeutic dialogue.* Hillsdale, NJ: The Analytic Press.

Knoblauch, S. H. (2005). Body rhythms and the unconscious: Toward an expanding of clinical attention. *Psychoanal. Dial., 15*(6), 807–827.

La Barre, F. (2001). *On moving and being moved: Nonverbal behavior in clinical practice.* Hillsdale, NJ: The Analytic Press.

La Barre, F. (2005). The kinetic transference and countertransference. *Contemp. Psychoanal., 41,* 249–279.

Lorenz, E. (1993). *The essence of chaos.* Seattle: University of Washington Press.

Lyons-Ruth, K. (1999). The two-person unconscious: Intersubjective dialogue, enactive relational representation, and the emergence of new forms of relational organization. In L. Aron & A. Harris (Eds.), *Relational psychoanalysis: Volume 2, Innovation and expansion* (pp. 311–349). Hillsdale, NJ: The Analytic Press. 2005.

McLaughlin, J. T. (2005). *The healer's bent: Solitude and dialogue in the clinical encounter.* Hillsdale, NJ: The Analytic Press.

Orbach, S. (1999). *The impossibility of sex.* London: Allen Lane, Karnac 2004.

Orbach, S. (2003). The John Bowlby Memorial Lecture Part 1: There is not such thing as a body. *Brit. J. Psychother., 20,* 3–26.

Orbach, S. (2004). What we can learn from the therapist's body? *Attachment and Hum. Dev., 6*(2), 141–150.

Orbach, S. (2006). How can we have a body: Desire and corporeality. *Stud. in Gender & Sexuality, 7*(1), 89–110.

Piers, C. (2005). The mind's multiplicity and continuity. *Psychoanal. Dial. 15*(2), 229–254.

Scarry, E. (1985). *The body in pain.* New York: Oxford University Press.

Seligman, S. (2005). Dynamic system theories as a metaframe for psychoanalysis. *Psychoanal. Dial. 15*(2), 285–319.

Shapiro, S. (1996). The embodied analyst in the Victorian consulting room. *Gender Psychoanal., 1,* 297–322.

Sonntag, M. E. (2006). I have a lower class body. *Psychoanal. Dial. 16*(3), 317–331.

Stern, D. B. (1997). *Unformulated experience: From dissociation to imagination in psychoanalysis.* Hillsdale, NJ: The Analytic Press.

Stern, D. N. (2004). *The present moment in psychotherapy and everyday life.* New York: W. W. Norton.

Stern, D. N., Sander, L., Nahum, J., Harrison, A., Buschweiler-Stern, N., & Tronick, E. (1998). Non-interpretive mechanisms in psychoanalytic therapy. *Internat. J. Psychoanal., 79,* 903–921.

Thelen, E. (2005). Dynamic systems theory and the complexity of change. *Psychoanal. Dial. 15*(2), 255–283.

Winnicott, D. W. (1960). Ego distortion in terms of true and false self. In *The maturational process and the facilitating environment* (pp. 140–152). Madison, CT: IUP, 1965.

10

"We" Got Rhythm

*Miming and the Polyphony of Identity
in Psychoanalysis*

Gianni Nebbiosi and Susanna Federici-Nebbiosi

Wahrheiten für unsere Füße,
Wahrheiten, nach denen sich tanzen läßt.
[Truths for our feet. Truths through which one can dance.]

F. W. Nietzsche, 1888

In this chapter, we intend to explore the value of the rhythmic experience—with its bodily and affective components—in perceiving, elaborating, and expressing emotions. We will try to show how the rhythmic experience is basically relational and how it plays a fundamental role in creating an implicit and explicit dialogue between ourselves and our bodies as well as between us and other people. Furthermore, we will explore the way in which the cocreation of rhythm is an extremely important element for the cocreation of meaning, as well as—through the use of miming—a factor promoting an ability to better get to know and understand the complex implicit languages of body movements and facial expressions to which contemporary psychoanalysis is assigning an increasing value.

Time, Body, Rhythm: The Dialectics Between Being and Not-Being

Philosophy discovered some important things about rhythm before psychoanalysis did. So let's start from Gaston Bachelard's and Friedrich Wilhelm Nietzsche's considerations. In our opinion, these two philosophers highlight the psycho-corporeal depth of rhythm: on the border between being and not-being. Bachelard (1932, 1936) believes that rhythm spreads across the plane on which matter is; the regularity of frequency that breaks the steady duration and spreads across matter deployed over time. Paraphrasing Bachelard, we say that rhythm spreads across the plane where the body is; the regularity that spreads across the body deployed over time. If rhythm plays on discontinuity, then the metaphor opens whereby the irregular breaks in between event and not-event, in the cadence between being and not-being. Rhythm is therefore a scan including stop, interval, rest as the pause interval between two events. Bachelard says rest is inscribed in the heart of being. Time is not datum, but building. Man builds the times with body and conscience: multiple and separate instants. Let us consider a fundamental rhythm of bodily life: The heart with its systole and diastole marks a rhythm in which the pause is as important as the beat. Therefore, thinking about rhythm entails not only *asserting* (the event, being), but also *questioning* (the pause, not-being). *Rhythm does not imply an answer, but always a further question.*

Nietzsche offers an extremely stimulating view whereby the world exists, it does not become, it does not pass. Or rather, the world never started becoming, nor did it ever cease to pass. It lasts in becoming and passing. Time is the motionless and the open at the same time. It is what has already been set and what is yet to be decided. As it is considered *Eternal Return*, time has a wavy, light, and dancing nature. In time, everything must have been lived and everything must return. *Therefore, repetition—rhythm—does not rise in time, it is time* (Nietzsche, 1883–1885). That is the reason why we put as an exergo to this chapter his illuminating posthumous extract: "Truths for our feet. Truths through which one can dance" (Nietzsche, 1888).

It is surprising how the thoughts of these philosophers find a correspondence—after about a century—in contemporary empirical research on human interactions. In their recent book on the rhythms of dialogue in childhood, Jaffe, Beebe, Feldstein, Crown, and Jasnow emphasize how the study of the alternation of sound and silence reveals completely new dynamics: "Our rhythmic approach explores the proposal that the patterns of sound and silence provide additional information about the organization of communication not evident in the separate components of sound and silence" (2001, pp. 3–5).

Rhythm as Quantity and Rhythm as Quality

Rhythm is linked with repetition; however, in order to talk about rhythm and repetition, we should deconstruct their everyday meaning and propose a meaning that is closer to both the artistic experience (music, dance, acting, mime, etc.) and the clinical experience.

In the Western culture, the instinctive perception of rhythm is apparently helped, but actually hindered, by calculating time values, subdividing them in regular successions of pulses. This *quantitative* perception of rhythm is an obstacle, so far as it interferes with the *qualitative* perception of rhythm. Different rhythms, considered as qualities, cause different reactions in our bodies and psyches. We all know that waltzing means not simply doing some rhythmic steps on an accent every three pulses; indeed, the subdivision into three has an acoustic and bodily quality—meant as the way in which our bodies react to it—which is qualitatively different from that of a subdivision into four (for example, rock and roll). Therefore, if we think that different rhythms express different qualities, our perception of and/or reaction to a certain rhythm refers to a different experience. It's about surrendering (Ghent, 1990) to a rhythm perceiving and living its quality, and not counting a rhythm with precision (unless counting it is preparatory to surrendering). If rhythm concerns the qualitative perception of a repetition, it immediately appears to be very different from the meaning that is commonly attributed to it: When we walk, talk, eat, we live a rhythm. When we feel an emotion, we live a rhythmic experience in our bodies and psyches. And when we relate to somebody, there is always the cocreation of rhythm in our interactions.

To introduce a crucial theme of our discourse, we would like to start precisely by the fact of surrendering to a rhythm and not controlling (counting) our movements to adhere to it. The rhythmic experience always entails surrendering to something other than us and which may become part of us only if we surrender to it. Indeed, a controlled rhythmic activity always has something mechanical and schematic about it. As we said elsewhere (Federici & Nebbiosi, 2006), the idea of recognizing in oneself an absolutely autonomous rhythm is one of the illusions that can be traced back to what Stolorow & Atwood referred to as the "myth of the isolated mind." Instead, we must recognize the absolutely relational value of rhythm ... there is a center of gravity we can revolve around by thinking, singing, talking, or acting, even if it practically escapes us. The presence and pull of this center are accentuated by the periodicity and trust with which we revolve around it. Periodic rhythm is not a linear and progressive succession of accented and unaccented pulses, but the rotation and fluctuation of two different values around a center that is out of time. Therefore, rhythm always implies a relationship with something that is outside of us and to which we can freely and trustfully surrender.

Fluctuating in continuous repetition, rhythm revolves around an elusive center, which, however, is the focal point of the relationship that is established between two qualities or two individuals, provided that each quality is clearly characterized and, consequently, allows the other to express itself. When, instead, one part interferes with the other, the relationship disappears. In its ultimate abstraction, rhythm is one of the most profound modes of spiritual life.

Consequently, it is never fundamentally a conscious phenomenon. Like all real experiences, it is lived originally unconsciously. "Having the sense of rhythm means living within a motion and a process without being aware of it at all" (Federici & Nebbiosi, 2006).

Rhythm: The Dialectics Between Symmetry and Asymmetry

Another aspect of rhythm we are interested in mentioning is the dialectics it establishes between symmetry and asymmetry. In the experience of a rhythm, we can never disregard both a certain symmetry of repetition and the fact that symmetry will never be complete. It is enough to watch a conductor to know that a good rhythm is never absolutely symmetrical. In all of living nature, there is no one rigorously symmetric active compound, for rigid symmetry inevitably leads to paralysis. Even the rhythm of inspiration and expiration is asymmetrical. In fact, theoretically perfect symmetry is a product of the mind more so than of nature, and a fine symmetry is never mathematically exact.

The dialectics between symmetry and asymmetry is a relational aspect of rhythm. Our individual rhythm of life is indissolubly tied to the rhythm of the environment, for we create our psychological world by interacting with others.

The dialectics of rhythm is extremely important because it is precisely when symmetry and asymmetry meet that form—and in particular, the form of emotions—comes into existence. A way to describe the form of emotions is that it is made of the rhythmic dialectics between symmetries and asymmetries that are established in our bodies. Subjective emotions all have special rhythms that give form to particular facial expressions, to a particular breath, heartbeat, muscle tension, and so on. These rhythmic forms have an exquisitely interactive value and—as we will mention later on—have a specific relational function. The experience of sharing a rhythmic/affective form with an other is a significant confirmation of the meaning of the relationship and produces activation and sense of cohesion at an individual level.

Bearing in mind this idea of rhythm, the results of the research carried out by Jaffe and collaborators can be better understood, and it can be emphasized that rhythm is something more than just the rules of interaction or expectations as to what the other will do. Jaffe and collaborators wrote in 2001: "When speakers coordinate rhythmic patterns such as sound-silence or look-lookaway, they are in fact exchanging important information regarding the perceived warmth, similarity, and empathy of their interaction" (p. 3).

Movement, Action, and Rhythm in Psychoanalysis

In order to talk about the rhythmic experience in psychoanalysis, it must be said at the outset that our discipline has been strongly suspicious about movement and acting from the beginning. Many of the most famous psychoanalytical models—e.g., Freudian, Kleinian, Bionian—consider thought as a function that originates from the ability to tolerate frustration and therefore ascribe to action a function of thoughtless burst that is antithetic of thought. This polarization has left its marks on some words used in psychoanalytical jargon, such as "acting out" or "enactment," which define something that is opposed to other expressions such as "insight," "introspection," "vicariant introspection" (Kohut's empathy), which ascribe to sight—in the metaphorical sense of the term—a quality that is closer to thought.

Observing (in oneself, in the other) and reflecting were considered activities intrinsically linked with thought and language, whereas action and movement were mainly considered activities to relieve tension and anxiety. Words and images (be they dreams, daydreaming, films, paintings, or drawings) were considered as bearers of symbolic meanings, which could be evolutional (think about Bion's reverie), whereas the symbolic value of deeds, movements, was often viewed in a regressive way. Body movements were rarely and marginally considered in evolutionary terms, and they were often considered in a regressive and symptomatic way.

It has been contemporary psychoanalysis—influenced by the research on early childhood—that recognized the importance of the body's motor activity and took an interest in the implicit language of movements (facial expressions, postures, etc.), which these days seems to play an important role in the psychoanalytic dialogue. Therefore, we must conclude that contemporary psychoanalysis takes movements and their language into greater consideration.

The Mirror Neuron System and the Perceptive/Cognitive Value of Motion

In the early 1990s—while psychoanalysis started recognizing and using more and more the research work on early childhood—in the field of neurosciences, something new and extremely stimulating happened: the discovery of the mirror neuron system. This discovery is of uttermost interest to psychoanalytic theory in general, and our topic in particular.

Thanks to these findings, a thorough revision was carried out whereby the motor system is no longer considered as a system playing a merely executive role according to the perception-cognition-movement scheme. It was noticed that the motor system is much more complex than previously hypothesized. It is formed by a mosaic of frontal and parietal areas that are closely interconnected with the visual, auditory, and tactile areas, and it has extremely complex functional properties. In this new picture, perception appears to be directly immersed in the dynamics of action, and it can be said that the brain that acts is also, and above all, a brain that understands. Rizzolatti and Sinigaglia (2006), studying some apparently simple acts such as taking a cup of coffee, discovered mirror neurons, which show how recognition of other people's actions and even their intentions depends in the first instance on our motor resources. Our brain is able to immediately understand the actions taken by others, without resorting to any kind of cognitive reasoning and based only on its own motor skills.

To be extremely concise, we might say that each individual has inscribed a sort of vocabulary of acts (which is the result of the evolution of the species) that serves to regulate and control the execution of movements. This vocabulary provides a range of potential actions. Seeing actions taken by others causes in the observer an immediate involvement of the motor areas that organize and carry out those actions. This involvement allows us to decipher the meaning of the "motor events" observed, namely understanding them in terms of actions—where this understanding appears independent of any reflexive, conceptual, and/or linguistic mediation, being based only on that vocabulary of acts and on that motor knowledge on which our own ability to act depends. "Such understanding involves not only individual actions but also entire chains of acts, and the different activations of the mirror neuron system show how it is able to code the meaning that each observed act acquires according to the actions in which it might be immersed" (p. 122). Having the mirror neuron system and the selectiveness of the answers determine a shared action space "within which each act and each chain of acts— either ours or other people's—immediately appear inscribed and understood, without this requiring any specific or deliberate 'cognitive operation (p. 127).'"

Therefore, the primary role played by the mirror neuron system is linked to the understanding of the meaning of other people's actions. As can be seen, this research on the neural bases of human interactions offers us the extraordinary discovery that thought originates in the body in movement. As the sequence of movements always gives rise to a rhythm, it becomes clear that the latter lies at the basis of the building of meaning. Every time that an attempt is made at understanding body and movement language, the rhythmic experience shows its unique function as a bridge between the movement of bodies and the building of the emotional meaning in the relationship.

Descartes and the Dichotomy Between Body (Movement) and Thought (Sight)

In his book on affects, Joseph Jones (1995) states that in psychoanalysis, it was not possible to formulate an exhaustive theory of affects owing to the general trend—initiated by Freud and continued by the other theorists—to separate psychoanalytic theory from philosophy. Descartes established the body/mind dualism that pervasively influenced the Western culture, so much so that it became the way in which mind is seen according to common sense. We recall that in Cartesian dualism, emotions (passions, as Descartes calls them) belong to the body, i.e., to the material world (*res extensa*), whereas reason (*res cogitans*) is the feature that distinguishes man from the other animals. Darwin—with his evolution theory—disrupted Cartesian dualism, pointing out that man is not so different from the other animals. In elaborating psychoanalysis, Freud tried to include the Darwinian perspective but he combined it—unintentionally, perhaps—with the philosophical-Cartesian vision. Says Jones, "This attitude set Freud's metaphysical agenda: his task was to maintain the dualistic perspective of Descartes, but at the same time to maintain the evolutionary continuity of Darwin. In other words, Freud's metapsychology represents his attempt to establish a scientific, non-Cartesian dualism, one that could ultimately be derived from an 'instinctual dualism' as the ground for his theory of mind. ... While rejecting Descartes's specific dualism of reason and feelings, Freud maintained the dualistic perspective, the hypothesis that the mind is best understood as being governed by two processes" (primary and secondary processes) (1995, p. 10).

Jones continues, summarizing Freud: "Drives push toward action ... if this is done, there is the appropriate alteration of reality. If the action is not completed, it goes to the interior of the body, leading to expressive movements and to manifestation of affect. In other words blocked action leads to affect. ... Action is primary ... in contrast affects are derivative, secondary, they have lost their process role and are now considered to be processes of discharge" (1995, p. 14).

These considerations on Freudian dualism lead Jones to conclude that:

> The model of the reflex arc, particularly when combined with the empiricist assumptions that linked thought formation to sensory input, created a formidable barrier to building a satisfactory theory of affects because of the assumption that efferentes were not sensory; therefore the regulation of motor activity could not be conceptualized in terms of affective processes. ... These assumptions were enough to prevent the exploration of the hypothesis that motor activity could be directly regulated by affective processes. (p. 31)

Going back to Jones's topic, we would like to highlight a further dualism, namely that between action and images. As we already mentioned above, the psychoanalytic thinking clearly privileged the value of images, giving them the status of primitive symbolic language. Chapters 6 and 7 of *The Interpretation of Dreams* are an eloquent example of this attribution of linguistic value to images. In Freud's opinion, the language of images is so multifaceted and complex—even though it is governed by the primary process—that it can be the translation of a verbal thought (dream work) and/or be translated again into a verbal thought (the interpretation of a dream). On the contrary, actions, movements, rhythms (if not those that refer to sexuality) in Freud's opinion only have the value of symptoms, but are far from being studied as language. A similar reasoning may be made with reference to the Kleinian concept of unconscious fantasy (Isaacs, 1952), where it is images as representations that are the building blocks of unconscious thinking. Bion more strongly uses the link of an emotion with an image as a watershed between the thinkable and the unthinkable. Neither Kleinian nor Bionian thinking sees movement as language.

In Winnicott's (1987) concept of holding, we find—perhaps for the first time—the symbolic attribution to an act, and it is by no mere coincidence a relational act. However, in spite of all this, we are still far from considering movement on an equal footing with a language, and more specifically an emotional language. Certainly, all this does not happen by chance. We are convinced that in order to understand movement in its linguistic function, it must be conceived as the language of a relationship, and not just as individual language. And it is precisely conceiving the psyche in a mainly intra-psychic and monopersonal way that moved classic psychoanalysis away from the vision of movement as language. In our opinion, the study of human interactions and a relational idea of the mind cannot disregard the study of movement as a privileged language for the creation and sharing of affective meanings, and that the study of movement as rhythmic experience is the *via regia* to understand implicit affective communication.

In order to stress the importance of the motor system in sharing and cocreation of emotional states, we believe it is useful to conclude this section by going back to the results of the recent research on mirror neurons carried out by Rizzolatti and Sinigaglia (2006). After defining the complex architecture of motor phenomena in contexts lacking an emotional connotation, in the last chapter of their book, they also investigate the emotional reactions considered—based on Darwin—as a set of answers that settled during evolution by virtue of their original adaptive usefulness. Taking into consideration a primary emotion such as disgust, they reached the conclusion that feeling disgust and perceiving other people's disgust have a common neural substrate, and that the involvement of the insula is crucial in both cases. "This seems to suggest that the 'real' understanding of other people's disgust, namely that in which one actually understands what the other feels in that particular moment, does not entail nor is it based on cognitive processes of the inferential or associative kind" (2006, p. 173–174). This is the way in which the two authors describe the process of sharing emotions through the visceral-motor system and mirror neurons:

> The information coming from the visual areas that describe faces or bodies expressing an emotion directly reaches the insula, where it activates an autonomous mirror mechanism, able to immediately code it in the corresponding emotional formats. The insula is the centre of this mirror mechanism as it is not only the cortical region where the inner states of the body are represented, but it is also a centre for visceral-motor integration, the activation of which causes the transformation of sensor inputs into visceral reactions. (2006, p. 180–181)

The strength with which we feel and communicate our emotions depends on the sharing of visceral-motor responses, which concur to define them. To summarize, "The mechanism of mirror neurons embodies, on the neural plan, that modality of understanding which—before any conceptual and linguistic mediation—shapes our experience of the others" (Rizzolatti & Sinigaglia, 2006, p. 183).

Based on these studies, therefore, it appears that the sharing and communication of emotions takes place largely through our patients' body movements, and that this process is mainly relational. All this raises the issue for us psychoanalysts (and for all those who deal with psychotherapy) of a different type of listening. We must be able to "listen" with all senses to our patients' movements, recognizing the rhythmic forms of postures, facial expressions, alternations of words, and silence. In short, understanding another person and ourselves in relation to another person is achieved not just through verbal and/or visual language, but also through the language of movements that gives form and allows to share the affects of a relationship. Rizzolatti and Sinigaglia say, "The origins of language should be sought—before looking for them in the primitive forms of vocal communication—in the evolution of a sign communication. … The progressive development of the mirror neuron system was a key component in the appearance and evolution of the human ability to communicate first with signs and then with words" (2006, p. 152).

Miming: Modalities of "Motor Introspection" and Empathic Listening With the Body

Generally, in the Western world, mimicking is an art used for humorous purposes. For a good impersonator, it is enough to catch a few features of the person he wants to mimic and exaggerate them a little, to obtain a sure comic effect on the audience. What makes people laugh at the impersonation is observing the sudden disclosure of a person's features, those that are always visible to everybody, but of which only a few are aware. The process is similar to that of caricatures, in which some facial features of a person are captured and highlighted by the caricaturist. Impression and caricature reveal to us what we already know but dissociate: the knowledge of somebody else's body. It is easy to know whether a friend of ours likes or dislikes drinking coffee; however, very few of us remember the way in which that friend drinks coffee.

If, in humorous mimicking, the thorough observation and identification work involved seems clear, this work is even vaster and more thorough in the art of miming. Indeed, the mime does not want to make us laugh; he is not content with some distinctive features. We love mimes because—like poets do with language—they enable us to look at the world and people more in depth and with greater attention. Through mimes, we discover the language of bodily rhythms: a world of meaning that would otherwise remain unrecognized. Mimes reveal to us what we have already observed in others, and they give back to us a modality of relational knowledge that we possess and practice, but that we are unaware of.

It is surprising how contemporary psychotherapists and psychoanalysts, who are so careful about implicit languages, did not attach any importance to the possibility of miming, even though in the clinical practice they sometimes pay a similar attention to nonverbal languages as that of mimes. We believe that the reason for all this, which is deeply rooted in the theoretical and clinical tradition of psychoanalysis, lies in the lack of trust we put in the body—and the excessive trust we put in the mind—as a tool for knowing ourselves, the others, and ourselves in relation to the others. Indeed in psychoanalytic literature, it's not unusual to find notations concerning the patient's body (expressions, postures, etc.); however, most of the time, these notations are matched by a reading that does not directly involve the knowledge process that the analyst's body develops by living these events.

For many years now, we have been using the tool of miming our patients in order to obtain a better understanding of them. This was done for the purpose of using a knowledge that resides in the analyst's body and of which he is completely unaware. However, to have access to this knowledge, we should try and suspend the will and surrender to the knowledge that our body has of the patient.

In doing so, we do not at all believe we rule out our subjectivity and we have direct access to the patient's subjectivity: We are suspicious of every idea that misleads the analyst into thinking that he can have an "immaculate perception" (Stolorow & Atwood, 1992) of other people's subjectivity. What we do want to do is surrender to the other's rhythmic movements, through the perception of his/her unique rhythmic quality, which we believe can be obtained by surrendering to the memory that our body has of the other, to what remains of him or her in our bodies and minds.

Of course, we do not mime patients in their presence, we do so in their absence. It's as if, besides writing some notes on the session, we

surrendered to the bodily memory linked with our relationship with
the patient.

The Case of Giuseppe

Giuseppe—a handsome 28-year-old man with dark eyes and long
hair, a thin face, a slightly prominent nose, and an intense gaze—
was referred to me by a colleague for a state of general anxiety and
because he was having trouble making progress in his career as an
opera singer. When he came to our first appointment he was very agitated and told me that he had had a terrible childhood. He was born
and raised in Catania (Sicily) in a middle-class family. His mother,
who was loving but very weak, was unable to contain her husband's
domineering attitude. His father, a doctor, inflicted upon the family unpredictable, bizarre, inconsistent, and violent behaviors. (The
father developed all-absorbing and sudden passions: For instance,
one day he showed up at home with five large cages and dozens of little birds, expecting everyone in the family to help take care of them;
the same happened when he became a radio amateur and filled the
house with electrical material and antennas and became furious if
anyone touched his equipment. The most serious episode occurred
when he moved the entire family into a flat on the upper floor in the
same building because in their house—where he continued to live—
he had to "accommodate a woman friend": an incredibly violent and
humiliating way for the whole family to "justify" a betrayal).

The only happy times in Giuseppe's childhood were the summers
spent in the country with his maternal grandparents. As a child,
when his father was not at home, Giuseppe would retreat to a small
room with an upright piano and play. But what he enjoyed most
was singing. And singing soon became his life. With his mother's
financial help, he started taking singing lessons from a maestro and
became very good, also thanks to a surprisingly sharp and exact ear.
At the age of 18, after yet another fight with his father, he left Catania and came to Rome to study singing at the Conservatory, working as a waiter in order to support himself. He studied very hard
and achieved good results. At the age of 25, he graduated with flying
colors and began working as a musician at the Teatro dell'Opera in
Rome. He had had some short-lived, sentimental relationships. At
the time, life seemed wonderful to him: He could make a living out

of singing, he had a home, and his father and the family, with its absurd and violent dynamics, were a distant memory. He finally felt free and self-fulfilled. Then he met Irene, a young woman who fell deeply in love with him and who, after some time, he fell in love with too. That is when the problems began.

"Irene immediately proved to be extremely jealous," Giuseppe said to me. "She was always suspicious that I was betraying her with other women. But I had actually fallen in love with her and was very faithful."

At the end of our conversation, we decided to meet twice a week. I had immediately taken a liking to Giuseppe, for the way he talked, his Sicilian accent, his background as a musician (I studied music myself at Rome's Conservatory).

Giuseppe dedicated the first sessions entirely to telling the story of the events that had turned his life into a complete disaster. Although the tale of his life was very dramatic, I always looked forward to our meetings with pleasure and curiosity. With great insight, he had understood that in his relationship with Irene he had had—and continued to have—a reaction very similar to the one he experienced with his father. Deep inside, he had started to hate her, feeling terribly offended, thinking it was impossible that she wanted to or indeed could understand him, and seeking shelter in music. But in his relationship with her, he behaved passively and was very "obedient" and meek, and when she made jealous scenes, most of the time he remained calm and patiently tried to persuade her that her suspicions were unfounded. This behavior was very similar to his mother's when his father had his outbursts. But Giuseppe often let his anger out on other people with whom he had become more and more disagreeable and intolerant: "I began to think that no one understood me."

One day, after being with Irene for a few years and just before starting therapy, he had flown into a rage with her. There had been no physical violence, but he had insulted her harshly and was then overwhelmed by guilt feelings and became more and more convinced of the fact that he could be safe only on his own. After this dramatic fight, Giuseppe began to engage in self-defeating behaviors: He quit his job as a chorus singer at the Teatro dell'Opera, he almost completely stopped moving in musical circles, he spent more and more days without leaving the house. He spent most of his time talking to himself, acting out long imaginary fights with his father and with

Irene. After he made up with her, he became passive once again. He gradually began to think that everyone was selfish, incapable of showing the least bit of sensitivity, ready to step over other people just to satisfy their every whim. After he quit his job, he started having financial problems and was forced to leave his home and move into a very small basement flat in a very poor area on the outskirts of Rome.

At this point, he sought help and decided to begin the analysis with me, thanks also to the financial support offered by his mother, who was frightened by his condition.

During the first months of Giuseppe's analysis, the sessions had a precise rhythm and form that repeated themselves regularly. He arrived at the session looking very worried, he walked rocking to and from, and once he was seated in front of me (he had chosen the face-to-face setting), he would begin to slowly describe the injustices inflicted by Irene, by some colleague, by people on the underground, and so on. As the minutes passed, he got more and more worked up, he gesticulated noticeably, he raised his voice a little, and, most importantly, his face became extraordinarily expressive.

Several times I caught myself watching him with great involvement, almost fascinated by his "acting skills." I experienced the very odd feeling of being caught up with the things he was saying and at the same time being completely hypnotized by the way he moved and spoke. It was as if I were watching a monologue performed by a great actor who moved me and worried me, but toward whom I somehow remained in the position of an observer. I found it very hard to interrupt him and say something because I did not want to disrupt the flow of his fascinating monologue. I soon realized that Giuseppe and I were cocreating a condition in which he could repeat in the analysis his solitary and imaginary dialogues, while I merely served as a witness.

Toward the end of the session, Giuseppe usually calmed down, relaxed, and ended the session saying, "Well ... I don't know, I don't know." He always left the office with a very friendly smile and a strong handshake.

Clearly, this situation stirred up many urgent questions in me. Why was I reacting that way toward Giuseppe? Why—above and beyond what he was saying (it was certainly not the first time that I heard a patient tell this type of story)—was I so struck and almost hypnotized by the way he spoke, the way he moved, his expressions?

How could I help him if during the session I could not reflect on the profound affective meaning of what he was saying?

One day, as I reflected on these questions, I spontaneously mimed Giuseppe. Alone in my office, I started to talk and move like him. It was an intense and very peculiar feeling. I felt that Giuseppe's expressions, his Sicilian accent, his manner of moving had slowly "rubbed off" on my body.

After asking myself, "Am I going completely crazy?" I thought that maybe there was some sense in this, and I decided to continue. As I went on with my imitation, I felt two increasingly precise sensations rising inside of me. First of all, strength. It was a strength that came from the extreme assertiveness of those behaviors and bodily rhythms. A strength that reminded me of how, when I was a child, I was fascinated when I listened to the farmers speak. (I spent most of my childhood and adolescence living in an area on the outskirts of Rome where the city bordered with the countryside. When the farmers talked about their work, they often complained about something that was not going right, but they did so with the same composure and determination with which they worked their land.) The other sensation I clearly felt was that of fighting destiny, a negative destiny that cannot be changed, but which one fights nonetheless. Something very similar to the sense of tragic that I had felt the first time I a saw a Greek tragedy: One must face terrible events that are beyond our control and yet resist and persevere.

During the session that followed my "mimed reflection," I had the powerful feeling that I was no longer listening to Giuseppe as a spectator. I felt closer to his emotions, and at the same time I was able to think and make associations without being hypnotized by his "performance." During a pause, as he was talking about his childhood, I asked him, "You told me that the only happy times you experienced as a child were in the country with your grandparents. Would you tell me a little about those times?" Giuseppe's face lit up and he began to talk to me about his relationship with his maternal grandfather. He was a strong, determined man who never lost his temper, in spite of the fact that he had many problems to solve. He was tall and sturdy, with big, strong hands. When he was with him, Giuseppe felt completely safe. His grandfather did not talk much, but when he spoke, everyone listened. I asked him whether he had ever felt he was like him or whether he ever wished to be like him. "Someone told me that I walk like him." And after a pause, he added, "When

I sing well, I feel confident, like him." I then asked him whether he had ever seen his grandfather lose his temper or become insecure. "Never!" he replied. "But you see, back home, in Sicily, that's the way it is. A man who loses his temper, or shows insecurity, is worthless."

Before the next session, I tried to imitate the expression of pride followed by a quick moment of desperation with which Giuseppe had pronounced this last sentence. At that moment, I really understood that Giuseppe had not felt guilty for his aggressive behavior with Irene: He had felt deeply and tragically ashamed. I was surprised by the intensity of the sense of failure that overwhelmed me as I imitated him. I noticed that during the previous session I had really listened to Giuseppe with my eyes, feeling on my face and in my entire body the power of the rhythm of his speech, of his facial expressions, of his way of alternating a position in which he sat up straight in his chair and another position in which he leaned on the desk that stood between us.

I continued to imitate those changes in his expressions, posture, tone of voice, and after a while, I began to feel the rhythm of these changes. Every episode was introduced, reached an expressive peak, after which its intensity declined, and it reached its conclusion. At that point, he would move on to another episode. During every session, there were at least four or five such episodes, alternated with short pauses during which Giuseppe would look at me lost, confused. The rhythm of these brief moments of loss and those in which Giuseppe regained a tremendous expressive ability and much greater strength and cohesion (the telling of the episodes) made me think of musicians who, even if they are able to perform written music beautifully, feel confused and anxious when they are asked to improvise a few bars. Did the alternation of episodes and brief moments of confusion in Giuseppe's stories mean something similar? In his affective states, were there perhaps scores, scripts on the one hand, and, on the other hand, moments when, having to improvise, he did not know what to do?

During the subsequent session, following this line of thinking, I asked Giuseppe, "When you tell me about your imaginary fights with Irene, with your father, or with someone who has hurt you, do you think or feel you are like someone in particular?" Giuseppe looked at me in surprise: "How did you figure that out?" I replied, "I was thinking of your grandfather." "No, Doctor, you haven't understood, then. I think I'm Al Pacino in *The Godfather*, or one of those boys I knew where I lived in Catania and were mobsters. When they were 15, they were mugging people already. They were confident and tough, they knew the 'law of the streets.'" As he spoke this last sentence, Giuseppe had a tough, almost challenging expression, like someone who feels invincible. But seconds later, his face turned into a grimace that revealed for the first time a pain I had never seen before. "But I'm not like that, unfortunately. And I know I'm wrong, because a man, a real man who had a father like mine, would have killed him."

I said to him, "It must be very hard and painful for you to have to deal with these terrible situations in your life, always thinking that you should be different than you are, better than you are, much more strong, confident, and aggressive than you are." Giuseppe answered with a great sense of relief and with deep sincerity, "But Doctor, if I'm myself, I don't know what to do. For instance, now I'm very confused because my father has communicated to me through my mother that he wants to buy a house in Rome. He doesn't say that it's for me, but I know it is. He's doing it for himself. He wants to be forgiven! And what am I supposed to do? Can I forget how much he hurt me? Because if I help him to buy the house, it's as if I've forgiven him." "I understand," I said. "And this is what your mother has always done with your father, isn't it?" "That's right, Doctor," he replied with a resigned, tired look I have seen many times on the faces of women from southern Italy.

On the one hand, Giuseppe felt strong and competent when he identified with some of the strong male figures—even if very different from one another—in his life (the young mobsters, his grandfather); these characters had a different way of being aggressive than his father because, unlike him, they had laws, order (even if the laws were Mafia laws), whereas his father followed no laws at all and was completely unpredictable in his behavior. On the other hand, if he experienced tender emotions, he felt incapable of reacting, fearful, like his mother; like the women in his culture and in his imagination. In the midst of all this, there was a lost and confused Giuseppe ("if I'm myself"), uncertain, anxious, and desperate, sometimes self-destructive, but especially filled with a tremendous sense of shame.

What was my rhythm as I listened to Giuseppe? During the sessions that preceded my imitation, the way I listened to him was absolutely symmetrical to his way of talking about himself. When he identified with the strong characters, I was fascinated and almost hypnotized by his story, just as I had been when I was a child and listened to the farmers speak. Instead, I perceived the moments when Giuseppe was more confused and scattered as pauses, interludes between the more significant events. My way of listening to his way of talking had coconstructed a rhythm, whose affective meaning was: We are interested in the identifications with strong men, the rest is nothing, and this nothing is cause for shame (I was ashamed, too, when I was not fascinated by his stories, for I felt that I was not being a good analyst). I was able to understand this coconstructed rhythm only thanks to my miming Giuseppe. After this "mimed reflection," I decided to dedicate myself more and more to feeling and miming Giuseppe when he was confused. It was very difficult to do because in those moments, Giuseppe no longer had the typical and evident traits that had so struck my bodily attention. Furthermore, by miming his confusion, I struck some painful personal chords. On one occasion, I remembered "in my body" an episode of my childhood when I was tested by a professor who found me unprepared and sadistically kept asking me questions, humiliating me in front of the class. On that occasion, I felt a terrible muscle contraction in my whole body and the irresistible desire not to exist.

But focusing on our moments of shame and nonexistence completely shifted my perception of the rhythm of our interactions. What I had previously considered as pauses were now significant events. I started to see our interactions as being characterized by long pauses (the identifications with strong characters) that alternated with significant events (the moments of shame and confusion). This way of listening on my part changed the way in which Giuseppe interacted with me. More and more, he spoke to me about his practical day-to-day problems: How could he go back to work? How could he react differently to Irene's jealousy? How could he solve the problem involving the purchase of the house?

Then an important and moving episode occurred between us. One day, Giuseppe told me that in a moment of weakness, but also of great intimacy, Irene had admitted to him that she was so jealous because she was ashamed to have small breasts. Giuseppe was very moved by this confession, and when I told him that he had been good in accepting Irene's confession with great affection, and that this was a very important gift he had, for the first time Giuseppe cried in front of me. As I said to him, "You see, Giuseppe, weakness and strength are not so far apart," I felt my body abandon itself, relax. I think that at that moment, we both felt it was possible to exist as we are, with our weaknesses and a new feeling of strength.

Conclusions

As we have seen, rhythm is, from the first days of our lives, a fundamental mode of interaction. Studies in infant research reveal the repetitive and rhythmic quality of the mother-child relationship. We believe that this repetitive and rhythmic quality that characterizes all human interactions is very important in the clinical interaction, whose effectiveness is based on the cocreation of a frame (repetitiveness) and on the activation of a transformative relational process for both participants; we could say that rhythm is the element with which our body is in relation with the process.

As we have seen in Giuseppe's case, a coconstructed rhythm contained a profound affective meaning. Patient and analyst had unconsciously shared the meaning that everything that had to do with the identifications with strong men was significant, while all the rest did not matter. It was precisely the process of transforming this rhythm—perceived through miming—that allowed both to reverse the accent placed on the value of strength, weakness, shame, thus coconstructing a new rhythm—that is, a new dialectic—between identifications with strong men in contrast to weakness on the one hand, and the perception of a new type of strength that included weakness on the other.

Two last remarks. Giuseppe's case can be interpreted on the basis of a wide variety of analytic models. Here, we simply wanted to point out the aspects of the treatment that are intrinsically tied to its rhythmic elements. It is evident that the affective meaning of a given rhythm of interaction must be integrated with many other aspects of the psychoanalytic technique. Here, we wanted to underscore its value and especially the possibility of introducing into the psychoanalytic technique an instrument that includes more directly the body of the analyst and the language of movements.

Finally, we wish to underline that bodily perception and "mimed reflection" do not represent at all a direct perception of the patient's subjectivity apart from the analyst's subjectivity. The analyst's body, with its rhythms and meanings, is inevitably infused with his subjectivity. We believe that the case has shown how the analyst's bodily perception was infused with subjective meanings. However, we feel it is important to underline how profound and rich is the language—often unheeded—of our body, mindful of E. E. Cummings' words, "so deep's the mind of flesh" (1950, p. 609).

References

Bachelard, G. (1932). *L'intuizione dell'istante. La psicoanalisi del fuoco* [The intuition of the instant. Psychoanalysis of fire]. Bari: Dedalo, 1973.

Bachelard, G. (1936). *La dialictique de la durée* [The dialectics of duration]. Paris: Bouvin.

Cummings, E. E. (1950). "Xaipe." In *Complete Poems (1904–1962).* New York: Liveright, 1994, p. 609.

Federici, S., & Nebbiosi, G. (2006). It don't mean a thing (If it ain't got that swing): Rhythm and meaning in the analytic encounter. Presented at the Boston IARPP Conference 2006.

Ghent, E. (1990). Masochism, submission, surrender: Masochism as a perversion of surrender. *Contemp. Psychoanal.,* 26, 108–136.

Isaacs, S. (1952). The nature and function of phantasy. In Klein, M., Heimann, P., Isaacs, S., & Riviere, J. (eds.), *Developments in psychoanalysis.* London: Karnac Books, 1989, pp. 67–122.

Jaffe, J., Beebe, B., Feldstein, S., Crown, C., & Jasnow, M. (2001). Rhythms of dialogue in infancy. *Monographs of the Society for Research in Child Development,* 66 (2, Serial No. 265), Boston: Blackwell.

Jones, J. M. (1995). *Affects as process.* Hillsdale, NJ: The Analytic Press.

Nietzsche, F. W. (1883–1885). *Also Sprach Zarathustra, Opere Vol. VI, Tomo 1* [Collected Works, Vol. VI, 1st book]. Milan: Adelphi, 1979.

Nietzsche, F. W. (1888). *Opere Vol. VI, Tomo 4* [Collected Works, Vol. VI, 4th book]. Milan: Adelphi, 1977.

Rizzolatti, G., & Sinigaglia, C. (2006). *So quel che fai. Il cervello che agisce e i neuroni specchio* [I know what you do. The acting brain and the mirror neurons]. Milan: Cortina.

Stolorow, R. D., & Atwood, G. E. (1992). *Contexts of being.* Hillsdale, NJ: The Analytic Press.

Winnicot, D. W. (1987). *Babies and their mothers.* London: Free Association Books.

Part IV.

The Analyst's Body as Object and Subject

11

When a Body Meets a Body

*The Impact of the Therapist's Body
on Eating-Disordered Patients*

Jean Petrucelli

When a body meets a body, no formal introductions are made. What are the feelings and ideas, conscious and unconscious, that go through our minds when we are looking at another person? As therapists, we focus on words but our bodies also speak. And, in a manner of speaking, there are actually always four, if not more, bodies in the room. Each partner in the analytic dyad has both a body as a material entity and a body as it expresses and symbolizes psychic life. For each person, the expressive and symbolic meaning of her own body and the body of the other changes with changes in her self-state. Yet most accounts of therapeutic process mention very little of what the bodies mean to each other. In the literature on eating disorders (ED), for example, while the patient's body is a constant focus, little attention has been paid to the effects of the therapist's body on the events of psychotherapy and the process of treatment.

Shapiro (1996) wrote one of the earliest papers regarding the patient's and the therapist's experience of each other's body in analytic treatment. She persuasively demonstrated that, with few exceptions, "traditional psychoanalytic theory and practice was, and still is, quite removed from bodily experience" (1996, p. 298). Detailing some of the major cultural and scientific changes responsible for the analytic privileging of symbolic experience, she advocates that equal attention be paid to somatic experience within the consultation room.

Several therapists and analysts have courageously explored how their own bodies, whether overweight or affected by illness, affected treatment (Burka, 1996; Kahn, 2003; Pizer, 1998). Looker (1998) explored the analyst's attention to her own and her patient's body-based experiences and to connections and disconnections between the experience of psyche and soma. She believes that understanding the "disconnects" is critical in fostering the analytic holding environment and that the analyst's struggle is to remain consciously embodied. Lowell and Meader (2002) have explored the impact of the thin therapist's body on their work with eating-disordered patients. Lieberman (2000) writes about looking and being looked at in therapy. Tintner (2007) describes how different overweight patients reacted to her ample form and discusses its effect on the emotional life of her patients.

Orbach (2003), addressing the body on its own terms rather than solely for what the body symbolizes, suggests the need to retheorize the mind-body relationship and examine its impact on our clinical work. Orbach has found eloquent ways to spark our curiosity by raising questions about the impact of how we, as therapists, wear our clothes, how we talk, how our bodies may affect our patient's bodies, making us more or less aware of the degree of bodily comfort or discomfort we convey. She speculates as well on how body presence may sanction, confirm, disturb, please, or overwhelm, and how the perception of all of this affects the therapeutic relationship and the treatment itself.

Exploring the interaction between the therapist's body and the therapeutic process, this chapter builds on and extends growing knowledge concerning the significance of the therapist's body for the patient. It is not an attempt to present new theory. Instead, it presents what I believe are some new additions to this topic. I consider how, for example, an eating-disordered patient's habit of comparing and contrasting her appearance to the other's appearance, including that of her analyst, may be a vehicle for, not only a resistance to, fundamental change. Particularly with eating-disordered patients, who act on rather than articulate and share their feelings, I am interested in how feelings are put into words. In the therapeutic encounter, bodies interact in ways that can be either verbalized or played out. When those feelings are unarticulated, the impact of the therapist's body can be gauged through observations of patient actions and vice versa. I explore both articulated and unarticulated interactions between therapist and patient around body and appearance.

For certain patients, even verbal hints at the ways in which their thin therapist's "put together" demeanor makes them feel envious and inadequate may humiliate them, evoking self-conscious constriction, silence, and shame. In one vignette, I describe how, without verbalization of the process, a patient's responses to her body unfurl imitatively, expressively, and interactively, resulting in improvements in her self-care and presentation. In other examples, I demonstrate how unverbalized bodily enactments ultimately enabled the analyst and patient to engage in verbalized dialogues about aspects of these patient dilemmas, which previously had been inaccessible to examination, interpretation, and working through. This process helped these patients to attain insight into and greater control of aspects of their lives that had caused them suffering for years.

In the last 20 years of working in the therapeutic arena of eating disorders, I have found that my patients seem to ask me the same two questions. These questions help me articulate some of the ways we become more aware of our bodies and of body-to-body interaction in this work.

The first question is, "Do you or have you had an eating disorder?" The second, which I'm going to address first here, is, "Has anyone ever told you that you look like Cher?" I am often told by patients that my presentation of self is youthful, "rock-n-roll-ish," energetic, and unlike their idea of a "typical" analyst. Now, while I do have long black hair, bangs and a tall, lean athletic build, a part of me still believes that, given all the changes and metamorphoses Cher has gone through, this question about our generic resemblance might have stopped after all these years. It has not, and so I have learned to accept seeing myself in this way through the eyes of the other. So that you can fully appreciate how often, and in what ways, this occurs in my office, let me "cher" with you some of the exchanges. Patients have given me 45-rpm singles, a Cher album cover, a pair of black lace pants actually owned and worn by Cher, and the full-size and mini-Cher doll equipped with blonde and red wigs. I've been asked if I could sing my interpretations, and during an intense exchange, one male patient burst into song with "I've Got You, Babe."

The point of addressing my "Cher awareness" is that every patient
who comes into the room is making some assessment about how we
look. Our bodies are being reacted to in several different ways, and
we are reacting to their bodies, whether we know it or not. Sometimes patients make a comment, but usually they do not. How, then,
can we make more conscious what we are saying about our bodies
and our patients' bodies as well as what our patients are saying about
our bodies? How do we bring the body language into the room and
put words to what is often wordless? We need a heightened sensitivity to the body-to-body communication that is always happening in
the room which is often ignored.

With the Cher comparison, what are my patients doing with me?
Are they asking just because I "look like" Cher, or are they beginning
to wonder who I am? Are they superimposing "Cher" on me? In part,
saying I look like Cher can be the most comfortable or safest thing
some patients can say because, for them, it is a way of opening things
up without necessarily revealing themselves. In this sense, part of
their comfort comes from turning me into someone or something
already known. Thus, the Cher reference might be used for comfort
and for distancing. Sometimes the references are more incongruous
than not. It is not always clear, but I'm sure it is worth knowing which
Cher it is that is being referenced: early fawnlike Cher, sexy Cher,
songstress Cher, *Moonstruck* Cher, or scary, post-plastic-surgery Cher.
"Cher" can also mean "dear," as in "You are a dear" and as in "You are
expensive" (Samstag, personal communication, June 2006).

This Cher phenomenon has been with me for the last 30 years,
and my feelings about it have changed in response to my personal
history and life experiences. Sometimes when the question is asked
and I am filled with a generosity of spirit, I focus on the meaning
behind the question, the idea of "Why now?" I understand the question to be a diagnostic indicator of patients' relatedness; it reveals
their level of comfort in asking, their playfulness, fondness, and
attachment—and, in some cases, their anger or aggression. I have
noticed that when I am feeling aggressively playful, I answer, "No,
as a matter of fact, you are the first person to ever ask me that." This
is a moment when I am most in touch with my sadistic impulses as
I watch my patients initially feel delight, surprise, and then foolish-
ness when they see me grin—and they give me the "Aw, come on …
you're pulling my leg" response.

I am reminded of an episode of the TV show *Will and Grace*, in which the punch line was Cher playing Cher. In this episode, Jack, a gay character who idolizes Cher, is convinced on meeting the real Cher that, in fact, he is in the presence of a female impersonator. Cher, who has the reputation of being rather narcissistic, has the confidence and sense of humor to allow herself to be mistaken by a fan for a female impersonator. So, if Cher can have this much fun with her own image, shouldn't I simply enjoy being linked to her?

What I realize, and what is essential, is that I am reacting to the comparison being made between my bodily appearance and Cher's. Is my reaction based on my perception of who she is and how I feel about her, or am I simply reacting to the fact that I am being compared? Just as the fake Cher or the "idea of Cher" becomes more believable and expectable to the fan than the real Cher is, I may be reacting to my body and appearance being used transferentially. I have learned that this is important information to pay attention to. I also might wonder if my patients are comparing me to this larger-than-life figure because, in some way, this comparison distances us from the experience of our all-too-life-size bodies in the room.

My negative reaction has led me to realize that not only are bodies coming into the room, but also that therapists and patients are having subtle physical reactions to their bodies being compared, even when these comparisons are not being made aloud. Comparisons can be thought of as a vehicle for transference and countertransference. And contrast also can be one of the most important ways to interpret and understand transference because it often reflects our values as human beings (Buechler, 1994). Levenson (personal communication, May 2006) highlights this idea when he fondly quotes Marshall McLuhan, who said, "We don't know who discovered water, but we know it wasn't a fish." Sometimes it is only by experiencing something new that we become able to see the assumptions we have always lived with but have not yet recognized. These moments offer us a chance to provide a contrast, catalyst, and relational challenge, in response to which the patient has to try to figure out how to deal with us. With the eating-disordered population, comparing and contrasting is an ongoing way of interacting in the world.

Sometimes it is through the "using" of my body and their fantasies about it that patients begin to speak about their bodies. Even if I did not look like Cher, what matters is that we allow our bodies and our patient's perceptions of our bodies, in whatever ways they appear, to be used transferentially. We all think or talk about transference in our work, but we usually don't do it visually.

As Orbach (2003) writes, "Our patients use our bodies just as they use our psyches" (p. 31). The therapeutic issue is how to help them use our psyches actively, consciously, and meaningfully. If this is to happen, attention has to be paid to the subtle nuances and not-so-subtle invitations to look, listen, and feel. Sometimes a patient invites us in; sometimes we have to invite the patient. It is often challenging when a patient confronts the therapist about her body. Patients are hypervigilant, scrutinizing, searching, comparing, not just how we look but also how we experience ourselves in our bodies. Do we feel safe enough to let patients use our bodies? And, when they do, are we giving up our sense of privacy? What happens when the body can be addressed on its own terms rather than solely for what it symbolizes?

How patients feel about their bodies, and how they respond to their therapists' bodies, may involve fear, attraction, objectification, idealization, devaluation, envy, curiosity, or any combination of these feelings. On one hand, appearance can evoke attraction and positive identification within an idealized transference. Optimally, in the course of the work, this identification will enable the patient to deidealize the therapist and to begin to value herself. On the other hand, a patient's responses also speak to dangerous aspects of the therapist or the therapeutic relationship that may be cumbersome and very hard to address. For example, when patients feel envy, they feel that the other has "it" and they want to destroy the other person's pleasure in "it" (whatever "it" is). The destructive wish is an attempt to relieve their psychic pain. Once a patient knows (and she always knows) that she has made me feel uncomfortable about the "thing" I have, she stops because she feels temporary relief. Envy is intolerable precisely because one believes that one must have "it" to survive, and yet one can never have "it" (because only Cher does), and so one feels devastated by the fantasy of this ideal's loss.

Many patients often ask for what they need with their actions rather than their words. By bringing a consciousness of the therapist's body into the therapeutic dialogue, we have a chance to recognize how patients disown their bodies: their feelings of insecurity, shame, humiliation, self-hatred. The parts of the body that feel most hated—like the "bulimic self-state" or the "anorexic moment" or the "garbage-eating dissociated state"—must be welcomed literally bit by bit, morsel by morsel. Sometimes a patient's body and her unintegrated body parts have to be brought into the room before she can even acknowledge the therapist's body. I hope to illustrate these ideas in the following vignettes.

Here is an example of how bodies concretize internal and historical experience. N, a 19-year-old anorectic woman, on medical leave from college, identified her "thighs" as the "culprit" for all that ailed her. One day, she commented how she felt that my thighs looked good in pants. An in-depth exploration of her feelings about my thighs and her thighs and a discussion of the function and many shapes of thighs in general uncovered in N a memory of being 9 years old and being held over her grandfather's head to see above a crowd. She remembers feeling his fingers creep around her thighs, into her genital region. She remembers feeling physically unable to move and emotionally frozen. She remembers how he thrust his fingers into her. She said she had never spoken these words out loud.

When faced with the horror of N's experience, as well as that of many others, we sometimes unwittingly find ourselves wanting to offer reassurance and comfort rather than holding their distress and hearing their pain, which would then allow these body parts to come into the room. N compared my "idealized" thighs to her thighs so as to bring in her "damaged/defective" thighs and to address her pain about this frightening, hated body part, which filled her with shame, anger, and disgust. Without our directly addressing her thighs, her pain could not begin to lessen. This example touches also on N's disowned body experience in which she could not connect to her thighs. In a sense, my thighs became her "safe haven" because they had not been "damaged" by abuse. One could say that in the room, she was having an "out-of-thigh" experience with me!

Sometimes we need not listen for the moment when the body (actual or symbolic) enters the room. Sometimes the patient literally tells us. M, a male patient with disordered-eating and body-image issues, was married but having affairs. He was told by a friend to seek therapy because he might have "some intimacy issues." In passing, the referring colleague commented to me, "I think you and he would be a good match. He's having all these affairs and he wants to see if he'll fall in love with his therapist." I did not think much of that remark until one day, M walked into the room and said, "Hey Doc! How's it going with you, babe?" BABE? (I could feel the hair on the back of my neck prickling.) I realized that he wanted to play, but I found myself wanting to set him straight about the frame of the treatment. I wanted to defend myself in reaction to feeling objectified.

The combination of my feeling objectified and the air of cocky, impenetrable bravado with which he sauntered in—without the "nervousness" a patient usually feels during a consult—was somewhat disarming. I entertained the idea that his bravado was a counterphobic response to his anxiety, and although my experience of feeling like an object had to occur, I was aware I did not like it. Nonetheless, knowing that an enactment had begun and aware that, in response, my questions were probing and penetrating, I took it all in.

I quickly discovered, though, how anxious, insecure, and antsy he was about his body. By the third session, the climate in the room changed. He "told" me of this change when he sat down. His first comment was, "Doc ... I really like this CHAIR ... MY BODDDYYYY ... feels comfortable in this chair." Clearly, that exclamation was really about his evolving feeling of being more comfortable with me; he used his physical sense sensation to talk about his internal state. Something had changed, and his body was representing his sense of being. In response to his anxiety, I had become more aggressive in my questioning, which resulted in M's feeling more comfortable with me. Was he testing my ability to play with him but conveying this intent through the experience of his body in the room?

In the first example, the patient, N, mentions my body part and then hers to get to a dissociated memory. The second example shows a male patient objectifying my body, then using his body to express his internal nonverbal experience of our interactions. In the next example, I highlight the fact that sometimes patients deal with bodies by not dealing with the obvious.

Often, when patients are asked directly about their feelings toward the therapists' bodies, they deny noticing or feeling anything at all. One overweight patient, E, could begin losing weight only when I gained weight. I gained 30 pounds; she lost 35. I, however, was 7 months pregnant before my patient referred unconsciously to the changes in our bodies. I had been waiting for an opportunity to tell her I was pregnant and gave her many chances to comment, but she seemed oblivious. When finally I could no longer withhold disclosing my pregnancy, she gasped in disbelief and said she felt horrible for not noticing.

At that point, E was able to acknowledge her secret feelings of superiority and envy, which now could surface and enter the room. In her fantasy, I was now the messy, gluttonous one, and this fantasy had motivated her to eat healthily. In her family of origin, her sister was "the thin one" with whom my patient felt she could "never compete," and so she relegated herself to the role of "the fat one" in the family. That way, she never had to acknowledge her internal conflictual feelings.

E was able to acknowledge the jealousy contained in her idealization of me. She thought I could always eat freely, whereas she had to eat in a controlled, restrained manner. I was able to acknowledge with her the complicated mix of feelings I had had about our bodies. Given her troubled history with her poor body image and being overweight, she had invoked in me a contrasting sense of my body's reliability, consistency, and steadiness, which could serve as a temporary external body or holding container for her. E had a mother and sister whose bodies were unstable and disorganized. E did not feel that she fit into her own body or her own skin. Her sister, identified by E as "the thin one," had had polio, was always sick, and had had many operations. E's mother was neglectful of her own body and dysregulated in her eating, sleep, and hygiene. E associated her "fat body" with her ability to stay robust and "healthy" and insulated from her own body concerns. The changes in my thin body had allowed a myriad of feelings to emerge. But E also associated thin bodies with illness even though thinness was also seen as desirable. With my pregnancy, my weight and body size shifted. My body when thin had been stable, as her body when overweight had been equally stable although devalued. When I became pregnant, my increased weight could be thought of as my being in a destabilized state because my weight was not holding steady. There was a system in the room; therefore, while our respective weights destabilized, the split in the room stayed stable. One of us was large and the other was small, and in some way it did not matter which of us was which.

The dissociated aspects of self emerging through the body and variously entering the room occur with all patients. With the eating-disordered population, however, these issues are going to be especially piercing and to the point. They comprise the language of eating-disordered patients.

Let us turn now to the second of the two questions that I am often asked: "Do you or have you had an eating disorder?" Or "How can you be someone who specializes in ED if you are thin?"

There are many beliefs held and assumptions made about a therapist, if she is thin. Her body can be idealized or devalued. These assumptions can be either barriers to, or tools for, recovery. Embedded in them are questions about the therapist's morality, competence, and physical and mental health (Lowell & Meader, 2002). For example, one patient who restricts and then binges said to me, "Part of me wants to idealize you as a perfect person and the other part has to break you down to make you feel more normal so I can feel better about myself."

When the question of whether I have had an eating disorder comes up in the course of a treatment, I explore patients' fantasies of what it would mean if I had had an eating disorder and what it would mean if I had not. The complexities of responses are always rich and meaningful and reveal some aspect of the work previously unknown and not yet shared between us. I have experimented with answering the question directly, and although patients are generally relieved that I have not had an eating disorder, all kinds of other complicated feelings ensue. It has been my experience that answering this question directly opens one door but inevitably closes off another. So I prefer to think of this question as an analytic "moment," allowing me to bring to bear all the clinical considerations I would give to other moments of possible self-disclosure. For me, it is more important to be open to a process in which, together with the patient, the unspoken can be discovered.

I often wonder what the silent question is behind the spoken question. Is it, "How do you stay so thin?" implying that I take some action toward this end. Or is it, "If you are a thin therapist specializing in this field, then you are in recovery from your eating disorder. And exactly how far into recovery are you?"(This assumption comes from the addiction model and assumes that all therapists must have personal experience with the disorder.) Would the fantasy, then, of my having recovered from an eating disorder enhance or revitalize the hope for the patient's own recovery? Other patients need the therapist to be healthy from the start, because any other possibility would simply be too terrifying. Or is the question behind the question, "Tell me exactly what you eat?" as if I could reveal a secret that would "cure" the patient. Another part of my experience has to do with "thin prejudice," which holds many assumptions, including that one cannot be naturally or genetically thin and healthy.

These questions are often the only language that eating-disordered patients can use to talk about what it's like to be in the world, even in the room, with another person. The point is not the answer, which I seldom give, but the fantasies and the resulting dialogue that brings the body-to-body interaction out into the open.

Some patients feel relieved if the therapist is in shape and not over-weight. A professional, "put together" demeanor may make it safe for them to feel a sense of connectedness because they assume that the "thin" therapist has her act together. If a patient perceives a therapist's "look" as particularly desirable, the idealization and accompanying envy may be intensified. In my experience, the idealization serves as a defense not only against hostility, competition, and shame but also against potential experience of a shared vulnerability. The patient perceives the therapist as being so polished that she can experience herself only as a spectator rather than a player on the field.

Sometimes issues open up and unfold because of the patient's experience of seeing the therapist appear not so "together." Some-times issues are overlooked because the patient, the therapist, or both need things to look polished and that outward finish makes everyone feel safer. Sometimes, however, events occur that level the playing field.

When I was working with a patient who was ambivalent about treatment, the leveling of the playing field occurred both literally and figuratively. C would compulsively overeat and binge. Her body type was the direct opposite of mine: She was less than 5 feet tall and overweight. Although our body types were dissimilar, we had simi-lar tastes in colors and clothes, as well as an appreciation of details and the nuances of color shadings. The colors of my clothes were often the first thing she would comment on in our sessions.

In our work together, C, struggling with issues of attachment, trust, and dependency, protected herself by figuratively keeping one foot in the door and one foot out. For the first year of treatment, she needed to tell me she felt absolutely no connection to me and that it was better that way. She was not sure the therapy was going anywhere, anyhow. At the end of every session, she would laugh and announce that she was not sure if she was coming back. Each week she returned, never late, never missing, always paying her bill on time. I was seeing her twice a week. C thought I was "nice, smart, sane, not crazy like her last psychiatrist," but the real and only reason she was staying was that she "liked my clothes and they looked good on my body." She was sure that she must not be getting anything out of therapy because, after all, she was "still fat." She would constantly remind me of that. This idea of being "still fat" implies that C did not want me to think that she was getting better because she needed me to keep looking for what was wrong inside her. I, on the other hand, felt that C was progressing quite nicely. Clearly, we were not having a meeting of the minds. This situation was about to change but in an unexpected way.

C had made an appointment, which she mistakenly thought she had confirmed. I did not think she had made the appointment so I did not expect her to come in. I happened to be in my waiting room when C walked in unexpectedly. Surprised, I told her I would see her, but I was expecting a call on my cell phone. Five minutes into the session, someone began pounding on my office door. I jumped up, startled, still a little off balance by her presence, and in my haste my pants got stuck on my high-heeled boots. In one rather fluid motion, I stood up, tripped, and took a belly flop dive across my office floor, landing at C's feet. I clearly "floored" her! She looked at me in horror and disbelief. Hearing a loud crash, one of my suitemates, an elderly psychiatrist, alarmed, barged into my office thinking I was on a break. "Is everything OK? And by the way, do you have an extra key to my office as I just locked myself out while in the bathroom?" I got up from the floor and, fumbling through the box of keys, desperately tried to find his, which I found 5 minutes later. Meanwhile, C, still sitting on the couch, said not a word. As I began apologizing for the interruptions, my cell phone rang and I answered that I could not meet the person as planned. C huffed loudly. My next patient buzzed me. It was a comedy of errors.

C was furious and shocked at having seen this untogether side of me and my newfound level of disorganization: my body lacking its usual "athleticism," failing me. This experience, however, opened up the door for C to express a wealth of feelings buried under her layers of protection. She told me that, because I had always seemed so polished and put together, she could not imagine me with any fallibilities or untogether aspects. She said she got a secret kick out of my lack of athleticism of the moment. On some level, C needed me to "demonstrate" my vulnerability so that she could share hers. In the weeks that followed, she disclosed events and feelings she had never talked about before, and she began exercising and following a food plan.

That series of mishaps, which literally enabled my body to be viewed from a new position—horizontally on my office floor—allowed C and me to cross a therapeutic divide in our work. Her idealization of me shifted dramatically as she was shaken by a forced encounter with my spontaneous humanness. This change stood in contrast to her perception of me as a physically poised, polished, "together" analyst. My most simply being human, with *a body that could be out of control*, allowed C to bring into the room split-off parts of herself, and she was able to let down her own guard and experience a vulnerability that she had been keeping under wraps.

Not all patients are able to respond to novel patient-therapist interactions as well as C was. Because of their histories, some patients have more complicated responses to the analyst's body becoming an explicit part of the dialogue. For example, K, a 38-year-old woman with a history of anorexia that fluctuated in severity over time, had been in an analytic treatment with me for several years. In the course of the treatment, she had progressed from being a loner to dating, getting married, and having a child; she was now pregnant with her second. Some of K's hiding stemmed from a long-standing fear of competing in the real world. Her food patterns involved denying herself food throughout the day, and then late at night she would eat secretly, loading up on raw vegetables and artificial sweeteners. Her night eating was a "love affair" that never disappointed her.

One day as she walked into my office, she commented, "I like your shoes." It was odd for her to notice something about my physical presence; she had never remarked on anything like that before. Now, I could have asked her, "Well, what makes you say that now?" or "What is it about my shoes you like?" But instead, I replied, "Didn't you used to have a pair of shoes like these, too?" She answered sullenly, "I don't remember," and became quiet.

"You know," I said, "we never talk about our bodies or our clothes and how you dress and how you feel about my physical presence." She gave me the "face."

"OK, I'll start." I said that, despite her being the beautiful woman she is, she dresses in a depressed way that draws attention to her not wanting to be seen. She then let loose. "I'm hiding. If I pay attention to myself, I realize I'm hiding. I know things would shift for me if I looked good, but I would feel more vulnerable for being admired

and wanting it … and then having to deal with the disappointment.
Clothes accentuate this desire. When I feel best about my body, it's
when I feel I have to put the least effort in my appearance because
I should look good naturally. But then when I look in a mirror and
I don't look gorgeous, I'm so shocked and disappointed. So, if I try
and it doesn't work, it's even worse. I feel so bad that even the clothes
can't hide it."

Without skipping a beat, she continued, "My mom would come to
school on parents' day. She would be all decked out in a suit with her
hair done. I had one of those *Charlie's Angels* moms. She seemed like
the perfect mom at these school events. I'd bask in reflective glory,
thinking that others were now thinking there's something good about
me because this is my mom. Then at home, she would go back to wearing schleppy clothes, not focusing on me, she would not act like the
mom wearing those polished clothes. She would wear revealing clothes
in front of my friends … the other moms were more conservative.
Things would feel shameful. I would think my mom must have secret
flaws that she's hiding because she was so much prettier than the other
moms. My mom was always cooking up a scheme—the Scarsdale diet,
the liquid diet, the no-carb diet, etc., etc. I became hypervigilant to
always keep looking … and to look closer to find the flaws …."

Hearing all this transferentially, I asked her how that played out
with me. She said, "When I first met you, I thought, 'No way can I
see her. She's too fancy, too pretty, too fashion model-ly.' I felt so self-
conscious about my looks."

I said, "You never said anything. How did it shift?"

She replied, laughing, "I'm not sure it has completely, but the one
thing I recognize now is that you have fun with it. That's apparent.
I admire and aspire to be able to be as playful with my body and
clothes as you seem to be. But then this voice kicks in and says she
can do that because she's naturally thin and naturally proportioned.
Me and my mom can't. I know when I ask my husband, 'Do I look
fat?' that I'm really communicating something else to him. He knows
too, so he rolls his eyes. He reacts like you do, catching me when I
try to get away with something. I know now that you both know that
all I really want to feel is closeness and a connection, and sometimes
reassurance. But instead, I push people away. It would be nice to feel
good about my looks freely."

The bind for K was that her mother's perfection, and therefore
transferentially my "perfection," were seen as hiding hypocrisy:

Behind the perfection was lack of concern and neglect. So for K to feel good about her looks would mean she would be as much of a hypocrite as her mother. K's "truth" was expressed in her plainness, her look of being neglected. In the process of helping K to own and publicly and verbally acknowledge her beauty, I had to find a way to help her realize that being beautiful does not make her a "copy" of the bad object Mother.

The point of these vignettes is similar. We need to pay attention to the unexpected, the accidental, particularly when it concerns the body. We need to stay mindful of how our patients are already using our bodies just as they use our psyches. There are times that, for example, you almost miss your seat when you sit down; or you fumble; there is that moment when your foot falls asleep or your eye starts to twitch. These unexpected moments bring something disso-ciated into the room, and these are ways of shaking up the treatment. These are often features that we do not pay attention to as much as we could. In C's case, my body was accidentally brought into the thera-peutic encounter in a new configuration, whereas in K's case, her unexpected notice of my shoes led to the emergence of new material and thus a new transference-countertransference configuration.*

In this chapter, I have attempted to add to the growing body of knowledge concerning the body in clinical work. My focus has been my experiences of the interplay of bodies in analytic dyads composed of an eating-disordered patient and myself, as a female analyst. I highlighted some of the feelings, as well as defensive and protective splits, evoked in and by this clinical relationship: envy and idealiza-tion, objectification and identification, attachment and distancing, "perfection" and "imperfection." Additionally, I pointed out the cen-tral importance to these patients' transferences of comparing and contrasting bodies and appearances, which is the language of eat-ing disorders. Working with—and through—this range of feelings meant struggling with the various enactments about my body and their bodies through which these feelings were initially expressed. A major part of the work with these patients is helping them put into words their feelings about our bodies together in the room. In

---

* I realized when writing this section that there are places I haven't gone, such as the sexualized aspects of looking at someone else's body or how idealization of another's body may also cover sexual feelings. Issues related to bodies in the room can evoke a particularly guilty kind of anxiety, which, like anything else, needs to be welcomed into the room.

that way, they learn that they no longer have to hide their feelings about, and their experiences of, bodies—mine, theirs, or others'. Instead, they can now consciously claim self-states and aspects of their histories that they formerly were compelled to keep split off from consciousness, including what they feel about themselves, physically (Bromberg, 1998). They, and we, hope that "when a body meets a body," our patients can do this without hiding, diminishing themselves, or relinquishing relationships.

Let me conclude with some words that one of my patients faxed me, some of her not-so-nice thoughts about me and about herself. She made me think about the fact that there is so much that makes people feel uncomfortable, that none of us want to see. Sometimes it is the parts of the patient that feel disgusting, sometimes it is the parts of us that feel disgusting, the parts of us that make us feel like we have to hide something. In different ways, don't we all have pieces of ourselves that we don't want to be seen?

The following is what this patient wrote:

> There's got to be some place to feel equal. There is no place with J (the patient is referring to her therapist). She is more beautiful, intelligent, financially secure, confident, etc. I'm left consistently a mess up. I find J's approach provocative and exciting—intimidating and empty. Her clothing is provocative—how can someone dress in costume without wanting to be the center of attraction and of attention. It is hard to not stare smilingly at her ability to put together an outfit that is so unique. Yet it is distracting, it makes me feel schlumpy, old, fat and ugly. I am. The frequent smell of perfume (once called a candle another time a bottle of cleaning fluid) what is it covering—bulimic smells, bathroom smells. None of my business? Yes, … my business … how do you talk to someone about eating disorders if she has an active one going on?
>
> I am ambivalent.
>
> I am disgusting.
>
> I need to be punished for what a defective rodent I was.
>
> I question a lot who you are as a person. After all I am entrusting you with my fragile very moldable soul. I need to know if she too has a genuine respect/understanding of/belief in the ability to heal for pain and for emptiness. Has she ever healed? Or hurt? I don't want sympathy ever. I do need to know though when I can no longer carry the load, that someone, you, can temporarily hold it until I get the strength myself.

I've included this to illustrate my conviction that, if you can be yourself as a therapist and if you encourage your patients to be open about themselves and about how they perceive you, then the things they say about you, things you may not want to hear, enhance their ability to be themselves in more ways than they could before they began therapy. Now they do not have to protect the connection by throwing parts of themselves away. It helps them know what they see and say what they know. Tolerating having your body "used" as an object in the Winnicottian (1971) sense does not break the relationship apart but makes the patient and the therapeutic relationship stronger. For someone with any eating disorder or disordered eating, this may be the greatest gift we can give them.

References

Bromberg, P. (1998). *Standing in the spaces*. Hillsdale, NJ: The Analytic Press.

Buechler, S. (1994). *Clinical values: Emotions that guide psychoanalytic treatment*. Hillsdale, NJ: The Analytic Press.

Burka, J. (1996). The therapist's body in reality and fantasy: A perspective from an overweight therapist. In B. Gerson (Ed.), *The therapist as a person* (pp. 255–276). Hillsdale, NJ: The Analytic Press.

Kahn, N. (2003). Self-disclosure of serious illness: The impact of boundary disruptions for patient and analyst. *Contemporary Psychoanalysis, 39*, 51–74.

Lieberman, J. (2000). *Body talk: Looking and being looked at in psychotherapy*. Northvale, NJ: Jason Aronson.

Looker, T. (1998). "Mama, why don't your feet touch the ground?" Staying with the body and the healing moment in psychoanalysis. In L. Aron & F. S. Anderson (Eds.), *Relational perspectives on the body* (pp. 237–262). Hillsdale, NJ: The Analytic Press.

Lowell, M. & Meader, L. (2002). My body, your body: The thin therapist and the treatment of eating disorders. *The Renfrew Perspective*, Fall, 10–12.

Orbach, S. (2003). There is no such thing as a body. In K. White (Ed.), *Touch: Attachment and the body* (pp. 17–34). London: Karnac Books.

Pizer, B. (1998). Breast cancer in the analyst: Body lessons. In L. Aron & F. S. Anderson (Eds.), *Relational perspectives on the body* (pp. 191–214). Hillsdale, NJ: The Analytic Press.

Shapiro, S. A. (1996). The embodied analyst in the Victorian consulting room. *Gender & Psychoanalysis, 1*, 297–322.

Tintner, J. (2007). Bypassing the barriers to change: *Bariatric surgery, case material. 43*(1), 121–134.

Winnicott, D. W. (1971). *Playing and reality*. London: Tavistock/Routledge.

12

The Analyst's Vulnerability

Preserving and Fine-Tuning Analytic Bodies

Adrienne Harris and Kathy Sinsheimer

In this chapter, through clinical examples and theoretical reflections, we will explore the very underdeveloped concept of analytic vulnerability. Here we concentrate on the impact of clinical work on the body, on embodied cognition, and on the analyst's psyche-soma. Although great space has been made over a century of thinking about transference and increasing space made for complex countertransference, there is not yet a clear, full registering of analysts' vulnerability (long term and short term, macro and micro). We want to make a contribution to that project here. Analytic vulnerability, we will argue, is both our greatest gift and our Achilles' heel.

In a way, we are simply extending the emerging recognition that the penetration and colonization of psychic functions in the analyst is an inevitable aspect of analytic work. Equally inevitably, we feel that the analyst's body is one key element in the analytic instrument, both crucial to analytic functioning and insufficiently cared for, at a theoretical as well as practical level. The analyst's body, perhaps for obvious reasons, is often a matter of anxiety or erasure. Although there are many ways to read the phrase "evenly hovering attention," it is a strikingly disembodied concept.

Introduction: I. The Personal in the Clinical

AH: One day, many years ago, in my own analysis, I was recounting a weekend event when I had gone to visit a friend with a sick cello. The cello
had become ill from a misjudged coat of varnish. The treatment was to
lie in a bed in Sag Harbor while Bach was piped electronically into the
instrument. Hooked up to CDs and mics, the cello lay for hundreds of
hours until the varnish cracked and eased. I was halfway through this
story before I had the thought, "Oh no, perhaps this is about me." But I
tell this story now and conjure up this image to urge seriously the care
of the analytic instrument, particularly now when we have to play so
many astonishing difficult and atonal tunes. Let us take seriously that
we are/have an instrument and that the artistry of analysis requires
attunement of and to this instrument (see Anzieu, 1990, and Grosz,
1994, for discussions of materiality and psychic functioning). As sing-
ers, actors, musicians preserve and care for their voices and bodies, we
too might see preservation as a worthy task.

I began to think seriously about this topic several years ago for quite
personal reasons. Reflecting back now, I can see a number of converg-
ing rivers. Two years ago, I had a serious health problem. It was the
second and different demanding body crisis I had experienced over
the preceding decade. It was illuminating and sobering to realize
the help I needed, the clinical trouble I got into and inevitably only
partially got out of, the web of care provided by family, colleagues,
consultants, analysts, and, no doubt, my patients. It takes a village to
sustain an analyst. Perhaps that's really the point.

Then, over a year ago, in California, I was teaching a course, based
on papers by Melanie Suchet (2003) and myself (Harris, 2003) concerning an analysis of a young woman with many early and terrible
losses, a treatment radically affected by Melanie's pregnancy, during
a time in which I had supervised her. Over several years, with a lot
of sadness and regret and enigma, Melanie and I worked over what
had happened, between patient and analyst, and between analyst
and supervisor. We came to feel that so many factors in our histories,
about abortion, pregnancy, childbirth, death, and loss, were always
in play in one if not all three of us. Not atypically, analyst, analysand,
and supervisor carried various ghosts and specters in relation to our
reproductive lives. How long the shadow of the unconscious is and
how much unconscious material, really at a bodily level, slips under
the radar, even when the analyst and the supervisor were deploying
powerful reflection and dialogue.

One of the students in the California class said, memorably, to me,
"I know who to read to take care of my patients; I do not know who to

read to take care of myself." It is to that statement that we are devoting this paper. That student was Kathy Sinsheimer.

KS: When I met Adrienne, I was a fourth-year candidate at the Psychoanalytic Institute of Northern California (PINC). I had reached a point in my training where I was able to work increasingly deeply with my patients. One consequence of this was that I felt the transference/countertranference intensely and had begun to wonder how it was going to be possible to metabolize the vast quantity of emotional and fantasy experiences I was involved with each day in my consulting room. I wondered if this struggle to metabolize was the experience of a beginning analyst or if a seasoned analyst would experience this as well. What I have come to understand is that the issue of self-care is of concern to many analysts, but that it seems to be something that few talk about openly. One possible explanation for this is that self-care often seems to involve the body. Analysis is often viewed, from the perspective of the analyst, as a primarily mental activity, rather than a fully embodied experience.

I may be especially vulnerable as an analyst, in that I listen in a particular way. What happens is that as I listen, I begin to imagine the patient's experience as it is being described to me. Or, if projection is the key mode of communication, I feel the impact of the projection. If my patient is telling me about a horrific scene, I inevitably picture it in my own mind. If the projection of the moment is rejecting and depreciating, in that moment, and perhaps afterward, I feel rejected and depreciated. The upside of these forms of listening is that I have access to a deep well of contact—emotional and fantasy—with my patients. The downside is that I am left with the experience of having been mutilated in a horror scene, or having been painfully rejected and depreciated. I wondered, "How does one make it through each day intact?" Not entirely intact, because one must be touched by one's patients in order to work with them, but adequately constituted to have one's own life outside the consulting room. This can include family, friends, other commitments, or communion with other aspects of one's self.

Introduction II: The Institutional and the Theoretical

This chapter comes at an interesting time. There is the bewitching, even tempting question of the legacy of relational thought—from Steve Mitchell onward. Relational theory is maturing and deepening (Aron, 1995, 2006; Aron & Harris, 2005; Bromberg, 2006; Corbett, 2001; Davies, 2003a, 2003b; Dimen, 2003; Dimen & Goldner, 2002). This chapter has been germinating in a moment in relational psychoanalysis of critical self-reflection and expansion. But we see the problem of analytic vulnerability as independent of any one theoretical orientation. The revolution in the understanding of countertransference has flowed into every nook and cranny of this field. Whatever you do about and with your countertransference, its presence is irreducible.

Perhaps another influence on this work is Joyce Slochower's (2006) essay on analytic crimes and misdemeanors, a paper that has produced a lot of creative and painful talk about the vicissitudes and temptations of clinical work. Our view is that the kind of analytic rigor and regulation Slochower is proposing and wanting us to aspire to will be aided by bodily and psyche-somatic self-care of the kind we are considering. Again, we strive to keep the tension between self-care and rigor.

Last year at Division 39, Adrienne was seated between two men on a panel on working with disturbed patients. These colleagues were and are extraordinary clinicians with attentive skills and capacity for containment. And indeed they reported work from the trenches, stimulating in the audience a deep and powerful discussion of the porousness of body and mind in analytic encounters, the primitive fears of being possessed, colonized, inhabited, of having one's own life and process leaking, spreading, and transmuting.

Pride and the need for affirmation and witnessing of our genuine heroism is an important element in our work and in our collective life together, and these habits and practices would, from our point of view, be included in self-care. Writing also is a form of self-care. But we should remember that trenches produced shell shock. And although the panel and the audience's discussion contained many really startling and striking comments and vignettes attesting to the power of unconscious transmission, there was not quite the available space to talk about the rigors of countertransference and the necessity of careful self preservation. So today, in highlighting analytic vulnerability, in particular the vulnerability of the body, we want to hold a tension between heroism and self-care.

AH: In fact, as the panel went on, I felt, with quite considerable shame, that I was turning into the Paris Hilton of psychoanalysis, advocating manicures and massage and yoga to manage the stress of clinical work. My shame is instructive. Speaking out about this topic of self-care and vulnerability is experienced (by me and others) as a kind of confession. I think in calling for theorization of this matter, I am seeking to address and diminish the presence of shame that adheres to the very idea of limits and weakness in the analyst, in particular the analyst's body.

The Contemporary Dilemma of the Analytic Body

We begin by setting a context for this way of thinking. Four factors play a role in considering analytic bodily and psychic vulnerability.

First, we have had a really dramatic reframing of countertransference (see Harris, 2005, for review of this history). This is the liberation and also the burden of relational theory, because central to our psychoanalytic attitude is a commitment to the idea of unconscious process. However you use your countertransference, there is an assumption that it is both crucial and only ever imperfectly masterable. That is actually a terrible combination: The mix of powerlessness and demand is a prescription for dissociation and trauma. This may be one of the indissoluble, irreducible conditions of analytic work.

Second, we are well into a profound revolution in neuroscience. We can now see how entrained we are—as dyads and as systems. At the level of body, soma, affect, and representation, people in dialogue and interaction actually are profoundly enmeshed (Damasio, 1999; Gallese, 2004; Olds, 2006; Schore, 1994). Mirror neurons, affect contagion, work like that of Myron Hofer (1984, 1986) on the biology of loss and separation, all argue for a deep enmeshment at the body/metabolic/physiological level. Mind and body turn out to be transpersonally organized, and this is not just a metaphor.

Third, there is a combustive mix of ego ideals in the profession, on the one hand, and the impact of the feminization of the profession, on the other hand, that has produced a powerful imago of the good analyst: invulnerable, all giving, maternal, containing, being of heroic service. Many of our cherished figures—even those with increasingly visible clay feet—manifest work lives and practices of service, devotion, and care that veer into masochism. Our goal here is to aspire to rigor without masochism. Self-care, at the bodily, interpersonal, and social levels, is a mode of self-regulation.

Fourth, most analysts are mindful that one of the developmental stories that often underwrites a career, as an analyst, is some early precocious caretaking of others, often parents. So, perhaps as a group, we are primed to have omnipotent fantasies about ourselves at work. Precocity, often the hallmark of the parentified child (the ur-analyst nestled deep in so many of us), is actually a terrible burden and one that falls often on the body, perhaps particularly because the origins of ego precocity are preverbal. Early implicit knowing as a body-based and affect-based schema may be the earliest proto-representation of the task of the ego precocious child: the care, the overwhelming demands for containment and management of parents and/or siblings, and the accompanying self-beratement that most parentified children feel deeply.

AH: Personally, I am a late convert to self-care. Growing up against a background of wartime, with an idealized and absent soldier father, and a mix of family dynamics and childhood illness, I came to be characterized in my family as "the good little soldier," an unironic epithet that took me two analyses and far too many enactments inside and outside treatment before I could begin to consider this designation as problematic. Perhaps, here I can speak also about the gendered aspect of our situation. The feminization of our field, along with the pretty solid sociological data about the degree to which women still do the bulk of the reproductive work (including care of aging parents, children, domestic life, etc.), means that women are likely to be carrying the particular ordeals of the professional domain in concert with demanding personal and family lives. But, men, too, may be ill-served by gender ideology. We might consider the barriers to self-care in the analyst as multifaceted, including elements of character, gender-driven processes, historical situations and contexts, and the demands of the economy.

KS: In response to an assignment that came late in my training, I brought a child's doctor's kit to class. The idea for bringing the kit came from knowing that Freud began as a physician who worked at the level of the body, and then had evolved to working at the level of the mind and the symbolic. I passed the doctor's kit around, asking classmates to take out an instrument (stethoscope, thermometer) and to name an idea from analytic theory that the instrument might represent. We had a lot of fun, and at the end, I gave everyone a red clown nose, which I also added to the doctor's kit, to include the necessity for a sense of humor.

My personal "doctor's kit" was filled with supplies from living in a home similar to the one Adrienne describes above, where the child is asked to take up the task of "precocious caregiving" for members of the family. I am no different from those who have gone before. I have certain capacities to palpate the internal state of the other, to anticipate needs, prevent disasters, and provide emotional goods that children develop when growing up in these circumstances. What is unfortunate, typically, in these scenarios is that there is no one to care for the small caregiver. He/she divines his/her care from the fact that he/she can bring pleasure or relief to the other. This creates and perpetuates a cycle for the child of only receiving through giving. Clearly, these capacities can be applied to the role of psychoanalyst. As the analyst, the level of projection I would need to absorb and the terrifying experiences I would need to undergo in order to offer useful interpretations to some of my patients are difficult to bear. It was in this state of awareness, as well as confusion, that I broached the question to Adrienne regarding analyst's self-care.

So now, briefly, four notes toward a view of analytic vulnerability.

Note 1: The Analyst as a Sick Cello

KS: One morning that I became a "sick cello" was a morning that projections were flying thick and fast in my consulting room. To my successful but aggressive and primitive male patient, I was the rejecting, overcharging bitch. In my next hour, I was the disappointing, infertile therapist to a couple who had not conceived during an IVF cycle. The third hour of the morning, I was assaulted with horrific images of mutilation, and the fourth, I was the disappointing, inadequate mother to a talented but masochistic patient who could not perceive that there were sufficient resources in her life.

By the end of that morning, I had become like the sick cello. I was either lacquered so heavily that I could not breathe, or I was engulfed with the projections that had been effectively inserted into me both by successful attempts at projective identification as well as my openness to receive and attempt to metabolize said projections. What was my cure? I actually think that extended listening to/feeling the vibrations of music, such as the cello experienced, might have done the trick. However, on short notice, I tried my favorite move for shedding projections: a yoga headstand. There is something incredibly reorganizing and rejuvenating in a few minutes of what yoga teachers call an "inversion." This does not work like the treatment of the cello—which sounded like it could be permanently cured. However, it is a great temporary cure for the colonization that can and possibly should occur in any given clinical day.

Given that self-care is often bodily care, it seems we think or speak about it in a different way. When a colleague tells me he went on a long bike ride or had a massage, is it stated between us that we are talking about his processing his work at the level of the body? I can't recall this occurring. Yet, because we are registering our work at the level of the body, it is inevitable that recreation or self-care is intertwined with the aspects of our physical selves in which we experience body-to-body communication.

Self-care is an integral part of our training system. As candidates, we have supervisors, our own training analyses, and advisors. All of this is in place for didactic and practical learning, but it is also to help us learn to function as analysts, on our own, and in our analytic communities. It is encouraged for analysts to continue to seek care through further analyses and consultation as they proceed in their professional lives. It seems that conventional support and care is directed at the mind. As we are uncovering the inevitable bodily links that we experience daily with our patients, and the work that takes place in that realm, it seems essential to add bodily awareness and care into our ongoing support of our analytic instrument.

An additional thought regarding our resistance to letting in the body came from my response to beginning my yoga class this morning. I was reminded of some of the motivation for ignoring the body, or relegating it to a secondary role. In class, I resisted settling in, letting go, allowing myself the kind of contact I have to have with my body in order to make my way through a 2-hour class. I have to be in touch with sensations in my body that I can often ignore, especially when I am thinking with my mind, or carefully observing the other, or even scanning my body for bodily sensations that could be clues to the communication of the other. It can be painful to be in touch with my own body—its aches and pains as well as emotions and tumult. All this becomes much more palpable, although not necessarily palatable, when one chooses to undertake self-care at the level of the body.

Note 2: Heroism and Care: Melodrama and Clinical Narrative

Analytic work is written about through the particulars of cases or vignettes. This narrative trope in analytic writing sidesteps analytic work as work, done over a day of seeing other patients. Our case histories disguise the working reality of analytic life—its movements through the day and the week, the sort of day Kathy describes as she becomes an increasingly lacquered cello. Paying attention to countertransference must include attending to the rhythm and tempo of work, its relation to exhaustion, depletion, and the almost altered states in continuous daily analytic sessions, states that over a whole work day often give a particular intrapsychic sheen or state. Paying attention to the moments when the analyst is alone in the room, the choices about multitasking, when to conduct personal and professional business, how to preserve the instrument in downtime—all these preoccupations are the layered experience and reality of analytic work. We need to make these concerns more explicit in our theories and not the private offstage whispers. It is as though we are ashamed to need help.

In the past few years, two different clinical accounts have appeared (Morrison, 2006; Silverman, 2006) in which a phone call between sessions triggered states in the analyst that entered and affected the clinical process. The probing and exploration of countertransference, the capacity for honesty, and both the courage and responsibility by the analysts were absolutely exemplary. Somehow, though, attention to self-care could also be part of the story. Theoretical concerns about self-care are not in opposition to the idea of suffering for service but in dialogue with it.

AH: Tracing the complex management of personal and professional matters is likely to be very tied to one's place in the life cycle. At my age and stage, the challenging preoccupations often involve worries over aging, illness both in family and in my generational cohort. Eriksen had an interesting constellation in respect to this life stage: generativity versus despair. But this stage brings up fears of bodily integrity, of mortality, and of aging that can get displaced into despair about the profession and about psychoanalysis. How are aging analysts incorporating their own fear of separations (death, retirement, etc.) at a very embodied level? There is another point of intersect of family and profession, not focused so much on duties and split loyalties and responsibilities but on private pleasures and happiness. Slochower (2006) chides herself for taking a difficult moment in an analysis to look at and think about a beloved child. A removal from the immediate immersion with the patient, to be sure. But is respite, even within a session, always to be criminalized? Is this not one of the reparative potentials of Thirdness?

After a difficult surgery and too-short absence from patients, I was conducting a session in which the analysand was very angry at my absence. I could feel the right and need with which she spoke, and I understood the issues behind her rage. And I could also feel how frequently this person has defeated her own wishes for closeness through anger. But I was compromised in allowing myself the full immersion in her experience. I met the letter of the law of clinical focus but perhaps some respite, some oxygen, some space would have made me more fully available. And in that instance, the mental constriction was very consciously, to me, related to the bodily experience of surgery. Something (psychic or somatic) about the cutting open of the body made me not so able to absorb more aggression.

KS: Adrienne's example of her self-protection following a serious surgery is very poignant to me. I think she characterizes a view of oneself as a professional that is commonly held—that one is to be, at all times, an object available for projection, mentally primed and emotionally strong, yet supple and accessible. Given the inherent horrors of undergoing surgery, followed by one's return to practice and one's inevitably angry patients, this produces an inevitable setting for a struggle with self-care.

In a similar vein, I have recently been grieving the sudden death of a close friend. When grief arises in my consulting room, I immediately experience my own feelings, including, at times, tears. These are tricky moments, because many things are occurring simultaneously: 1) I am resonating with the patient's emotion. This should be informative and useful for the treatment. 2) I am experiencing a moment in my own grieving process, which is personal and theoretically best experienced when I have more space to attend to my own reactions. 3) I am having to struggle to find a middle ground between my awareness of the feelings of grief while primarily focusing on the patient and her associations. If I do not give my own emerging feelings any space, I may pay the price of becoming somewhat emotionally flat, which will not only negatively impact the analytic hour, but will leave me in a dissociated spot within myself, making it difficult to contact myself and my own response to the feelings of grief later, when I have an opportunity for privacy.

These are the difficult spots one can wind up in, as one seeks to remain awake, alive, and healthy (Winnicott, 1965), while retaining an analytic stance. I believe these moments are often where unfelt feelings begin to be expressed at the level of the body in the analyst. These unfelt feelings seem to me to be one of the phenomena that begin to accrue at the level of the body and may set in motion physical symptoms as a form of expression.

Note 3: Dissociation as Creative, as Point of Preservation, as a Necessary Aspect of Thirdness

We often take the ideal of "evenly hovering attention" as a directive toward total immersion, attunement, and containment, alongside a discrete and scrupulous restriction of the self. We want to add to that definition, not amend it. "Evenly hovering attention" may be a kind of meditative state, a place of deep receptivity. We also think that sometimes it is necessary, clinically useful, and illuminating to think of "hovering attention" as containing some form of dissociation. Some dissociated states may provide buffers, resting points, safety zones, and protected landscapes that are an inevitable part of clinical work (Bromberg, 1998). Perhaps it is useful to think that analytic work occurs in a kind of state of doubled consciousness. Ron Britton (1995) used a clinical example in which a patient's intrusion and colonization of the analyst's mind was manifest in her determined rageful shout, "Stop that fucking thinking." But the thought, the moment of reflection, in which Britton took up an aspect of Bion's (1961) maternal reverie, surely, can be a life raft for analyst and therefore for patient. This can take form in a number of ways, some brilliant, some problematic. Analytic or supervisory fogs may be necessary protection and then useful guides to clinical process (Harris & Gold, 2003). Simple things can function as the Thirdness that is respite and self protection: breathing, reverie, dream states. Landscapes of safety may be large or tiny.

AH: Many of my landscapes of Thirdness involve dogs. In a phone call with a desperate patient one weekend day, I was finding myself caught in a familiar bind: I must offer help. Any wrong step and she/we are doomed. I feel myself, along with the patient, grinding down in terror. Suddenly Rosie, my dog, barked in the background. The patient stopped sobbing and said, "Rosie, is that Rosie?" This patient was deeply connected to dogs, had been very bonded with her own dog in childhood—decidedly a refuge for her—and she knew of my dog by name. In that moment, that bark, she and I could pause and I could then get to a safer place. I could think, could frame a way of naming our dilemma. But the landscaped Thirdness was a crucial way station. Another patient was describing to me a fantasy of stuffing a dog. Taxidermy was mentioned. I flinched and said something that stopped the conversation. He does not know consciously of my connection to dogs, but I assume that is more permeable than I sometimes imagine. The clinical moment was one of reversal. I refused to hold his terror and disgust. It is a moment I would deem to be a clinical failure, a dissociative moment that haunts me in the treatment, an eclipsed Thirdness that has not received its due. So I speak of dissociation as a complex process, both a failure and a necessary step. The difficulty is deciding which is which. So nothing in this chapter is an argument for throwing away books, or that anything goes, and so on. But psychic time-outs may have their clinical relevance.

Safety and space that have aspects of Thirdness can in certain cases be crucial. In a treatment conducted by one of the authors (KS), the preserving capacity in the analyst brought her paradoxically closer to her patient. It is not unlike what the Baranger et al. (1983) describe as "bastion," a potential site of impasse or mobility.

KS: In the case described below, I have often been the witness to horrific scenes of torture, violent rage, and descriptions of grotesque primitive states. My initial response to this witnessing was often to cringe, with revulsion or disgust. This interfered with my listening and left my body vulnerable to states of nausea and overwhelm. Slowly, I developed a method of listening in which I created a slender, soft surround for my mind and body. One substance that this is something like is the cotton batting one places in a quilt between the two layers of fabric. The batting keeps the layers of fabric from touching one another, while also keeping them connected. It provides warmth as well as adding softness (Sinsheimer, in press). I evolved this "batting" over time, unconsciously forming a space that was slightly removed from the horror. In the vignette below, I have somewhat limited access to the batting. When I can make use of it, the batting allows for listening and understanding without creating further dissociation or severely uncomfortable physical or mental states.

M: I'm in touch with my friend, the throat singer. I wish I could growl. It sounds like good digestion. It would clean through my guts. I imagine it being even more satisfying than hearing it. I want more.

I watched *Zombie* last night (a horror movie). It was good. I don't know if I saw the corpse I was looking for (*a corpse to represent the corpse that resides in his body and represents the dead or somewhat alive father*). I saw some corpses. The director's really into eye mutilation. It's his trademark. A zombie punches his hands through the door. He grabs a woman and pulls her head into the door. A splinter slowly goes into her eye. There are pieces in her eyeball. He pulls her head some more and the wood snaps off in her eyeball.

This may be a reference to me. Mutilating my eye: a splinter in my eye. Could I still see, understand, if he was violent with me? Can he growl at me, empty his guts for me, mutilate me, eat me? (See below.)

I feel interested, disgusted, threatened. As the object of the scene, I am painfully and explicitly mutilated. This is nauseating to picture. I can only partially do it. I can tell that I am dissociated from it, as I sense I am cutting myself off from feeling.

There was lots of flesh eating. Eating a body. Zombies sitting around a person picking meat off. It was really satisfying.

K: How so?

I want him to extend his image. To articulate the satisfaction. I may also be getting some respite for myself. If he extends the image without further attacks, I may get some distance and be able to think.

M: I don't know. I felt like I wanted to see some kind of death. Dying. I guess I like the way he (the director) does it. I'm trying to think how that's so ... I don't know. There's something about it. It's not boring! It's an older film ... like listening to an old record. It has depth to it. It's not so realistic that it's cold and boring. He's working on a really low budget. His work is very honest.

I am hoping for a sense that it is not real as well. That the woman who has splinters in her eye will not be me, and that I will continue to be able to see.

I'm trying to see ... trying to watch his movies. What is it about him? I'm new to his stuff. I'm not sure what it totally is. It goes along with that throat singing and in this case flesh eating. Somehow those connect. After hearing that guttural singing I feel so cleansed. Through my guts. But it feels kind of temporary. If I can do it myself (*singing*) I can do it on my own. Hearing it and seeing images like that pulls it out of me. Because it's visual and hearing it is temporary. It assists but the stuff is still there. Being able to sing like that, it's much more thorough. Long lasting.

K: If you could sing, not just watch, you could find the right voice. What would that pull out?

M: Darkness that's here (points to solar plexus). Dark oily sludge.

When it builds up I feel much less grounded and more afraid. I feel clogged up. I feel I have food rotting in me or something rotting in me.

If I am able to use the batting, I can keep the "food" from rotting in me. I can consider it as an image and an action without experiencing the mutilation. Without getting the splinter in my own eye. I begin to make a transition at this point in the session. The imagery is enough at a distance that I can see and somewhat experience it without having to shield myself from my own images of being mutilated.

K: Something?

M: A substance. I see black oily tarry shit. Stuff. I also see rotting matter. Clogged rotting matter. It won't pass through my bowels. It's all over. I'm not sure it's in my bowels, but that's where I imagine things like that. Swelling, rotting things.

K: These rotting things take different shapes—a corpse, dead babies ...

M: Yeah.
        Dead babies, dead father, dead self. ...
        Like I hold on to all the dying pieces of myself. I didn't let them exfoliate. I left them there.
        Yeah, rotting flesh. That definitely sounds like one of the things it is. Death.

K: You're a cannibal, eating parts of yourself. Then you can't excrete what remains.

M: Yeah, and they won't pass.
        Man, I want to be able to throat sing like that! I want to patch a cord to my head like the iPod and download a thousand songs.

K: You want to sing; you can't sing.

M: I don't have the natural talent. I'm not good enough. I don't have what it takes. If it was so easy, so doable, lots of people would be doing it. I admire those people. I feel like I can't do it.

K: Be someone you admire.

M: Yeah. Maybe I don't want to be. The singer, he sounds like what he's been through. It's not like his aggression and anger, it's very clean. It sounds exactly like what he's been into.
        I feel that on a certain level. His level, no. I understand it. I'm not on that level. You have to be, to understand that. I guess that's my reasoning I've come to. Does that mean I can't do it at all? That's my question.
        I see a heightened interest in that expression as I see myself investigating how my father died. I see this as a way to deal with that.
        I'm reaching out in that direction as much as I'm reaching out in the direction of _____ (dead father).

In this session, I may have been in both spots that M describes. In the beginning, I am a victim of the torture. Halfway through, I recover and begin to use my batting. In the end, M can feel both urges, to torture as well as to let go. This may reflect my having been able to reside in both spots during the hour. Even as I reread the hour, I can feel myself dissociate during the first images of the torture of the woman. This recedes until a portion of the hour, which occurs following the above vignette, where M speaks of mutilation and torture of a penis. It is so shocking as to overwhelm. In this case, to invoke my "batting," I have to wait. Let some time elapse from the original telling. I also, following the hour, employ theory to bring me back to, as well as aid, in thinking.

Note 4: Training and Institutional Life

Self-care is not solely a personal or even solely a professional matter, let alone just a political one. We will need to theorize on a social as well as personal level. This is likely to be a delicate matter as the interface between privacy, solo practice, entrepreneurial ambitions, pride in accomplishments, and the social and institutional life of psychoanalysis is complex. Different psychoanalytic cultures parse this differently, with North Americans particularly loading the dice on the side of individuality and privacy. Here, we protect individuality and privacy with the collateral costs in loneliness, isolation, alienation, costs that are particularly heavy on newer practitioners.

Sandra Buechler (2006), in a beautiful and moving paper, recently outlined the costly presence of shame in our institutes, which through training leave us very myopic in regard to shame in general and countertransference shame in particular. What might be the techniques for diminishing shame and creating contexts of trust where difficulties and needs within the community might have space for recognition? Could we as collectivities explore self-care and collaborative care?

Obviously, one area of greatest difficulty involves our collective responsibility for errors and failures of colleagues. Gabbard and Lester (1995) have written about this in the context of boundary violations. With boundary violations, we are in the realm of embodied action, not symbolization, even as this divide is not perfectly or sharply delineated. In assessing the history of boundary violations in institutional contexts, Gabbard and Lester make us aware of the complex networks of collusion and intergenerational transmission of trauma and predation within the field. Our complex reactions to these undeniable facts and the vague miasma that surrounds them (in the life histories of Khan, Ferenczi, Jung, etc.) are part of this story of analytic vulnerability. Victims of trauma inflicted within treatments are as traumatized as family members in any group where power can be wielded in mad and terrifying ways. The strange mix of professional ethics ("First, do no harm"; abstinence), as well as victim shaming and blaming, makes plain talk impossible and, we would say, invades the psychoanalytic body/bodies collectively and individually.

In Gabbard and Lester's (1995) careful and steadfast exploration of the institutional and individual response to boundary violations, one hears the anxious refusal in the community to fully take on this matter. Margolis (1997), commenting on his own efforts to open up discussion of boundary violations, reports that merely entertaining the topic made many colleagues question his motives. Gabbard and Lester, very interestingly, tie embodied violations to other levels of seductiveness and control by the analyst. Boundary violations are a body/mind problem or, perhaps, a body/speech problem (Lakoff & Johnson, 1999).

In the wake of a serious boundary violation that had radically disrupted an analytic institute, members of that institute contemplated but have not yet enacted a system of buddies, whereby each person chose some peer to whom they assigned the right and the role of intervention if the analyst were in some trouble—personal, social, professional. In such a process, the norms of individual private practice, of entrepreneurship, and of clinical responsibility are poised against the capacity of a community to aid its members and to protect the reputation of psychoanalysis, a matter we all have a stake in.

KS: Potential boundary violations can pose a threat from either direction between patient and analyst. These can be frightening concerns, raising the question of how one finds focus and a way to move forward. Recently, while treating a male patient who had rape fantasies about me, I became scared. I needed a collaborator, not because I was worried that I would violate a boundary, but because I felt on the verge of being so emotionally violated that I became unable to do good clinical work. Fortuitously, I had begun consultation with Charles Spezzano, who functioned as a powerful male "Third" and enabled me to find safety as well as a renewed ability to think. I could mentally bring Charles with me into the consulting room, as an adjunct mind, as well as a male force for protection. This provided me with adequate mental space to think and then interpret.

Jeff Sandler, former chair of the Ethics Committee at PINC, recently stated in conversation that, simply by the nature of what we undertake daily in our consulting rooms, we are at risk for boundary violations. He felt that the most protective position for any analyst would be to say to him/herself, "I am at risk by the very nature of this work." Since the time of Freud, we have taken up the work of, among other things, talking with people about their sexualities. As described in this chapter, discussion of sexuality would inevitably lead to bodily responses as well as potential body-to-body communication, whether or not bodies touch. What Sandler endorsed was to accept that problems with boundaries are inevitable in this work. He recommended a greater freedom among analysts to speak with one another about problems (potential or actual) that they are having with boundaries while in their consulting rooms. Sandler felt that this freedom might be more accessible if one were to start from the position stated above: That simply due to the nature of our work, we are inevitably at risk for our fantasies, as well as our realities, to be affected by our contact with others, perhaps especially our patients. This view of the evocative nature of our clinical situation explains a significant difficulty of self-care and makes clear the need for greater collective attention to the problems of boundary violations.

Conclusion

Since we have begun to pay attention to this matter, the issues appear everywhere. We still write about the heroic aspects of psychoanalysis, not about the costs. We create an ego ideal of the good analyst as a person with a perfectly functioning and regulated body, a potential to survive aggression and damage that can easily border on the omnipotent or hypomanic presented as normative good work.

We hope here to have begun a train of thought that links analytic vulnerability and analytic care with analytic responsibility, analytic self regulation, attunement, and other virtues perhaps easier to see and affirm. We consider that all these processes require a renewed and evolved attention to the analyst's body, as an instrument of work, as a repository of stress and life demands, and as a site of great potential knowledge of self and others. We need to apply to ourselves what we routinely communicate to patients: that narcissistic injuries, crimes, thefts, and abuses are less likely when you yourself are fed, contained, given to. We also need to apply to ourselves what we routinely communicate to patients regarding self-care: that, when cared for, the analyst is more able to offer the requisite, multileveled attention in order for analytic work to proceed.

References

Anzieu, D. (1990). *The skin ego.* New York: Academic Press.
Aron, L. (1995). *The meeting of minds.* Hillsdale, NJ: The Analytic Press.
Aron, L. (2006). Analytic impasse and the third. *International J. of Psychoanal. 87*, 1–19.
Aron, L., & Harris, A. (2003). *Relational tradition.* (Vol. 2). Hillsdale NJ: The Analytic Press.
Baranger, M., Baranger, W., & Mom, J. (1983). Process and non-process in analytic work. *Int. J. Psycho-Anal., 64*, 1–15.
Benjamin, J. (1997). *The shadow of the other: Intersubjectivity and gender in psychoanalysis.* New York: Routledge.
Bion, W. (1961). A theory of thinking. *Int. J. of Psychoanal., 43*, 306–310.
Britton, R. (1995). Psychic reality and unconscious belief. *Int. J. of Psychoanal, 76*(1), 19–23.
Bromberg, P. (1998). *Standing in the spaces.* Hillsdale, NJ: The Analytic Press.
Bromberg, P. (2006). *Awakening the dreamer: Clinical journey.* Hillsdale, NJ: The Analytic Press.
Buechler, S. (2006, March). Paper presented at the PED CD-ROM conference on Shame, New York.
Corbett, K. (2001). More life: Centrality and marginality in human development. *Psychoanal. Dial., 11*, 313–335.
Damasio, A. (1999). *The feeling of what happens: Body and emotion in the making of consciousness.* New York: A Harvest Book Harcourt.
Davies, J. (2003a). Falling in love with love: Oedipal and post-oedipal manifestations of idealization, mourning, and erotic masochism. *Psychoanal. Dial., 13*(1), 1–27.
Davies, J. (2003b). Reflections on Oedipus, post-Oedipus and termination. *Psychoanal. Dial., 13*(1), 65–75.
Dimen, M. (2003). *Sexuality, intimacy, power.* Hillsdale, NJ: The Analytic Press.
Dimen, M., & Goldner, V. (Eds.). (2002). *Gender in psychoanalytic space: Between clinic and culture.* New York: Other Press.

Gabbard, G., & Lester, E. (1995). *Boundaries and boundary violations in psychoanalysis.* New York: Basic Books.

Gallese, V. (2004). "Being like me": Self-other identity, mirror neurons and empathy. In S. Hurley & N. Chater (Eds.), *Perspectives on imitation: From neuroscience to social science.* Cambridge: MIT Press, 61–80.

Grosz, E. (1994). *Volatile bodies: Toward a corporeal feminism.* Bloomington: University of Indiana Press.

Harris, A. (2003). Discussion of M. Suchet's Whose mind is it anyway. *Studies in Gender and Sexuality, 5,* 289–302.

Harris, A. (2005). *Gender as soft assembly.* Hillsdale, NJ: The Analytic Press.

Harris, A., & Gold, B. (2003). When the fog rolled in. *Psychoanalytic Dialogues, 11,* 357–384.

Hofer, M. (1984). Relationships as regulators: A psychobiologic perspective on bereavement. *Psychosom. Med., 46,* 183–197.

Hofer, M. (1996). On the nature and consequence of early loss. *Psychosom. Med., 58,* 570–581

Lakoff, G., & Johnson, M. (1999). *Philosophy in the flesh.* New York: Basic Books.

Margolis, M. (1997). Analyst-patient sexual involvement: Clinical experiences and institutional response. *Psychoanalytic Inquiry, 17,* 349–370.

Morrison (2006). Shame in the transference and countertransference. Paper presented at the PEP CD-ROM conference on Shame, March 2006. New York.

Schore, A. (1994). *Affect regulation and the origin of the self,* Hillsdale, NJ: Lawrence Erlbaum Associates.

Silverman, S. (2006). Where we both have lived. *Psychoanal. Dialogues. 16,* 527–542.

Sinsheimer, K. (in press). To dream, perchance to think: Making use of the analyst's reverie to help a disturbed patient symbolize his experience.

Slochower, J. (2006). *Psychoanalytic collisions.* Hillsdale, N.J.: The Analytic Press.

Suchet, M. (2003). Whose mind is it anyway? *Studies in gender and sexuality, 5,* 259–288.

Winnicott, D. W. (1965). *The Maturational Processes and the Facilitating Environment.* New Haven, Connecticut: International University Press.

Index

A

Active imagination concept, 30, 111
Addictions, 9, 30
Affect regulation, 15
Affective attunement, 55
Affective core, 58, 72, 137
Affects, 220–221
Alexander technique, 4–6, 43
Alone state, 32
Analytic process, 110
Analytic relationship, 14, 107, 110, 140
Analytic vulnerability, 255
    boundary violations, 269–270
    case notes on, 261–271
    dilemma of, 259–260
    dissociation, 265
    personal in clinic (case), 256–257
    self-care and, 258–260, 262, 269
    training and institutional life, 269–271
Anderson, F. S., 1
Anorexia; see also Eating disorders
    clinical illustration of, 114–121
    discussion, 121–123
Aron, L., xv, xxi
Arousal, 69–70
Attachment theory, 81, 83–84
Attention deficit hyperactivity disorder
    (ADHD), 129–130
Atwood, G. E., 152, 216
Auerhahn, N., 17
Authentic Movement (AM) discipline, 36,
    43, 110–111
Authentic self, 107–108
Autobiographical memory, 74
Autobiographical self, 61
Autonomic regulation, 133–134
Awareness. see Body awareness

B

Bachelard, G., 214
Barlett, F. C., 57
Bass, G., 13, 18, 20, 151
Beebe, B., 81, 215
"Being Joan Didion" (Robertson), 2
Benjamin, J., 96, 183
Biofeedback, 17–18
Bion, W. R., 181, 265
Birth trauma, 10, 23
Blocked trauma response, 79–80
Body awareness, 5, 36, 52; see also Sensory
        awareness
    family and cultural norms, 6
    in psychoanalysis, 31–32
    self-experience and, 107–110, 114
Body-centered psychotherapy, 3, 31, 33, 36
Body image, 117
    anorexia patient, 114–121
Body memories (implicit/procedural), 40
Body-mind centering, 43
Bodywork; see also Craniosacral Therapy;
        Polarity therapy; Yoga
    affect processing by, 105
    authentic awareness of self, 108
    body as unconscious mind, 152–153,
        155, 164–165
    boundaries in, 19–22
    clinical vignettes on, 39–43, 193–197
    energy concept and, 13–14
    experiences of, 17–19
    historical perspective on, 34–37
    meditation and, 6
    micro-moment body meanings,
        197–201
    ownership and, 16
    resistance to self-care, 9

therapeutic process and, 33, 43–44
therapist's body and, 237–243
training for psychoanalysts, 112–114
transference/countertransference in, 8,
   15, 44
Bosnak, R., 159, 162
Boston Process of Change Study Group, 83
Boundary violations, 269–270
Brain anatomy and process, 84–85
Britton, R., 265
Bromberg, P. M., 8, 14, 56, 62, 70, 114, 160,
   164
Brosschat, J. F., 133
Brown, R. P., 128
Bucci, W., 2, 23, 51, 136
Buechler, S., 269

C

Cartesian dualism, 220
Chefetz, R. A., 70
Chodorow, J., 111
Cimino, C., 130
Civilization and Its Discontents (Freud),
   146
Clinical technique. see Therapeutic work
Cole, G. W., 79
Communication; see also Language
   psychological functions of, 51
   symbiotic communication, 162
   verbal communication, 2–3
Communicative treatment, 71, 74
Conscious, 52
Core self, 40
Cornell, W. F., 18
Correale, A., 130
Cortical loop, 65–68
Counter-projection, 160
Countertransference, 57, 201, 208, 255,
   258–259, 263
Craig, A. D., 133
Craniosacral Therapy, 18, 153–154
   case examples, 154–162
   significance detector, 158
   theoretical considerations, 159–160,
      162–164
Creativity, as expression of self, 103–107
   psychoanalysis and, 110–112
Cross-cultural experiences, 195
Crown, C., 215
Cunningham, M., 105

D

Damasio, A. R., 61, 64, 133
Dance and dance therapy, 36, 43, 109
   authentic self and, 107–108
   creative process and psychoanalysis,
      110–112
   as expression of self, 103–107
Dance movement therapy (DMT), 110–112
Dancing self, 114
Darwin, C., 60, 220
Davies, J. M., 159
Descartes, 220
Developmental trauma, 16–17
Directiveness, 86–87
Disconnection syndromes, 139
Disorganized attachment, 84
Dissociation, 71, 139, 159, 265
Double consciousness, 159
Dream analysis, 14–15, 30, 164, 194
Dunbar, F., 4
Dynamic system, 202

E

Eating disorders, 113–123
   case studies, 243–253
   therapist's body impact, 237–243
Edelman, G., 81
Ego, 52
Eldredge, C. B., 79, 89
Emotion schemas, 57–58
   affective core and, 72
   clinical and theoretical implications,
      71–74
   contents of, 59
   cortical loop, 65–68
   development of pathology, 61–62
   direct route, 65
   dissociation vs. repression, 71
   emotion circuitry, 64
   emotion execution sites, 65
   integration of, 60
   interpersonal context and, 58–61
   neurophysiological model of, 63–68
   self and others, 61
Emotion triggering sites, 65
Emotionally competent stimulus (ECS), 64
Enactments, 57, 85, 88–89, 91, 152
Energy concept, 13, 163, 172; see also
      Polarity therapy

involution/evolution flow of, 178–179
polarity relationship, 182–182
tracking sensation and energy change, 185–187
Environmental transference, 89
Experience, symbolic mode of, 2
External resources, 87

F

False self, 8–9
Family and religious traditions, 195–197
Father transference, 12–13
Federici-Nebbiosi, S., 213
Feldstein, S., 215
Ferenczi, S., 34–35, 82
Fisher, J., 79
Fogel, A., 40
Fonagy, P., 81–83
Freud, S., 33, 52, 82, 146, 172, 220–221
Fromm, E., 36

G

Gabbard, G., 269–270
Generativity, 53
Gerbarg, P. L., 127–128
Gergely, G., 81
Ghent, E., 176, 181, 202
Gindler, E., 36–37
Graham, M., 108
Groddeck, G., 34–36

H

Hands-on body treatment, 5
Hare, D., 3
Harris, A., 255
Hess, E., 84
Hippocampus/hippocampal dysfunction, 66–67
Hofer, M., 259
Holotropic Breathing, 128
Horney, K., 34
Human development, 33

I

Id, 52
Imagery, 53–57
as sensory specific, 55
Implicit languages, 224
Internal resources, 87
Interpersonal context, 58–61
Interpersonal resources, 87
Interpretation of Dreams, The (Freud), 221
Intuition, 55
Involuntary muscles, 95–96
Iteration, 70–71

J

Jacoby, H., 36
Jaffe, J., 215, 217
James, W., 60
Jasnow, M., 215
Johnson, D. H., 35, 37
Jones, J., 220–221
Jung, C., 30, 37, 111, 172, 183
Jurist, E., 81

K

Keller, H., 55
Kemple, C., 4
Kinesthetic empathy, 109
Knoblauch, S. H., 193
Kohut, H., 109, 120
Kruger, D. W., 35, 117
Krystal, H., 5, 9, 15

L

Laban, R., 36, 104
Lachman, F., 81
Language, 53, 181
as arbitrary and abstract, 53
implicit languages, 224
nonverbal language, 114
role in therapeutic work, 73–74
talking therapies, 21, 31, 34, 51, 71, 83, 112

thought and, 218
  use of, 87
Larsen, S., 139
Laub, D., 17
Learning disabilities, 129–130
LeDoux, J., 64–65
Lester, E., 269–270
Letting go, 7, 9, 18
Levine, P., 79, 81
Lieberman, J., 238
Limbic resonance, 177
Lindenberg, E., 36
"Listening with the third ear," 55
Loewald, H., 82
Lorenz, E., 203
Lowell, M., 238
Lyons-Ruth, K., 81, 83

M

McDougall, J., 9, 15
McFarlane, A. C., 81
McLuhan, M., 241
Main, M., 84
Margolis, M., 270
"Massage and Psychotherapy" (Groddeck),
  36
Meader, L., 238
Meditation, 6
Memory, 29–30
  autobiographical memory, 74
  body memories (implicit/procedural),
    40
  memories, as sensate experiences, 30
  participatory memory, 40–41
  procedural memory, 95
  verbal memory (explicit/narrative), 40
  working memory, 61
Memory schemas, 57
Mimed reflection, 223–224, 228, 231–2
Mind-body connection, 4, 15, 32–33, 51, 82,
    143, 220, 238
Mindful Mediation, 128
Minton, K., 79
Mirror neurons, 59, 111, 218–220, 222, 259
Mitchell, S., 110
Modell, A., 81
Mother-child relationship, 117, 232
  separation-individuation, 142
  separation trauma, 15–16, 23
Motor events, 219

Movement and movement therapy, 37; see
    also Dance and dance therapy
  moving freely, 7
  ongoing psychotherapy, 39–40
  as selfobject, 106
Multiple code theory, 52, 55
  components of system, 55
  emotion schemas, 57–61
  referential process and, 53–63
  subsymbolic system, 55–56
  symbols, words, and images, 53–55
  yoga and, 136–137
Musculoskeletal pain, 5–6
Musical Edge of Therapeutic Dialogue, The
    (Knoblauch), 202

N

Narrative, 30
Nebbiosi, G., 213
Neural networks, 133–134
Neuronal Darwinism (Edelman), 81
Neurophysiological models, 132–134
Newman, H. M., 13, 169
Nietzsche, F. W., 214
Nonlinear dynamic system, 202
"Nonlinear Systems Theory and
    Psychoanalysis" (Ghent), 202
Nonlinear thought, 56
Nonpersonalized transference, 92
Nonrecognition, 8
Nonverbal forms, 32, 53, 111
Nonverbal language, 114
Nonverbal symbolic, 3, 74, 136–137
Now moment, 202

O

Ogden, P., 79–81
Open-ended inquiry, 187–188
Orbach, S., 238, 242
Ownership of one's body, 16

P

Pacifici, M. P., 103
Pain, C., 79

Participatory memory, 40–41
Pathology, 63
Perfectionist behaviors, 11–12
Perls, F., 36
Perls, L., 36
Personality development, 84
Pert, C., 152
Petrucelli, J., 237
Phaedrus (Plato), 107
Phenomenology, 30
Physical rehabilitation medicine, 3
Physical sensations, 29
Piers, C., 202–203
Plato, 107
Playing and Reality (Winnicott), 9
Polarity therapy
    applying methods of, 184–188
    basics of, 171–173
    case scenario, 183–184
    elemental patterns of, 174–175
    energy movement, 182–183
    evolutionary process, 180–182
    holding polarities, 182–183
    involution and evolution, 178–179, 183
    maintenance of form, 178–180
    open-ended inquiry, 187–188
    psychoanalytic relationship and, 173–174
    psychosomatic wholeness, 175–178
    reasons for, 170–171
    sensation and energy change, 185–187
Polyvagal theory, 134
Porges, S., 81, 95
Post-traumatic stress disorder (PTSD), 67,
    128–132
Posture, 4–5
Preconscious, 52
Press, C., 114
Procedural memory, 95
Projective identification, 43
Projective techniques, 4
Psycho-education, 86, 91
Psychoanalysis; *see also* Therapeutic work
    body in, 31–32, 37
    dance and creative process, 110–112
    evolutionary process and, 180–182
    fundamental concepts of, 51
    healing process of, 151–152
    historical perspective of bodywork and,
        34–37
    movement, action, and rhythm in,
        217–218
    polarity therapy and, 173–174, 184–188
    sensory awareness and movement
        interventions, 39–40, 43

training in bodywork, 112–114
traumatology and, 79, 82
yoga and, 127–128, 137–146
Psychomotor development, 33
Psychosomatic disorders, 4, 114
Psychosomatic wholeness, 175–178

R

Referential process, 52–53, 56–57
    arousal, 69–70
    iteration, 70–71
    multiple coding and, 53–63
    phases of, 69–71
    reorganizing, 70
    symbolizing, 70
    therapeutic work and, 69–71
Regression, 72
Rehabilitation medicine, 6
Reich, W., 34–36
Reik, T., 55, 60
Relational imagery, 17
Relational perspective, 169
Relational Perspectives on the Body (Aron),
    xiii, xv, xxii
Relational thought, 257–258
Reorganizing, 70
Repression, 71
Resistance, 72–73
Resources, 86–87
Rhythm, being and not-being, 214–215
    body movement and thought, 220–223
    case study, 225–232
    motor introspection, 223–225
    perceptive/cognitive value of motion,
        218–220
    in psychoanalysis, 217–218
    as quantity and quality, 215–216
    symmetry and asymmetry, 216–217
Ringstrom, P. A., 106
Rizzolatti, G., 219, 222–223
Robertson, C., 2
Rosen Method Bodywork, 43
Rotenberg, C., 106
Rusk Institute, 3, 5

S

Sandler, J., 271
Sarno, J. E., 5–6, 11

Scarry, E., 207
Schore, A. N., 8, 81–82, 84, 88
Self, false self, 8–9
    multiplicity of, 114
Self agency, 32
Self-care of therapist, 81, 258–260, 262
Self-experience, 107–110
    shame and, 8
Self-healing, 5, 122
Self-investigation, 33
Self-learning, 33
Self-organization, 33, 40
    bodily experience, 35
Self-regulation, 84, 95
Self-resources, 89
Self-states, 5, 21–22, 114, 152, 165–166
Selfobject, 106, 118, 120
Seligman, S., 203
Selver, C., 36
Sensate experience, 100, 185
Sensitive dependence on initial conditions,
    203
Sensorimotor Psychotherapy, 21
Sensory awareness, 36–37, 43
    ongoing psychotherapy and, 39–40
    physical sensations, 29
Sensory thalamus, 65
Separation-individuation, 142
Separation trauma, 15–16, 23
Shame, 8, 269
Shapiro, S. A., 35, 237
Shaw, R., 32
Significance detector, 158, 165
Sills, F., 178
Sinigaglia, C., 219, 222–223
Sinsheimer, K., 255, 257
Slochower, J., 258
Somatic Experiencing, 21
Somatic marker hypothesis, 133
Somatic resonance, 43
Somatic sensations, 6, 9–10, 12–17, 30, 177
Somatosensory phenomena, 35
Stern, D. N., 55–6, 58, 81, 108, 160
Stolorow, R. D., 152, 216
Stone, R., 171, 188
Stress-related disorders, 128
Stressor events, 66
Subsymbolic modes, 2–3, 37, 53, 55–56, 74
Suchet, M., 256
Sudarshan Kriya Yoga (SKY), 127, 129
    case analysis, 129–132, 138
    effects of, 134–135
    neurophysiological studies, 135–136
    nonverbal visceral messaging, 136–137

Superego, 52
Symbiotic communication, 162
Symbolic system, 53
Symbolic verbal/nonverbal, 53
Symbols, words, and images, 53–55, 70
Symptomalogy, 62
System, 202

T

Talking therapies, 21, 31, 34, 51, 71, 73–74,
    83, 112
Target, M., 81
Termination dream, 10–11
Thayer, J. F., 133
Thelen, E., 202
Therapeutic work; see also Analytic
        vulnerability
    affective core, 72
    clinical and theoretical implications,
        71–74
    dissociation vs. repression, 71
    goals of, 68–69
    illustrations of, 89–99
    organizing principles for, 86–88
    referential process in, 69–71
    regression and resistance, 72–73
    role of language, 73–74
    therapist's body and, 237–243
Therapist's self-care, 81, 258–260, 262
Thompson, C., 36
Tintner, J., 238
Tipping point, 201–209
Tomkins, S., 81
Transference, 22, 40, 57, 85, 241, 255
    in bodywork, 8, 15, 44
    deflection of, 160
    environmental transference, 89
    father transference, 12–13
    nonpersonalized transference, 92
    transference enactment, 88, 91
    yoga teacher and, 141
Trauma and traumatology, 79, 82
    abuse and, 61–62
    affect regulation, 15
    birth process, 10, 23
    blocked trauma response, 79–80
    bodywork and, 21–23
    clinical examples, 89–99
    developmental trauma, 16–17
    impact on body, 11
    separation trauma, 15–16